Frommer's®

New York City
day BY day
1st Edition

by Hilary Davidson

Wiley Publishing, Inc.

Contents

Published by:

Wiley Publishing, Inc.

111 River St.
Hoboken, NJ 07030-5774

ISBN-13: 978-0-7645-7931-8

ISBN-10: 0-7645-7931-2

Editors: Alexis Lipsitz, Margot Weiss

Special Thanks to Stephen Bassman and Aliyah Vinikoor

Production Editors: Donna Wright & Heather Wilcox
Photo Editor: Richard Fox
Cartographer: Roberta Stockwell
Production by Wiley Indianapolis Composition Services

Savvy Traveler illustrations by Rashell Smith, Karl Brandt, and Kelly Emkow

For information on our other products and services or to obtain technical
support, please contact our Customer Care Department within the U.S. at
800/762-2974, outside the U.S. at 317/572-3993 or fax 317/572-4002.
Wiley also publishes its books in a variety of electronic formats. Some content that appears in print may not be available in electronic formats.

Manufactured in China

10 9 8 7

A Note from the Publisher

Organizing your time. That's what this guide is all about.

Other guides give you long lists of things to see and do and then expect you to fit the pieces together. The Day by Day guides are different. These guides tell you the best of everything, and then they show you how to see it in the smartest, most time-efficient way. Our authors have designed detailed itineraries organized by time, neighborhood or special interest. And each tour comes with a bulleted map that takes you from stop to stop.

Hoping to discover the treasures of the Metropolitan Museum of Art, or to see some of Brooklyn's highlights? Planning a walk through Greenwich Village, or a whirlwind tour of the very best that New York City has to offer? Whatever your interest or schedule, the Day by Days give you the smartest route to follow. Not only do we take you to the top sights and attractions, but we introduce you to those special moments that only locals know about—those "finds" that turn tourists into travelers.

The Day by Days are also your top choice if you're looking for one complete guide for all your travel needs. The best hotels and restaurants for every budget, the greatest shopping values, the wildest nightlife—it's all here.

Why should you trust our judgment? Because our authors personally visit each place they write about. They're an independent lot who say what they think and would never include places they wouldn't recommend to their best friends. They're also open to suggestions from readers. If you'd like to contact them, please send your comments my way at mspring@wiley.com, and I'll pass them on.

Enjoy your Day by Day guide—the most helpful travel companion you can buy. And have the trip of a lifetime.

Warm regards,

Michael Spring,
Publisher
Frommer's Travel Guides

About the Author

Hilary Davidson first moved to New York City in 1995 to intern at *Harper's Magazine.* She returned in October 2001 thanks to her persuasive Manhattan-born husband, Daniel, with whom she shares an apartment in the shadow of her favorite New York landmark, the Chrysler Building. Hilary has written for *American Archaeology, Discover, Executive Travel, Fitness,* and *Martha Stewart Weddings;* she's also the author of *Frommer's Toronto.* She can be reached at hcdavidson@yahoo.com.

Acknowledgments

Thank you to my terrific editor, Margot Weiss, whose creativity, thoughtfulness, and resourcefulness made an impact on every page of this book. Thanks also to Myka Carroll for getting me involved in the project in the first place, and to all of the Frommer's team for their dedicated work. Heartfelt thanks to my husband, Dan, who helped me plan—and walk—the tours in this book, and who read every page at least twice. Finally, thank you to the many New Yorkers who were, for reasons both professional and personal, so generous in sharing their observations and ideas.

An Additional Note

Please be advised that travel information is subject to change at any time—and this is especially true of prices. We therefore suggest that you write or call ahead for confirmation when making your travel plans. The authors, editors, and publisher cannot be held responsible for the experiences of readers while traveling. Your safety is important to us, however, so we encourage you to stay alert and be aware of your surroundings.

Star Ratings, Icons & Abbreviations

Every hotel, restaurant, and attraction listing in this guide has been ranked for quality, value, service, amenities, and special features using a **star-rating system.** Hotels, restaurants, attractions, shopping, and nightlife are rated on a scale of zero stars (recommended) to three stars (exceptional). In addition to the star-rating system, we also use a **kids icon** to point out the best bets for families. Within each tour, we recommend cafes, bars, or restaurants where you can take a break. Each of these stops appears in a shaded box marked with a coffee cup–shaped bullet 🍵 .

The following **abbreviations** are used for credit cards:

AE	American Express	DISC	Discover	V	Visa
DC	Diners Club	MC	MasterCard		

Frommers.com

Now that you have the guidebook to a great trip, visit our website at **www.frommers.com** for travel information on more than 3,000 destinations. With features updated regularly, we give you instant access to the most current trip-planning information available. At Frommers.com, you'll also find the best prices on airfares, accommodations, and car rentals—and you can even book travel online through our travel booking partners.

A Note on Prices

In the Take a Break and Best Bets section of this book, we have used a system of dollar signs to show a range of costs for one night in a hotel (the price of a double-occupancy room) or the cost of an entrée at a restaurant. Use the following table to decipher the dollar signs:

Cost	Hotels	Restaurants
$	under $150	under $15
$$	$150–$250	$15–$25
$$$	$250–$400	$25–$40
$$$$	over $400	over $40

An Invitation to the Reader

In researching this book, we discovered many wonderful places—hotels, restaurants, shops, and more. We're sure you'll find others. Please tell us about them, so we can share the information with your fellow travelers in upcoming editions. If you were disappointed with a recommendation, we'd love to know that, too. Please write to:

Frommer's New York City Day by Day, 1st Edition
Wiley Publishing, Inc. • 111 River St. • Hoboken, NJ 07030-5774

16 Favorite
Moments

16 Favorite **Moments**

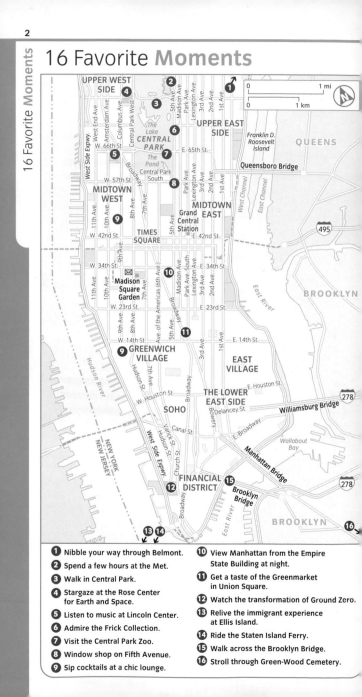

1. Nibble your way through Belmont.
2. Spend a few hours at the Met.
3. Walk in Central Park.
4. Stargaze at the Rose Center for Earth and Space.
5. Listen to music at Lincoln Center.
6. Admire the Frick Collection.
7. Visit the Central Park Zoo.
8. Window shop on Fifth Avenue.
9. Sip cocktails at a chic lounge.
10. View Manhattan from the Empire State Building at night.
11. Get a taste of the Greenmarket in Union Square.
12. Watch the transformation of Ground Zero.
13. Relive the immigrant experience at Ellis Island.
14. Ride the Staten Island Ferry.
15. Walk across the Brooklyn Bridge.
16. Stroll through Green-Wood Cemetery.

Every New Yorker has a lengthy list of places to visit and things to see. Here's mine. Visitors often wonder how residents like myself put up with the city's crowds and frenetic pace, not to mention the tiny apartments. But when we're out enjoying any of the 16 attractions below, we wouldn't be anywhere else.

1 **Nibble your way through Belmont.** This historic Italian community in the Bronx is redolent with bakers, cheese-makers, and other vendors, most of them happy to have you sample their goods. *See p 62.*

2 **Spend a few hours at the Met.** You can't go wrong here. The Greek, Roman, and Egyptian collections are among the finest in the world. The Impressionist paintings are just about everyone's favorite. Go on a Friday or Saturday, and stop by the Great Hall Balcony Bar after 4pm for cocktails and live classical music. *See p 32.*

3 **Walk in Central Park.** Manhattan's backyard offers endless variety: formal gardens, rustic rambles, Victorian buildings, ornate statuary, even its own lake. *See p 100.*

4 **Stargaze at the Rose Center for Earth and Space.** The planetarium usually has several shows available, but the perennial favorite is "Are We Alone?" Not only is it thought-provoking, it's narrated by Harrison Ford. *See p 13.*

5 **Listen to music at Lincoln Center.** Dancers, singers, musicians, actors—some of the world's most talented performers get standing ovations in the various theaters and performing halls here. The sets at the Metropolitan Opera can be reason alone to visit. I particularly enjoy listening to tomorrow's great artists at a Juilliard School recital. *See p 26.*

The interior of the Frick Museum.

6 **Admire the Frick Collection.** This former robber baron's mansion is as close to an ideal museum as you can get. Its size is manageable and its carefully selected art is a "best of" collection by the likes of Rembrandt, El Greco, and Gainsborough. *See p 37.*

7 **Visit the Central Park Zoo.** There's something slightly unexpected but entirely delightful about seeing playful monkeys and chunky penguins frolicking in the middle of the city. My favorite sight, however, is the toucan. Tucked away in a dark corner, he's all bright colors and oversize beak. *See p 103.*

8 **Window shop on Fifth Avenue.** If you've got the cash, by all means indulge yourself at Takishimaya, Saks, Henri Bendel,

A red panda at the Central Park Zoo.

Ellis Island's "Treasures from Home" exhibit contains more than 1,000 items donated by descendents of immigrants.

Tiffany & Co., Cartier, Harry Winston, Bulgari, and the rest. Everyone else can browse or enjoy the elegantly clever window displays. *See p 28.*

⑨ Sip cocktails at a chic lounge. Whether it's Hell in the Meatpacking District or Kemia Bar in Midtown West, you'll find a wealth of sexy spots that will remind you why New York was the *real* star of *Sex and the City. See p 125.*

⑩ View Manhattan from the Empire State Building at night. The city that never sleeps begins to glitter at dusk, with millions of lights keeping it aglow. You won't see any stars in the New York sky, but this view is unique. Romantics, take note: The Observatory is open until midnight. *See p 18.*

⑪ Get a taste of the Greenmarket in Union Square. Local farmers come here to sell produce, cheese, cider, plants, and flowers. The quality is high, and getting to talk face-to-face with the people who grow these products is a treat. Open year-round Monday, Wednesday, Friday, and Saturday during the day. *See p 18.*

⑫ Watch the transformation of Ground Zero. Millions have made a pilgrimage to the site of the World Trade Center since September 11, 2001. *See p 7.*

⑬ Relive the immigrant experience at Ellis Island. Whether or not your family entered America through Ellis Island, a visit here is extremely poignant. The on-site museum does an excellent job of bringing the experience to life from the point of view of a new arrival to our shores. *See p 9.*

⑭ Ride the Staten Island Ferry. The free 25-minute ride takes you past the Statue of Liberty. From the water, you can imagine how new arrivals must have felt when they first entered New York Harbor. *See p 9.*

⑮ Walk across the Brooklyn Bridge. I love the Gothic bridge itself, but the view from here is the biggest selling point—on a clear day you'll see both the towering spires of Midtown Manhattan and Lady Liberty on Liberty Island. And it's entirely possible to ignore the roar of traffic when you're walking above it. *See p 108.*

⑯ Stroll through Green-Wood Cemetery. If you love walking in peaceful, bucolic, historic surroundings near a major city, there is no better place. This 1938 Brooklyn cemetery is filled with life—it's a favorite spot for bird-watchers—and its countless statues, monuments, and mausoleums are works of beauty themselves. *See p 104.* ●

The Best
Full-Day Tours

The Best **in One Day**

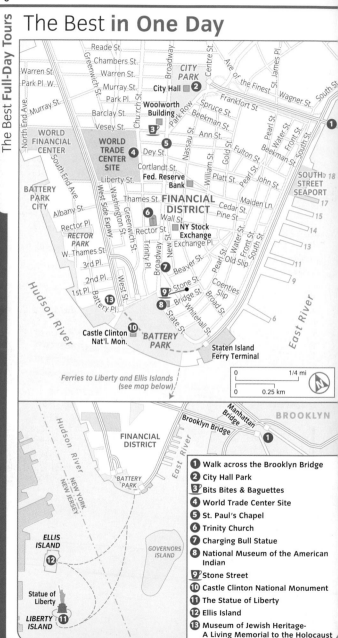

1 Walk across the Brooklyn Bridge
2 City Hall Park
3 Bits Bites & Baguettes
4 World Trade Center Site
5 St. Paul's Chapel
6 Trinity Church
7 Charging Bull Statue
8 National Museum of the American Indian
9 Stone Street
10 Castle Clinton National Monument
11 The Statue of Liberty
12 Ellis Island
13 Museum of Jewish Heritage-A Living Memorial to the Holocaust

The most wonderful—and maddening—thing about New York? The endless number of choices. My first love is history, and to explore the city's beginnings, head first to Lower Manhattan, with its Dutch roots and cobblestoned streets. But this area of New York is not limited to centuries-old structures frozen in time; it's also the dynamic center of city government and world finance. START: **Subway A or C to High St. in Brooklyn.**

❶ **★★ Walk across the Brooklyn Bridge.** For a glorious view of New York City, you can't beat the 30-minute walk across the Brooklyn Bridge. The celebrated suspension bridge is a wonder in itself, with its Gothic-inspired towers, Maine granite, and intricate web of steel cables. *See p 108. Subway: A/C to High St. in Brooklyn.*

❷ **City Hall Park.** City Hall has been the seat of NYC government since 1812. Security concerns prevent visitors from touring inside, but you can get close enough to appreciate the handsome French Renaissance exterior, built from 1803 to 1811. Abraham Lincoln was laid in state in the soaring rotunda. Equally grand is the colossal **Municipal Building** (1 Centre St. at Chambers),

The Municipal Building straddles a busy city street.

built on the other side of Centre Street in 1915 by McKim, Mead and White; it was the celebrated firm's first "skyscraper." Across Broadway at no. 233 is that temple of commerce known as the **★ Woolworth Building.** Built on the back of a nickel-and-dime empire in 1913, this neo-Gothic masterpiece is the work of Cass Gilbert. At press time, the public was not allowed inside the building. *City Hall Park: btwn Broadway & Park Row.*

❸ **Bits Bites & Baguettes.** Grab a sandwich here, or one of the hearty salads. *22 Park Place (btwn Church & Broadway).* ☎ *212/374-1111. $.*

❹ **★ World Trade Center Site.** The Twin Towers once dominated the city's skyline, and visitors from around the world have made pilgrimages to the vast, gaping hole left after their destruction during the September 11, 2001, terrorist attacks. The Wall of Heroes lists the names of those who died that day; there are also photos of the construction of the World Trade Center in the 1960s (it opened in 1972). Daniel Libeskind's proposed 1,776-foot-tall Freedom Tower will eventually stand here, along with a permanent memorial entitled *Reflecting Absence.* Work on the site is expected to last till 2015. *Bounded by Church, Barclay, Liberty, & West sts.* ☎ *212/484-1222. www.nycvisit.com or www.downtownny.com. Subway A/C to World Trade Center; N/R to Cortland St.*

⑤ ★ St. Paul's Chapel. This is Manhattan's only surviving pre-Revolutionary (1766) church. Built to resemble London's St. Martin-in-the-Fields, with an elegant Georgian interior, the chapel was a refuge for rescue workers after September 11, and is now home to the **Unwavering Spirit** exhibit, which honors those who died and those who tried to save them. ⏱ *45 min. 209 Broadway (at Fulton St.).* ☎ *212/233-4164. Mon–Sat 10am–6pm; Sun 9am–4pm. Free concerts Mon 1–2pm. www.saintpaulschapel.org. Subway: 2/3 to Park Place; 1/9/4/5/A to Fulton St/Broadway Nassau.*

⑥ ★★ Trinity Church. This neo-Gothic marvel was consecrated in 1846 and is still active today. The main doors, modeled on the doors in Florence's Baptistery, are decorated with biblical scenes; inside are splendid stained-glass windows. *Broadway (at Wall St.). 7am–6pm daily. www.trinitywallstreet.com. Subway: 4/5 to Wall St.*

⑦ Charging Bull Statue. This Wall Street statue is a favorite photo op for visitors. It's across from the **Museum of American Financial History,** where you can explore New York's titanic growth as a financial capital (the Stock Market itself is closed to visitors for security reasons). ⏱ *45 min. 28 Broadway (at Bowling Green Park).* ☎ *212/908-4100. www.financialhistory.org. Tues–Sat 10am–4pm. $2 admission. Subway: 4/5 to Bowling Green; 2/3 to Wall Street.*

⑧ ★★ kids National Museum of the American Indian. This Smithsonian Institution museum is a little-known New York treasure. Not only does the collection span more

Founding Father Alexander Hamilton is buried at Trinity Church.

than 10,000 years of Native heritage, it's housed in a glorious 1907 Beaux Arts building designed by Cass Gilbert. ⏱ *1 hr. 1 Bowling Green.* ☎ *212/514-3700. www.americanindian.si.edu. Free admission. Daily 10am–5pm (Thurs 8pm). Subway: 4/5 to Bowling Green; 1/9 to South Ferry.*

⑨ ★ Stone Street. This is a historic cobblestoned street filled with restaurants. One of the best is **Cassis,** a charming bistro where you can enjoy a salad or pasta dish. *52 Stone St. (btwn William & Pearl sts.)* ☎ *212/425-3663. $–$$.*

⑩ Castle Clinton National Monument. The fort was built between 1808 and 1811 to guard New York Harbor from British forces—but it never had to defend itself. It has served as everything from an immigration landing center

National Museum of the American Indian.

to an opera house to an aquarium. *Southern tip of Battery Park.* ☎ *212/344-7220. Subway: 4/5 to Bowling Green; 1/9 to South Ferry.*

⑪ ★ kids The Statue of Liberty. For the millions who arrived in New York by ship, Lady Liberty was their first glimpse of America. A gift from France to the United States, the statue was designed by sculptor Frédéric-Auguste Bartholdi and unveiled on October 28, 1886. Visitors now have access to the base of the statue and can explore the Statue of Liberty Museum, peer into the inner structure through a glass ceiling near the base of the statue, and enjoy views from the observation deck. *Tip:* The Staten Island Ferry (a free 25 min. trip) provides spectacular skyline views of Manhattan) and is a wonderful way to see the harbor. You'll pass by (though not stop at) the Statue of Liberty and Ellis Island. Check www.siferry.com for more information. ⏱ *1 hr. (ferry ride: 15 min.). On Liberty Island in New York Harbor. Buy tickets online or in Castle Clinton National Monument (see above).* ☎ *212/363-3200 (general info), or 212/269-5755 (ticket/ferry info). www.nps.gov/stli or www.statueofliberty ferry.com. Free admission; ferry ticket to Statue of Liberty & Ellis Island $10 adults, $8 seniors, $4 children 3–17. Daily 9am–5pm (last ferry departs around 4pm); extended hours in summer. Subway: 4/5 to Bowling Green; 1/9 to South Ferry.*

⑫ ★★★ kids Ellis Island. For 62 years (1892–1954) this was the main point of entry for newcomers to America. Today it's one of New York's most moving attractions—particularly for the 40% of Americans whose ancestors passed through the immigration center here. Among the points of interest: the Immigration Museum, which skillfully describes coming to America through the eyes of the immigrants; the American Immigrant Wall of Honor, which commemorates more than 500,000 immigrants and their families; and the American Family Immigration Center, where interactive exhibits can help you research your own family history. ⏱ *90 min. (ferry ride: 10 min. from Liberty Island)* ☎ *212/363-3200. www.nps.gov/elis or www.ellisisland. org. For tickets, see Statue of Liberty, above. Subway: 4/5 to Bowling Green; 1/9 to South Ferry.*

⑬ ★★ Museum of Jewish Heritage—A Living Memorial to the Holocaust. Dedicated to teaching people of all backgrounds about 20th-century Jewish life, this award-winning museum was designed in a six-sided shape to symbolize the Star of David and honor the six million Jews who died in the Holocaust. Inside are photos, artifacts, and moving accounts from survivors. A second-story stone garden —where each of the hollowed-out boulders has a tree growing out of it—overlooks New York Harbor. ⏱ *90 min. 36 Battery Place.* ☎ *646/437-4200. www.mjhnyc.org. Admission $10 adults, $7 seniors, $5 students, free for children under 5. Sun–Wed 10am–5:45pm; Thurs 10am–8pm; Fri & eves of Jewish holidays 10am–3pm. Subway: 4/5 to Bowling Green; 1/9 to South Ferry.*

The Museum of Jewish Heritage.

The Best **in Two Days**

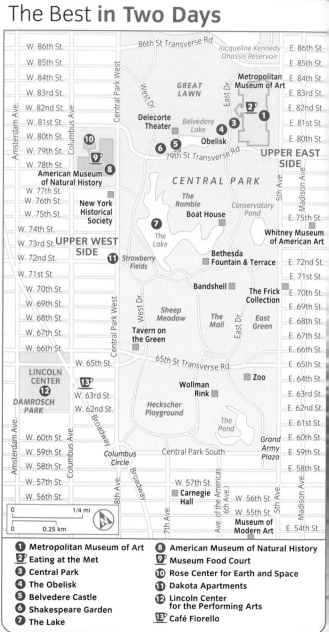

W. 86th St. · 86th St Transverse Rd. · Jacqueline Kennedy Onassis Reservoir · E. 86th St.

W. 85th St. · E. 85th St.

W. 84th St. · **Metropolitan Museum of Art** · E. 84th St.

W. 83rd St. · E. 83rd St.

W. 82nd St. · **2** · E. 82nd St.

W. 81st St. · **3** · E. 81st St.

W. 80th St. · **4** · E. 80th St.

W. 79th St. · **10** · **6** **5** · **Obelisk** · **UPPER EAST SIDE**

W. 78th St. · **9** **8**

American Museum of Natural History

W. 77th St. · **CENTRAL PARK**

W. 76th St. · **New York Historical Society** · The Ramble · Conservatory Pond

W. 75th St. · **Boat House** · E. 75th St.

W. 74th St. · The Lake · **Whitney Museum of American Art**

W. 73rd St. · **UPPER WEST SIDE**

W. 72nd St. · **11** · Strawberry Fields · **Bethesda Fountain & Terrace** · E. 72nd St.

W. 71st St. · E. 71st St.

W. 70th St. · **Bandshell** · **The Frick Collection** · E. 70th St.

W. 69th St. · E. 69th St.

W. 68th St. · Sheep Meadow · The Mall · East Green · E. 68th St.

W. 67th St. · E. 67th St.

W. 66th St. · **Tavern on the Green** · E. 66th St.

W. 65th St. · 65th St Transverse Rd. · E. 65th St.

LINCOLN CENTER · E. 64th St. · **Zoo**

12 · W. 63rd St. · **13** · **Wollman Rink** · E. 63rd St.

DAMROSCH PARK · W. 62nd St. · Heckscher Playground · E. 62nd St.

The Pond · E. 61st St.

W. 60th St. · E. 60th St. · Grand Army Plaza

W. 59th St. · **Columbus Circle** · Central Park South · E. 59th St.

W. 58th St. · E. 58th St.

W. 57th St. · **Carnegie Hall** · W. 57th St.

W. 56th St. · W. 56th St.

W. 55th St.

Museum of Modern Art · E. 54th St.

0 ____ 1/4 mi
0 ____ 0.25 km

Great Lawn · Delacorte Theater · Belvedere Lake · Central Park West · Columbus Ave. · Amsterdam Ave. · West Dr. · East Dr. · Broadway · 5th Ave. · Madison Ave. · 8 Ave. · 7th Ave. · Ave. of the Americas / 6th Ave.

① **Metropolitan Museum of Art**
② **Eating at the Met**
③ **Central Park**
④ **The Obelisk**
⑤ **Belvedere Castle**
⑥ **Shakespeare Garden**
⑦ **The Lake**
⑧ **American Museum of Natural History**
⑨ **Museum Food Court**
⑩ **Rose Center for Earth and Space**
⑪ **Dakota Apartments**
⑫ **Lincoln Center for the Performing Arts**
⑬ **Café Fiorello**

If Lower Manhattan is the city's historic heart, uptown is its artistic soul. It's also home to Central Park, an urban oasis that recharges body and mind. This part of town has a wealth of museums, so to avoid burnout, decide which ones you want to focus on before heading out. If you have kids in tow, I suggest heading to the American Museum of Natural History. START: **Subway 4, 5, or 6 to 86th Street.**

1 ★★★ kids **Metropolitan Museum of Art.** At 1.6 million square feet, this is the largest museum in the Western Hemisphere, attracting five million visitors annually. Nearly all the world's cultures through the ages are on display—from Egyptian mummies to ancient Greek statuary to Islamic carvings to Renaissance paintings to Native American masks to 20th-century decorative arts—and masterpieces are the rule. You could go once a week for a lifetime and still find something new on each visit. My suggestion: To avoid museum burnout, identify two collections to see, and browse other exhibits on

The glass-walled gallery containing the Temple of Dendur has striking Central Park views.

your way to them. Everyone should see the Temple of Dendur, the jewel of the Egyptian collection. But let personal preference be your guide to the rest. My favorite paintings are in the American wing: John Singer Sargent's portrait *Madame X* and Frederic Church's landscape *The Heart of the Andes*. For a full tour of the Met, see p 32. ⏱ *2½ hr. Fifth Ave. (at 82nd St.).* ☎ *212/535-7710. www.metmuseum.org. Admission $12 adults, $7 seniors & students, free for children under 12. Sun, Holiday Mon (Labor Day, Memorial Day, & so forth), & Tues–Thurs 9:30am–5:30pm; Fri–Sat 9:30am–9pm. Subway: 4/5/6 to 86th St. Bus: M1/2/3/4.*

2 **Eating at the Met.** If you're visiting between May and October, check out the Roof Garden's casual **café/bar** ($) and breathtaking treetop view of Central Park. Year-round you can get lunch at the ground-floor **cafeteria** ($) or at the elegant **Petrie Court Café** (☎ 212/570-3964; $$), which overlooks Central Park.

3 ★★★ kids **Central Park.** Manhattanites may not have yards, but they do have this glorious swath of green. Designed by Frederick Law Olmstead and Calvert Vaux in the 1850s, the park is 2½ miles long (extending from 59th to 110th sts.) and a half-mile wide (from Fifth Ave. to Central Park West). It encompasses a zoo, a carousel, two ice-skating rinks, restaurants, children's playgrounds, even theaters. See p 100 for a full tour.

4 **The Obelisk.** Also called Cleopatra's Needle, this 69-foot obelisk is reached by following the path behind the Met leading west. Originally erected in Heliopolis, Egypt around 1475 B.C., it was given to the city by the khedive of Egypt in 1880. Continue on the path to the **Great Lawn,** site of countless softball games, concerts, and peaceful political protests.

5 ★ **Belvedere Castle.** Built by Calvert Vaux in 1869, this fanciful medieval-style fortress-in-miniature sits at the highest point in the park and offers sweeping views. The many birds that call this area home led to the creation of a bird-watching and educational center in the Castle's ranger station. To get here, follow the path across East Drive and walk west.

6 **Shakespeare Garden.** Next to Belvedere Castle, you'll find this garden, where the only flowers and plants in evidence are those mentioned in the Bard's plays.

7 ★★ **The Lake.** South of the garden, you'll cross the 79th Street Transverse Road to reach The Lake, its perimeter pathway lined with weeping willows

The Lake, with Bow Bridge in the background.

and Japanese cherry trees. The neo-Victorian Loeb Boathouse at the east end of the Lake rents rowboats and bicycles; on summer evenings, you can arrange gondola rides. Walk back up to the 79th Street Transverse Road and follow it west; it exits the park at 81st Street and Central Park West.

8 ★★★ kids **American Museum of Natural History.** If you can get past the spectacular entrance—a *Barosaurus,* the world's largest freestanding dinosaur exhibit—you'll have plenty more to see. Founded in 1869, the AMNH houses the world's greatest natural science collection in a square-block group of buildings made of whimsical towers and turrets, pink granite, and red brick. The diversity of the holdings is astounding: some 36 million specimens, ranging from microscopic organisms to the world's largest cut gem, the Brazilian Princess Topaz (21,005 carats). If you only see one exhibit, make it the ★ **dinosaurs**, which take up the entire fourth

The dinosaurs and the Hall of Ocean Life are must-sees at the AMNH

floor. ⏱ *2 hr. Central Park West (btwn 77th & 81st sts.).* ☎ *212/769-5100. www.amnh.org. Admission (includes entrance to Rose Center, below) $12 adults, $9 seniors & students, $7 children 2–12; Space Show (see below) & museum admission $19 adults, $14 seniors & students, $12 children under 12. Daily 10am–5:45pm (Rose Center open Fri to 8:45pm). Subway: B/C to 81st St.*

9 kids **Museum Food Court.** The food court has a selection of fresh salads, pizzas, hot entrees, sandwiches, even sushi. Naturally there's a kids' menu. *$.*

10 ★★ kids **Rose Center for Earth and Space.** Even if you're suffering from museum overload, the Rose Center will lift your spirits. Attached to the American Museum of Natural History, this four-story planetarium is an astonishing sight: a giant sphere in a glass square. Of the Center's several shows, a perennial favorite is "Are We Alone?" narrated by Harrison Ford.

11 **Dakota Apartments.** With its dark and dramatic gables, dormers, and oriel windows, this 1884 apartment house is one of the city's legendary landmarks. Its most famous resident, John Lennon, was gunned down next to the entrance on December 8, 1980; Yoko Ono still lives here. *1 W. 72nd St. (at Central Park West). Subway: 1/2/3/4 to 72nd St.*

12 ★★ **Lincoln Center for the Performing Arts.** New York has countless performing arts venues, but none so revered as Lincoln Center. After a long day on your feet, you can relax on the outdoor plaza in front of the fountains. At night and at Christmas the light displays are particularly lovely, and on some summer evenings there's ballroom dancing. *See p 27.*

13 **Café Fiorello.** If you want to attend a performance at Lincoln Center, this bustling place across the street is a great place for dinner. Main courses can be pricey, but stick to the antipasti (head to the bar where you can drool over the extensive selection of fresh veggies, seafood, and meats) or the ultra-thin crusted pizzas (so large they flop over the edge of the plate) and you can get out of here without doing too much damage. *1900 Broadway (at 64th St.).* ☎ *212/595-5330 $$–$$$.*

The Rose Center for Earth and Space.

The Best **in Three Days**

CENTRAL PARK

Columbus — Central Park South
Circle

Carnegie
Hall — W. 57th St

Grand
Army
Plaza

❶

❷

Aerial Tram

E. 61st St.
E. 60th St.
E. 59th St.

E. 58th St. Sutton
Pl. Sutton
E. 57th St. Sq.

E. 56th St.
E. 55th St.
E. 54th St.
E. 53rd St.

❹❸

American ■
Craft Museum

■ ■ Museum of TV
& Radio

MIDTOWN
EAST

E. 52nd St.
E. 51st St.

Radio City **❺**
Music Hall

❼ St. Patrick's
Cathedral

E. 50th St.

Beekman
Pl.

❻

❽

E. 49th St.
E. 48th St.
E. 47th St.
E. 46th St.

MIDTOWN
WEST

ROCKEFELLER
CENTER

TIMES
SQUARE

W. 42nd St.
BRYANT
PARK

Grand Central
Station

⓫

❿

E. 45th St.
E. 44th St.
E. 43rd St.
E. 42nd St.
E. 41st St.

UNITED
NATIONS

■ Port Authority
Bus Terminal

❾

⓬

MURRAY
HILL

E. 40th St.
E. 39th St.

East River

Pierpont Morgan
Library ■

E. 38th St.
E. 37th St.
E. 36th St.
E. 35th St.

Macy's ■

Main Post
Office
✉

Penn
Station

Empire State
■ Building

⓭

E. 34th St.
E. 33rd St.
E. 32nd St.
E. 31st St.
E. 30th St.
E. 29th St.

Madison
Square
Garden

W. 28th St.

E. 28th St.
E. 27th St.

W. 27th St.
W. 26th St.
W. 25th St.
W. 24th St.
W. 23rd St.
W. 22nd St.
W. 21st St.
W. 20th St.
W. 19th St.
W. 18th St.

MADISON
SQUARE
PARK

■
Flatiron
Building

FLATIRON
DISTRICT

GRAMERCY
PARK

GRAMERCY
PARK

■ Theodore
Roosevelt
Birthplace

E. 25th St.
E. 24th St.
E. 23rd St.
E. 22nd St.
E. 21st St.
E. 20th St.
E. 19th St.
E. 18th St.
E. 17th St.

24TH
STREET
PARK

PETER COOPER
VILLAGE

STUYVESANT
TOWN

⓯

W. 17th St.
W. 16th St.
W. 15th St.
W. 14th St.
W. 13th St.

UNION
SQUARE

⓮

E. 16th St.
E. 15th St.
E. 14th St.

0   1/4 mi
0   0.25 km

❶ The Plaza	**❾** New York Public Library
❷ Fifth Avenue	**❿** Grand Central Terminal
❸ Museum of Modern Art.	**⓫** Grand Central food court
❹ Café 2	**⓬** Chrysler Building
❺ Radio City Music Hall	**⓭** Empire State Building
❻ Rockefeller Center	**⓮** Union Square Greenmarket
❼ St. Patrick's Cathedral	**⓯** Rubin Museum of Art
❽ Saks Fifth Avenue	

You've discovered downtown and uptown, and now it's time to hit midtown, the city's business and commercial center. But it's not all about corporate skyscrapers and designer shops; this tour will also introduce you to many quintessential New York landmarks. START: **Subway N, R, or W to Fifth Avenue/59th Street.**

① ★ **The Plaza.** There's no denying the glamour of the Big Apple's most famous hotel. This 1907 landmark French Renaissance palace has hosted royalty, celebrities, and a legion of honeymooners. Scott and Zelda frolicked in the Pulitzer Fountain out front. *768 Fifth Ave. (at Central Park South). Subway: N/R/W to Fifth Ave./59th St.*

② ★★ **Fifth Avenue.** New York's most famous style-and-shopping artery starts at the southeast corner of Central Park at 59th Street. Some landmarks to note: **FAO Schwarz,** at no. 767 (58th St.), the city's best toy emporium, **Tiffany & Co.,** at no. 727 (btwn 56th & 57th sts.), with its stainless-steel doors and Atlas clock; gilded **Trump Tower,** at no. 725 (56th St.), with a seven-story waterfall and pinkish granite walls; **Henri Bendel,** at no. 712 (btwn 55th & 56th sts.), the city's most whimsical department store; and **Takashimaya,** at no. 693 (btwn 54th & 55th sts.), a branch of Japan's popular department store. *Subway: N/R/W to Fifth Ave./59th St.*

③ ★★★ **Museum of Modern Art.** MoMA boasts the world's greatest collection of painting and sculpture from the late 19th century to the present, including everything from Monet's *Water Lilies* and Klimt's *The Kiss* to later masterworks by Frida Kahlo, Edward Hopper, Andy Warhol, and Jasper Johns. Add to that a vast collection of modern drawings, photos, architectural models and modern furniture, iconic design objects ranging from tableware to sports cars, and film and

The Museum of Modern Art.

video. A massive 3 year, $650-million renovation project—under the guidance of Japanese architect Yoshio Taniguchi—was completed in 2004. It's twice as big, and, many critics contend, better. Paul Goldberger, writing in *The New Yorker,* said "The old building looks better than it has in half a century, both inside and out. ⏱ *2 hr. 11 W. 53rd St. (btwn Fifth & Sixth aves.). ☎ 212/708-9400. www.moma.org. Admission $20 adults, $16 seniors, $12 students, kids 16 & under free when accompanied by an adult. Sat–Mon & Wed–Thurs 10:30am–5:30pm; Fri 10:30am–8pm. Subway: E/V to Fifth Ave./53rd St.; B/D/F to 47th–50th sts.*

④ **Café 2.** On the second floor of the new MoMA, a cafeteria style restaurant has Italian-inspired offerings. Rest your feet and enjoy pastas, panini, pizza, salads, and soups. *$–$$.*

The Rockefeller Center skating rink is open mid-October to mid-March.

⑤ ★★ Radio City Music Hall.

Designed by Donald Deskey and opened in 1932, this sumptuous Art Deco classic is the world's largest indoor theater, with 6,200 seats. Long known for its Rockettes revues and popular Christmas show, Radio City also has a stellar history as a venue for movie premieres, having opened more than 700 movies since 1933. **Insider tip:** The "powder rooms" are some of the swankiest in town. *1260 Sixth Ave. (at 50th St.).* ☎ *212/247-4777. www.radiocity.com. 1-hr. Stage Door Tour is daily 11am to 3pm (extended hours Nov 15-Dec 30). Tickets $17 adults, $14 seniors, $10 children under 12. Subway: B/D/F/V to 47th–50th sts/Rockefeller Center.*

⑥ ★★ Rockefeller Center. A

prime example of the city's sky-scraper spirit and historic sense of optimism, Rock Center was built mainly in the 1930s. Designated a National Historic Landmark in 1988, it's now the world's largest privately owned business-and entertainment center, with 18 buildings on 21 acres. The **GE Building,** at 30 Rock-efeller Plaza, is a 70-story show-piece towering over the plaza; walk through the granite-and-marble lobby lined with monumental murals by Spanish painter José Maria Sert

(1874–1945). The mammoth Rocke-feller Christmas tree is traditionally placed in the plaza fronting 30 Rock. *Bounded by 48th & 51st sts. & Fifth & Sixth aves. Subway: B/D/F/V to 47th–50th sts/Rockefeller Center.*

⑦ ★★ St. Patrick's Cathedral.

This Gothic white-marble-and-stone wonder is the largest Roman Catholic cathedral in the United States. Designed by James Renwick, begun in 1859, and consecrated in 1879, St. Patrick's wasn't completed until 1906. You can pop in between serv-ices to get a look at the impressive interior. The St. Michael and St. Louis altar came from Tiffany & Co. (also on Fifth Ave.), while the St. Elizabeth altar—honoring Mother Elizabeth Ann Seton, the first American-born saint—was designed by Paolo Medici of Rome. *Fifth Ave. (btwn 50th & 51st sts.).* ☎ *212/753-2261. www.ny-archdiocese.org/pastoral/cathedral_about.html. Free admission. Sun–Fri 7am–8:30pm; Sat 8am–8:30pm. Subway: B/D/F/V to 47th–50th sts./ Rockefeller Center.*

⑧ Saks Fifth Avenue. At this

quintessential New York luxury

The door to St. Patrick's Cathedral.

Occasionally the library lions don construction or baseball hats.

⑩ ★★ Grand Central Terminal. Another Beaux Arts beauty. The highlight is the vast, imposing main concourse, where high windows allow sunlight to pour onto the half-acre Tennessee-marble floor. Everything gleams, from the brass clock over the central kiosk to the gold-and nickel-plated chandeliers piercing the side archways. The breathtaking **sky ceiling** depicts the constellations of the winter sky above New York. *42nd St. & Park Ave.* ☎ *212/340-2210. www.grand centralterminal.com. Subway: 4/5/6/ 7/S to 42nd St.*

retailer even the elaborate window displays are a treat. *611 Fifth Ave. (at 50th St.)* ☎ *212/753-4000. www.saks fifthavenue.com/. Subway: B/D/F/V to 47th–50th sts/Rockefeller Center.*

⑨ ★ New York Public Library. The lions *Patience* and *Fortitude* stand guard outside the grand Fifth Avenue entrance of the library, designed by Carrère & Hastings in 1911 and one of the country's finest examples of Beaux Arts architecture. Sadly, architect John Mervin Carrère never got to enjoy the fruits of his labor; he was killed in a taxi accident 2 months before the library dedication. The majestic white-marble structure is filled with Corinthian columns and allegorical statues. Special exhibits inside have run the gamut, from Imperial Russia to Newtonian Thought. *Fifth Ave. (btwn 42nd & 40th sts.).* ☎ *212/ 661-7220. www.nypl.org. Open Tues– Wed & Sat 11am–6pm; Thurs–Fri 10am–6pm, Sun 1pm–5pm. Subway: B/D/F/V to 42nd St.*

⑪ ★ Grand Central food court. I know people who go way out of their way to eat on the lower level at Grand Central. From hearty Mexican (Zocalo) to Creole (Jacques Imo's) to top-notch soup (Hale & Hearty), Indian (Spice), and pizza (Two Boots), the choices are extensive and quick, and the seating plentiful. *$–$$.*

⑫ ★★ Chrysler Building. Built as the Chrysler Corporation headquarters in 1930, this local favorite is New York's most romantic Art Deco masterpiece. It's especially dramatic at night, when the lights in its triangular openings play off its steely crown. And don't overlook the gargoyles

The sky ceiling at Grand Central.

The Chrysler's Building's gargoyles resemble hood ornaments on a car.

reaching out from the upper floors. *405 Lexington Ave. (btwn 42nd & 43rd sts.). Subway: 4/5/6 to Grand Central.*

⑬ ★★ **Empire State Building.** King Kong climbed it in 1933. A plane slammed into it in 1945. After September 11, 2001, the Empire State regained its status as New York City's tallest building. Through it all, it has remained one of the city's favorite landmarks. Completed in 1931, the limestone-and–stainless steel Art Deco dazzler climbs 103 stories (1,454 ft.). The best views are from the 86th- and 102nd-floor observatories, but I prefer the former, from which you can walk onto an outer windswept deck. From here the citywide panorama is magnificent. ⏱ *1 hr. 350 Fifth Ave. (at 34th St.).* ☎ *212/736-3100. www. esbnyc.com. Observatory admission $10 adults, $9 seniors & children 12–17, $5 children 6–11, free for children under 6. Buy & print tickets in advance online to avoid lines. Mon–Fri 10am–midnight; Sat–Sun 9:30am–midnight; tickets sold until 11:25pm. Subway: 6 to 33rd St.; B/D/F/V to 34th St.*

⑭ ★★ **Union Square Greenmarket.** The farm comes to the city at Manhattan's largest greenmarket. You'll find fresh produce from upstate and New Jersey farms, just-off-the-boat fish from Long Island, artisanal cheeses and homecured meats, plants, and organic herbs and spices. I've seen celebrated chefs arrive here with wheelbarrows in tow. *In Union Square.* ☎ *212/477-3220. www.cenyc.org. Open year-round Mon, Wed, Fri & Sat during daylight hours. Subway: 4/5/6/N/Q/R/W to Union Square.*

⑮ ★★ **Rubin Museum of Art.** New York must have some good karma: In October 2004 it scored this stunning collection of Himalayan art. In the former Chelsea outpost of Barneys, the Rubin Museum features sculptures, paintings, and textiles. ⏱ *90 min. 150 W. 17th St. (btwn Sixth & Seventh aves.).* ☎ *212/620-5000. www.rmanyc.org. Admission $7 adults, $5 seniors & students, free for children under 12. Tues & Sat 11am–7pm; Thurs–Fri 11am–9pm; Wed, Sun, & public holidays 11am–5pm; closed Jan 1, Thanksgiving, & Dec 25. Subway: 1/9 to 18th St.* ●

The Empire State Building.

2 Special-Interest Tours

Romantic New York

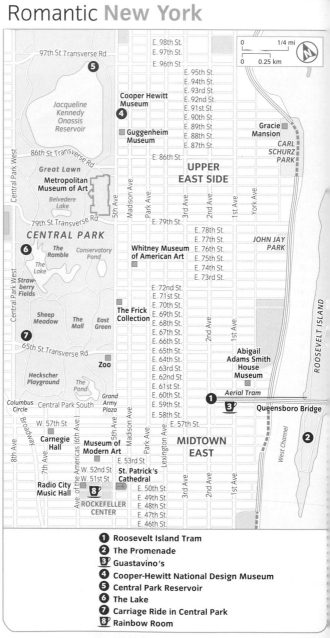

1 Roosevelt Island Tram
2 The Promenade
3 Guastavino's
4 Cooper-Hewitt National Design Museum
5 Central Park Reservoir
6 The Lake
7 Carriage Ride in Central Park
8 Rainbow Room

New York is revered for its high-energy, never-say-die attitude. But to my mind, the city harbors a romantic streak as wide as the Hudson River—it just takes a little longer to uncover. This tour introduces you to places that are perfect to discover as a twosome. START: **Subway 4, 5, 6, N, R, or W to 59th Street.**

❶ ★★ Roosevelt Island Tram. Roosevelt Island residents who ride the tram back and forth to the city every day are privy to one of the city's best-kept secrets: The view from the tram is one of the city's most dramatic. Each way is only 4 minutes long, but the panorama will leave you breathless: As you look down the East River, you'll see four bridges (Queensboro, Williamsburg, Manhattan, and Brooklyn). You can even see Lady Liberty on a clear day. Leave the tram station via the east exit and walk toward the water and Manhattan skyline. *Second Ave. & 59th St. Fare $2. Subway: 4/5/6/N/R/W to 59th St.*

❷ The Promenade. Roosevelt Island's beautiful East River walkway is famous for its romantic Manhattan views. But you'll have a very different experience depending on whether you walk north or south of the Queensboro Bridge. The south promenade is the most scenic, and

it's lined with wooden benches that are shaded by leafy trees; I love sitting here and taking in the view of the Chrysler Building. The only downside is that everyone else loves the view from here, too. The north promenade is much more private; after you pass the seawall and pier you won't see many people. There aren't any benches either, but this part of the promenade is just wide enough for two people to walk side-by-side. Either way, when you've finished admiring the skyline, take the tram back to Manhattan.

❸ Guastavino's. This dramatic setting under the Queensboro Bridge is perfect for romantics. From the upstairs bar (which serves lunch), diners have sweeping views of the restaurant's stone pillars, granite walls, intricate tilework, and soaring, vaulted ceilings. From May to October, you can dine on the

The Roosevelt Island Tram.

The Cooper-Hewitt is the only U.S. museum dedicated to design.

more casual menu at Guastavino Café ($–$$$) on the outdoor terrace. *409 E. 59th St (btwn First Ave. & Sutton Place).* ☎ *212/421-6644. www.guastavinos.com. $$$–$$$$.*

④ ★★ Cooper-Hewitt National Design Museum. Yes, museums can be romantic, especially when they are as richly appointed as this one. The 64-room mansion, with sumptuous oak paneling and a truly grand staircase (one, a critic noted, "you could drive a Sherman tank up"), was steel industrialist Andrew Carnegie's private home. After a $20-million renovation in 1974, the house became part of the Smithsonian Institution, with 11,000 square feet of gallery space devoted to industrial design, drawings, textiles, wall coverings, books, and prints. Spend time in the garden, quite possibly the most idyllic oasis in New York; Carnegie deliberately built his home farther north than his contemporaries in order to have room to create this spectacular, private space. Steal a kiss in the lovely glass conservatory—you won't be

the first. ⏱ *1½–2 hr. 2 E. 91st St. (at Fifth Ave.).* ☎ *212/849-8400. www.ndm.si.edu. Admission $10 adults, $7 seniors & students, free for children under 12. Tues–Thurs 10am–5pm; Fri 10am–9pm; Sat 10am–6pm; Sun noon–5pm. Subway: 4/5/6 to 86th St.*

⑤ Central Park Reservoir. You've probably already seen this oasis dozens of times on film and on television. The 106-acre body of water was created in 1862 to supply the city's water system, but was designed with beauty in mind: It's surrounded by bridle and jogging paths (the path that rings it is 1½ miles long) and has both east and west views of the elegant high-rises surrounding the park. *Central Park, 85th to 96th sts.*

⑥ ★★ The Lake. Ella Fitzgerald sang "I love the rowing on Central Park Lake" in "The Lady Is a Tramp," and when you see the shimmering waters edged by weeping willows and Japanese cherry trees, you'll understand why it inspired songwriters Rodgers and Hart. The green banks along the man-made lake slope gently toward the water—and are perfect for picnics. You can rent a rowboat for two at the neo-Victorian

The Reservoir is a great place for a stroll.

The view from the Rainbow Room.

Loeb Boathouse at the east end of the lake. The boathouse also has a seasonal outside bar with terrace seating overlooking the lake. It's a pleasant spot to enjoy a glass of wine, but can get quite crowded in the early evening. *Mid-Park from 71st to 78th sts.*

7 Carriage Ride in Central Park. Why resist? Although it sounds cheesy, it's actually a lot of fun, not to mention romantic. I think they're particularly special in winter, when the park is hushed by snow, and you can snuggle under a heavy blanket. Rides run roughly $40 for 20 minutes. To continue the tour, tell the driver to drop you off on Central Park South near Sixth Avenue, and then sit back and enjoy the scenery—and the company. You can usually find a carriage on Central Park South (near Seventh Ave.) or you can catch one at Tavern on the Green on the west side of the park at 68th Street (one or two are generally pulled up outside).

8 ★ Dinner & Drinks. A drink at the **Rainbow Room** is a classic way to appreciate the city at dusk. The cocktails may be pricey, but it's really the fabulous views you're paying for. As your sip your drink, gaze out the floor-to-ceiling windows onto millions of tiny lights twinkling in midtown, as well as the Empire State Building and the Brooklyn Bridge. When you're ready for your romantic dinner a deux, head to **One If By Land, Two If By Sea** (p 121) if money is no object, and **Cafe St. Bart's** (p 117) if it is. *Rainbow Room: 30 Rockefeller Plaza (at 49th St.).* ☎ *212/632-5000. www.rainbowroom.com. Cocktails: $$$.*

A carriage ride through Central Park.

New York for **Music Lovers**

1. Louis Armstrong House Museum
2. MTV Studios
3. Virgin Megastore
4. TKTS
5. Music Store Row
6. The Brill Building
7. Carnegie Hall
8. Lincoln Center for the Performing Arts
9. Cafe Vienna
10. Strawberry Fields
11. Dakota Apartments
12. Minton's Playhouse

New York is a world-class stage. Many famous musicians got their breaks in the Big Apple, and many others have called it home. No one-note town, this is a city with something for every musical taste, from classical to experimental, jazz to post–alt rock. If you want to extend your tour into the evening by taking advantage of New York's live music scene, check the listings in chapter 8, "Arts & Entertainment." START: **Subway 7 to 103rd Street-Corona Plaza, Queens. Walk north on 103rd Street, turn right on Thirty-Seventh Avenue, then left onto 107th Street.**

---

① ★ **Louis Armstrong House Museum.** Legendary jazz trumpeter Louis Armstrong was born and bred in New Orleans, but he lived in this unassuming house in working-class Queens from 1943 until his death in 1971. Unassuming, that is, until you open the door: Inside, the decor is exuberantly kitschy (turquoise kitchen! bathroom with floor-to-ceiling mirrors!), and a hidden sound system plays Satchmo's music as well as excerpts from his home-recorded tapes (in his famously gravelly voice, he tells jokes and has conversations with his wife, Lucille, who lived here until 1983). After their deaths, the house became both a National Historic Landmark and a New York City Landmark, and in 2003 it opened to the public as a museum. It's so intimate and personal that visitors get a real sense of how the Armstrongs lived. The house includes a gift shop and some of Armstrong's memorabilia,

Louis Armstrong's mirrored bathroom.

including two of his trumpets. ⏱ *1 hr. 34–56 107th St. (btwn 37th & 34th aves.), Corona, Queens.* ☎ *718/478-8274. www.satchmo.net. Admission $8 adults, $6 seniors & children. Tues–Fri 10am–5pm; Sat–Sun noon–5pm. Subway: 7 to 103rd St.–Corona Plaza. Walk north on 103rd St., turn right on Thirty-Seventh Ave., then left onto 107th St.*

② **kids** **MTV Studios.** Fans of "Total Request Live" can gather outside the studio where the show is filmed to catch a glimpse of whichever pop star is scheduled for that day. *1515 Broadway (btwn 44th & 45th sts.).* ☎ *212/398-8549 for advance audience tickets (must be 18–24). www.mtv.com. Tapings Mon–Fri 3:30pm. Subway: 1/2/3/7/9/A/C/E/N/R/S to 42nd St.*

③ **Virgin Megastore.** *See p 97.*

④ **TKTS.** For details on buying discount tickets to Broadway musicals, see "Getting Tickets" on p 147.

⑤ **Music Store Row.** If you're in the market to buy a new guitar (or just want to indulge your inner rock star) check out the stores on this block. (One of my favorites: **Sam Ash** at no. 160.) In window after window you'll see musical instruments, recording equipment, guitars, keyboards, drums, sheet music, and more. *W. 48th St. (btwn Sixth & Seventh aves.). Subway: 1/9 to 50th St; N/R to 49th St; B/D/F/V to 47th–50th St.*

6 The Brill Building. This 1931 Deco structure was the center of the music world in the early 1960s, providing office and recording space for 165 music businesses and many of the masters of '60s pop and early rock 'n' roll. It was here that producer Phil Spector worked, and several celebrated songwriting teams created a golden age of classics: Goffin & King ("Up on the Roof," "Will You Love Me Tomorrow?"); Mann and Weil ("You've Lost That Lovin' Feeling"); Leiber & Stoller ("Stand by Me," "Hound Dog"); Greenwich & Barry ("Be My Baby"). *1619 Broadway (at 49th St.). Subway: 1/9 to 50th St; N/R to 49th St; B/D/F/V to 47th–50th St.*

7 ★ Carnegie Hall. How do you get to Carnegie Hall? Practice, practice, practice, as the joke goes. Perhaps the world's most famous performance space, Carnegie Hall features everything from orchestral classics to solo sitar. The **Isaac Stern Auditorium,** the 2,804-seat main hall, welcomes visiting orchestras from around the world. There's also the intimate 268-seat **Weill Recital Hall,** and the ornate underground 650-seat **Zankel Concert Hall.** Tickets for the 1-hour tours are available at the box office. ⏱ *1 hr. (for tour). 881 Seventh Ave. (at 56th St.).* ☎ *212/247-7800, or 212/903-9765 for tour information. www.carnegiehall.org. Tours cost $9 adults; $6 children or seniors and are offered Mon–Fri 11:30am, 2pm & 3pm. Subway: A/B/C/D/1/9 to Columbus Circle; N/Q/R/W to 57th St./Seventh Ave.*

Isaac Stern Auditorium at Carnegie Hall.

8 ★★★ Lincoln Center for the Performing Arts. The world's largest performing arts center was built between 1962 and 1968 and is home to 12 resident arts organizations. *Note:* By the time you read this, work may have started on a major $475-million renovation; plans are underway to renovate the facades of many of the buildings described below and complete a landscape redesign. One of the best ways to get an overview is to take the daily hour-long tour (☎ **212/875-5350**), which must be reserved in advance.

9 Cafe Vienna. Grab coffee and a pastry or a sandwich here and, if it's a nice day, head outside to the reflecting pool in front of the Performing Arts Library. *Avery Fisher Hall. No phone. Lincoln Center. $.*

10 Strawberry Fields. At this memorial to John Lennon you'll almost always find an offering of strewn flower

The Brill Building.

Exploring Lincoln Center

While you're wandering around Lincoln Center, take some time to sit on **Josie Robertson Plaza,** which is particularly seductive at dusk with its fountains and floodlights. All summer long Lincoln Center holds events here and at **Damrosch Plaza**. Two popular ones are "Midsummer's Night Swing," devoted to ballroom dancing, and "Lincoln Center Out of Doors," with free music and dance performances. **The Juilliard School** (☎ 212/799-5000; www.juilliard.edu), the nation's premier arts education institution, presents free performances almost daily. **The Film Society of Lincoln Center** (☎ 212/875-5600), which hosts the New York Film Festival and screens films year-round, is inside the Samuel B. and David Rose Building. **The New York Public Library for the Performing Arts** (☎ 212/870-1630) has excellent arts-related collections and temporary exhibits. You can listen to music and watch films of dance and theatrical performances from the extensive archives.

petals and a guitarist strumming Beatles tunes (more or less on-key). *Just inside the 72nd St. entrance to Central Park. Subway: B/C to 72nd St.*

⑪ Dakota Apartments. This historic 1882 address has long been home to artists and musicians, including Leonard Bernstein and singer Roberta Flack. But it's most notorious as the site where John Lennon lived, and where he died, on December 8, 1980, when he was shot by a deranged fan near the entrance. Another musician, Madonna, tried to buy an apartment here but was famously turned down by the co-op board. *1 W. 72nd St.*

Subway: B/C to 72nd St. (at Central Park West).

⑫ Minton's Playhouse. Bebop reigned at this Harlem jazz club in the 1940s, where legendary Monday-night after-hours jam sessions attracted the likes of Dizzy Gillespie, Charlie Parker, and Thelonious Monk. After 30 years of being shuttered down, this designated city landmark is expected to reopen as a jazz club in 2006, complete with the original 1948 mural that some say shows Billie Holiday sleeping off a drunk. *210 W. 118th St. (at Seventh Ave.). Subway: A/B/C/D to 116th St.*

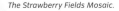

The Strawberry Fields Mosaic.

New York for **Fashionistas**

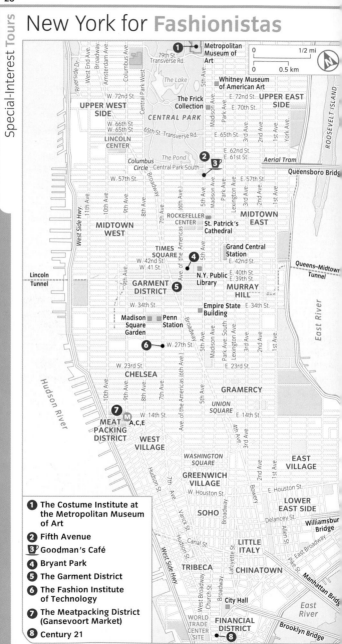

1 The Costume Institute at the Metropolitan Museum of Art

2 Fifth Avenue

3 Goodman's Café

4 Bryant Park

5 The Garment District

6 The Fashion Institute of Technology

7 The Meatpacking District (Gansevoort Market)

8 Century 21

Ｎew York is a fertile breeding ground for fashion. Inspiration is everywhere in this cross-cultural stew, where exotica from all over the world is rapidly absorbed into the fashion slipstream and then promptly disseminated through a wide variety of outlets, from the high-end retailers of Fifth Avenue to the gritty storefronts of the East Village. START: **Subway 4, 5, or 6 to 86th Street.**

❶ The Costume Institute at the Metropolitan Museum of Art. Fashion may be fickle, but this collection shows how knowing the past is essential to designing for the future. Among the hundreds of articles in the collection are a French silk corset from the 1700s (complete with baleen—whale cartilage—wire), a shoe buckle from 400 A.D., and 17th-century silk robes from Japan. Particularly inspiring are the early-20th-century pieces from such illustrious designers as Chanel, Schiaparelli, Lanvin, Dior, Givenchy, and Courrèges. 🕐 *1 hr. 1000 Fifth Ave. (at 82nd St.).* ☎ *212/535-7710. www.metmuseum.org. Admission $12 adults. Tues–Thurs & Sun 9:30am–5:30pm; Fri–Sat 9:30am–9pm. Subway: 4/5/6 to 86th St.*

❷ Fifth Avenue. New York's most famous shopping artery extends southward from the corner

"The Souper Dress" at the Costume Institute is made of paper.

of Central Park West and 59th Street. It's a great street to window-shop. Some landmarks: **Tiffany & Co.,** at no. 727, where you can browse for serious baubles; **Henri Bendel,** at no. 712 (56th St.), a department store known for its whimsical displays and cutting-edge cosmetics; **Takashimaya,** at no. 693 (54th St.), a branch of Japan's most famous department store; and **Saks Fifth Avenue,** at no. 611 (50th St.), the quintessential New York luxury retailer. Not every fashionable shop on Fifth is priced sky-high: Cheap-chic pieces for men and women are available at **H&M** at no. 640, and at **Mexx** at no. 650. *Subway: N/R/W to Fifth Ave./59th St.*

❸ Goodman's Cafe. Tucked away on the seventh floor of the luxury retailer **Bergdorf Goodman** is a snazzy cafe/restaurant crammed with ladies who lunch and shop. It's not just the convenient location that packs 'em in, but the food: It's really, really good, from sublime sweet-pea soup to mountainous veggie salads. *754 Fifth Ave. (at 58th St.).* ☎ *212/872-8708. Subway: N/R to Fifth Ave. $$.*

❹ Bryant Park. During most of the year, Bryant Park is a peaceful oasis of green in midtown, just behind the New York Public Library. But when the New York Fashion Week circus comes to town in spring and fall, the park is mobbed with designers, models, fashion editors, photographers, and dedicated fashionistas. Year-round the **Bryant**

Models strut the catwalk at Bryant Park during Fashion Week.

Park Grill (25 W. 40th St. [btwn Fifth & Sixth aves.]; ☎ 212/840-6500; $$–$$$) is a terrific spot for lunch, either indoors or on the garden patio. In summer, Bryant Park hosts a **Summer Film Festival** (☎ 212/512-5700) with classic film screenings on Monday evenings at dusk (usually between 8 and 9pm.) Tuesday is the rain date. The lawn opens at 5pm for blankets and picnics. Early risers can check out the *Good Morning America* concerts that take place at 7am on the Upper Terrace (see http://abcnews.go.com for details). *Bordered by 40th and 42nd sts. & Fifth and Sixth aves. Subway: B/D/F/V to 42nd St.*

❺ **The Garment District.** If Fifth Avenue is the city's shopping show-case, Seventh Avenue is the work-shop, where many of America's top fashion designers have offices. It's also the home of the knock-off, where so-called "garmentos" design cheap copies of couture or filter out the less commercial elements to make clothing for the mass market. Few clothes are actually made in the District, but you can shop here—and snatch up some great bargains. Most labels host seasonal sample sales in the neighborhood. (For more information, see the following page.) *Bordered by 41st St., Fifth Ave., 35th St., & Ninth Ave. Subway: 1/2/3/7/9/A/C/E/S to 42nd St.*

❻ **The Fashion Institute of Technology.** This school has pro-duced some of the country's best designers, and its stunning museum is one of New York's hidden gems. The small horseshoe-shaped gallery features changing exhibits that usually focus on the 20th century; subjects have included movie-star glamour, couture accessories, and a Manolo Blahnik retrospective. ⏱ *45 min. Seventh Ave. & 27th St. ☎ 212/217-5800. www.fitnyc.edu. Free admission. Open Tues–Fri noon–8pm; Sat 10am–5pm. Subway: 1/9 to 28th St.*

Shopping at Century 21.

Sample Sales

New York changed the way I shop. Forget trendy boutiques: I've fallen hard for sample sales, where designers unload last season's merchandise for a song. A sale can run for a day or a week, and discounts begin around 60% off (and may go as high as 80%). On any given day you might score a cashmere sweater, Italian leather shoes, even 400-thread-count linens. Some sample sales are held in designer showrooms, but the auditorium at the **Parsons School of Design** (40th St. and Seventh Ave.; ☎ **212/229-8987**) hosts many of the biggest sales, so don't be surprised if you see a queue here that stretches around the corner. Visit **www.newyorkmetro.com**, **www.topbutton.com**, or **www.dailycandy.com** before your trip for locations and hours. You can also cruise the Garment District along Seventh Avenue between 40th and 28th streets and pick up flyers for current sales. The ground rules: Forget modesty (few sales have changing rooms), go early (lines can stretch around the block), and avoid lunchtime (that's when sharp-elbowed New Yorkers arrive). And remember, *all* sales are final.

7 The Meatpacking District (Gansevoort Market). Not too long ago, only butchers had wares here. Now it's Manhattan's trendiest neighborhood, with countless designer boutiques. On 14th Street between Ninth and Tenth avenues, you'll find designers **Alexander McQueen** at no. 417 and **Stella McCartney** at no. 429. **Jeffrey New York** at no. 449, is an upscale department store with an amazing shoe collection. Wander south of 14th Street along the cobblestone streets and you'll find **Scoop** (873 Washington St.), a hip clothing boutique for men and women; **Boucher Jewelry** (9 Ninth Ave.), selling frothy necklaces, bracelets, and earrings in pretty pastels; and

Catherine Malandrino (652 Hudson St.), with handsome French-influenced women's designs. *Bordered by W. 15th St., Hudson St., Gansevoort St., & Eleventh Ave. Subway: 1/9 to 14th St.*

8 Century 21. This is a don't-miss spot for shoppers who love a deal. On its four floors of discounted merchandise—including clothes for women, men, and kids, as well as housewares and linens—you'll find designer names such as Diane Von Furstenberg, Tracy Reese, Giorgio Armani, Elie Tahari, and Jean-Paul Gaultier. *22 Cortland St. (at Broadway).* ☎ *212/227-9092. Subway: A/C to Fulton St.*

The Metropolitan Museum of Art & the Cloisters

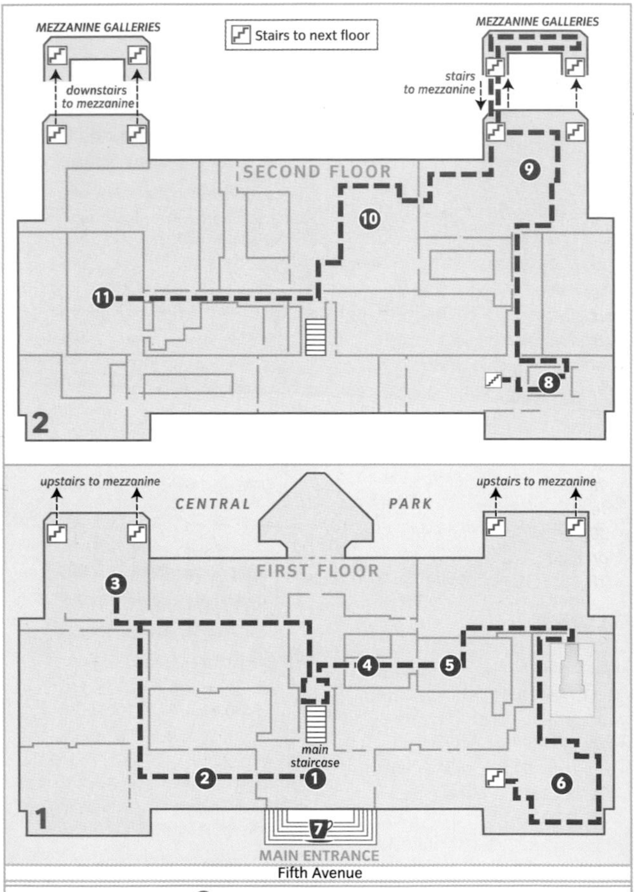

MEZZANINE GALLERIES

Stairs to next floor

MEZZANINE GALLERIES

downstairs to mezzanine

stairs to mezzanine

SECOND FLOOR

⑨

⑩

⑪

⑧

2

upstairs to mezzanine

CENTRAL   PARK

upstairs to mezzanine

FIRST FLOOR

❸

❹   ❺

main staircase

❷   ❶

❻

1

❼

MAIN ENTRANCE

Fifth Avenue

❶ The Great Hall
❷ Greek and Roman Galleries
❸ Modern Wing
❹ European Sculpture and Decorative Arts
❺ Arms & Armor
❻ Egyptian Art
❼ A Meal at the Met
❽ Asian Art
❾ American Wing
❿ European Paintings, The Old Masters
⓫ European Paintings, The 19th Century

In 1866 a group of New Yorkers decided their hometown needed a museum that would function as a living encyclopedia of world art. Today the Met fulfills that promise with a collection of more than two million objects dating from the Paleolithic period (300,00–75,000 B.C.) to the early 21st century (that is, now) and originating from every continent except Antarctica. START: **Subway 4, 5, or 6 to 86th Street.**

❶ The Great Hall. The main entrance to the Met is meant to make you feel like royalty. With its soaring domes, elegant balconies, restrained use of Greco-Roman motifs, it is a fine example of neo-classical architecture. ⏲ *3–4 hr. If you're in a rush, skip the main entrance on 82nd & enter through 81st St. The least crowded times are Fri & Sat nights or right at opening. Fifth Ave. & 82nd St.* ☎ *212/535-7710. www.metmuseum. org. $12 adults, $7 seniors & students, free for children under 12. Open Sun & Tues–Thurs 9:30am–5:30pm; Fri–Sat 9:30am–9pm. Closed Mon & holidays. Subway 4/5/6 to 86th St.*

The Met's Great Hall.

❷ ★★ Greek and Roman Galleries. These galleries take you from prehistory to the Roman Empire. Start with the Minoan *Seated Harp Player.* His open, upturned face and slightly lifted feet instantly convey that he is lost in his silent, ancient music. The many examples of black and red pottery will give you an idea of daily life in ancient Greece. Check out the statue of the Greek woman at the end of the sculpture gallery. The naturalistic display of her linen dress and wool shawl knocks me out.

❸ ★ Modern Wing. Head through the galleries of the Arts of Africa, Oceania, and the Americas to get to the Modern Wing, which is full of blockbuster artists. Must-sees include Picasso's *Gertrude Stein,* Jackson Pollock's *Autumn Rhythm,* and Edward Hopper's *The Lighthouse at Two Lights.* If you need a jolt of energy, seek out Charles Demuth's *The Figure 5 in Gold,* an iconic American image that radiates frenetic movement and was responsible for influencing the Pop artists of the 1950s.

❹ European Sculpture and Decorative Arts. My favorite spot in these galleries filled with period rooms is the astonishing **Studiolo Gubbio.** The walls of this small Renaissance study are covered in elaborate wood panels inlaid with thousands of pieces of wood to give the illusion of a room lined with cabinets containing books, musical instruments, and scientific tools.

5 ★ **kids** **Arms & Armor.** The full sets of European armor in the courtyard are dazzling, but make sure you pop into the smaller galleries that surround the court. Here you'll find curiosities like ceremonial saddles carved from bone and pistols inlaid with semi-precious stones. The late **Ottoman Empire sword** created in 1876 is a miracle of sparkling diamonds, smooth-as-ice jade, and rich gold work.

6 ★★★ **kids** **Egyptian Art.** The **Temple of Dendur,** built in 15 B.C., is arguably the most famous object at the Met. Inside, you'll find graffiti from Victorian-era travelers. For a glimpse of daily life in ancient Egypt, check out the 13 wooden models from the **tomb of Meketra.** These models represent Meketra's wealth on earth that is to be taken with him into the afterlife. They show his bakery, his dairy, his beer-producing facility, and boats.

7 **A Meal at the Met.** If it's a nice day, head outside the main entrance and get a snack from one of the carts ($) on the plaza. The food won't be gourmet, but eating a pretzel or hot dog while people-watching from the steps of the museum is a quintessential New York experience. For other dining options, see p 11, bullet **2**.

8 ★ **Asian Art.** The **Astor Court,** a Chinese scholar's garden based on a Ming Dynasty design, is a great place for a little R&R. The principle of yin and yang, or opposites, gives this space its sense of harmony and tranquillity. In the Indian galleries, I always pay a visit to **Standing Ganesha,** the Hindu god of wisdom. The Japanese galleries are filled with delicate scrolls, screens, kimonos, and tapestries. Don't miss the **Japanese tearoom**/study room.

9 ★ **American Wing.** This section of the Met is a museum inside a museum. The Hudson River Valley paintings are extraordinary in their scope, from the grandeur of Frederick Church's **The Heart of the Andes** to the delicate and refined **Lake George** by John Kensett. Head into the opposite gallery with the iconic **Washington Crossing the Delaware** by Emanuel Leutze. On the mezzanine level, you'll find John Singer Sargent's **Madame X,** Winslow Homer's **Northeaster,** and Mary Cassatt's **Lady at the Tea Table.** Take the stairs to ground level to check out **Frank Lloyd Wright's Living Room** from the Little House. It's an excellent example of his Prairie Style with the focus on open space and the dramatic horizontal lines that make you feel close to the earth.

The Temple of Dendur is the highlight of the Egyptian Collection.

Portrait of Don Manuel *by Goya.*

⑩ ★★ European Paintings, the Old Masters. To get to these galleries cross the Engelhard Court and go up the elegant Louis Sullivan staircase to the second level. As you open the door into the European paintings galleries you'll be face to face with Rembrandt's ***Aristotle with a Bust of Homer.*** Other highlights include Vermeer's ***Young***

Woman with a Water Jug, El Greco's ***Portrait of a Cardinal,*** Velazquez's ***Juan de Pareja,*** Goya's ***Don Manuel,*** Lippi's ***Portrait of Man and Woman at the Casement,*** Bruegel's ***The Harvesters,*** Titian's ***Venus and Adonis,*** and Duccio's ***Madonna and Child.***

⑪ ★★★ European Paintings, the 19th Century. These are the galleries that everyone comes to see and they are crowded, but patience will produce rich rewards. Here you can compare Courbet's controversial and explicitly sexual ***Woman with a Parrot*** with Manet's more discreet version. You can watch the emergence of Monet's loose, painterly style from his tightly composed ***Garden at Sainte-Adresse*** to the practically abstract ***Poplars.*** Finally, take a look at Cezanne's ***Still Life with Apples and Pears*** with its funky perspectives and innovative use of color to get a feel for the great changes in painting that came in the 20th century.

The Cloisters

If you still have some energy after visiting the Met, hop on the M4 bus at Madison and 83rd Street and head up to **The Cloisters ☎ 212/923-3700**). This museum is devoted to medieval art and architecture and is a branch of the Met (your Met button will get you in the door without paying an additional fee), but its location on Fort Tyron Park overlooking the Hudson feels worlds away. The building incorporates elements from five medieval cloisters in France, Spain, and Italy.

Even without the magnificent setting and extraordinary architecture it's worth coming to see ***The Unicorn Tapestries,*** a series of seven tapestries depicting a sometimes brutal hunt that ends with the resurrection of the unicorn enclosed in a garden under a pomegranate tree. ***Campin's Annunciation Alterpiece*** is another piece I always visit. It shows the Virgin Mary in a contemporary (here that means 1425) Netherlandish setting and it's filled with domestic details.

Note: The last stop on the M4 is directly in front of The Cloisters. The ride takes about an hour.

Power Brokers: The Robber Barons & Their Descendants

1. Trump Tower
2. Breakfast at the Regency
3. The Frick Collection
4. Daisy Mays BBQ
4. Michael's
5. Theodore Roosevelt Birthplace
6. Forbes Magazine Galleries
7. Federal Reserve Bank of New York
8. New York Stock Exchange
9. Museum of American Financial History

The city has long been a mecca for ambitious types, from artists to mercenaries—and some things never change. The robber barons of the 19th century, men like Henry Clay Frick and J. P. Morgan, thrived here. Their modern-day counterparts include such power titans as Donald Trump and Mike Bloomberg. START: **Subway B, F, or V to Fifth Avenue and 57th Street.**

① **Trump Tower.** Definitely not your average shopping mall. Bold and brassy, the gold signage on this 1983 building practically screams "Look at me!" Step inside to view the six-story mirrored atrium and the waterfall cascading down a pink-granite wall. Admire the glitzy displays of luxury shops like Cartier and Ferragamo as you glide upward on the escalators. *725 Fifth Ave. (btwn 56th & 57th sts.).* ☎ *212/832-2000. Subway: B/D/F/V to 57th St.*

Trump Tower.

② ★ **Breakfast at the Regency.** According to local lore, this is where the term "power breakfast" was coined. Come before 8am to see tycoons and politicians table-hopping, back-slapping, and making deals aplenty. You may not recognize some of the big players (many prefer to keep a low profile), but famous faces do materialize (or at least semi-famous—if you're a fan of Sunday-morning "talking head" programs like I am, you'll be in heaven). If you want to be guaranteed a seat, make a reservation. *540 Park Ave. (at 61st St.).* ☎ *212/759-4100. www.loewshotels. com. $$–$$$.*

③ ★★ **The Frick Collection.** Industrialist Henry Clay Frick, who controlled the steel industry in Pittsburgh at the turn of the 20th century, began collecting art after he made his first million. Architects Carrère & Hastings built this palatial French neoclassical mansion in 1914 to house both Frick's family and his art (Frick chose to live in Manhattan instead of his native Pennsylvania, legend has it, because of the soot from the steel mills). This living testament to New York's Gilded Age is graced with paintings from Frick's collection: works by Titian, Gainsborough, Rembrandt, Turner, Vermeer, El Greco, and Goya. A highlight is the **Fragonard Room,** which contains the sensual rococo series *The Progress of Love.* The house is particularly stunning dressed in Christmas finery. ⏱ *90 min. 1 E. 70th St. (at Fifth Ave.).* ☎ *212/288-0700. www.frick.org. Admission $12 adults, $8 seniors, $5 students. Children under 10 not admitted; children under 16 must be accompanied by an adult. Tues–Sat 10am–6pm; Sun 1–6pm. Closed Mon*

The Fragonard Room at the Frick.

& all major holidays. Subway: 6 to 68th St. Bus: M1/2/3/4.

4 ★ **Power Lunches.** You know your place in the pecking order when you are seated in this power palace—even though the fresh flowers, pretty paintings, sunny service, and California cuisine work to soften the blow. The New York media elite lunches at **Michael's** (24 W. 55th St. [btwn Fifth and Sixth aves.]; ☎ 212/767-0555; $$$–$$$$), a spacious spot in a landmark building—and we're talking *everybody,* from Barbara Walters to Bill Clinton. As *Vanity Fair* columnist Michael Wolff put it, "Michael's is as close as I've ever come to my dream of living in the

Manhattan of movies." If you want to spend a little less, grab lunch to go from a food cart such as **Daisy Mays BBQ** (52nd St. and Park Ave.; $), which dishes out some of New York's best barbecue.

5 ★ **Theodore Roosevelt Birthplace.** America's 26th president was born and raised here (the original house was destroyed in 1916 then faithfully reconstructed in 1923). It was decorated by Roosevelt's wife and sisters with many original furnishings. The reconstructed house contains five period rooms, two museum galleries, and a bookstore. Roosevelt was the nemesis of the robber barons. Known as the "Trust Buster," he broke up monopolies in industries like railroads and steel to protect the public interest. ⏱ *45 min. 28 E. 20th St. (btwn Broadway & Park Ave. South).* ☎ *212/260-1616. www.nps.gov/thrb. Admission $3. Tues–Sat 9am–5pm. Subway: 6 to 23rd St.*

6 ★ **kids** **Forbes Magazine Galleries.** The late magnate Malcolm Forbes was a passionate collector. Toy soldiers (10,000 or so), early-edition Monopoly boards, and toy boats (over 500) are the highlights here. (The real stars of the Forbes collection, 12 Fabergé

Over 10,000 miniature figures are on view at the Forbes Galleries.

The New York Stock Exchange.

Imperial Eggs, were sold, fittingly, to a Russian tycoon in 2004; he plans to return them to their Russian homeland.) Changing exhibits have included a selection of letters written by First Ladies, jeweled flowers and fruit by Cartier, and historically accurate miniature rooms. ⏱ *45 min. You can book a free tour in advance. 60 Fifth Ave. (at 12th St.).* ☎ *212/206-5548. www.forbesgalleries.com. Free admission. Tues–Wed & Fri–Sat 10am–4pm. Subway: 4/5/6 to 14th St.*

⑦ Federal Reserve Bank of New York. This is where they keep the gold—\$90 billion of it. It rests 50 feet below sea level. Tours are free, but you need to book at least 5 days ahead. (Realistically, because the tours are so popular, you should try to book at least a month in advance.) ⏱ *1 hr. 33 Liberty St. (btwn William and Nassau sts.). To schedule a tour, call*

☎ *212/720-6130 or e-mail frbny tours@ny.frb.org. www.newyorkfed. org. Subway: 4/5 to Wall St.*

⑧ New York Stock Exchange. The serious action is here on Wall Street, a narrow lane dating to the 18th-century. At its heart is the **NYSE,** the world's largest securities exchange. The NYSE came into being in 1792, when merchants met daily under a nearby buttonwood tree to trade U.S. bonds that had funded the Revolutionary War. In 1903 traders moved into this Beaux Arts building designed by George Post. The NYSE is surrounded by heavy security and is not open to the public. *20 Broad St. (btwn Wall St. & Exchange Place).* ☎ *212/ 656-3000. www.nyse.com.*

⑨ ★ Museum of American Financial History. This small but intriguing museum across from the famous *Charging Bull* statue explores key events in America's history from a financial perspective. It is housed in the former headquarters of **John D. Rockefeller's Standard Oil Company** (check out the 1885 building's main lobby to get a taste of old-time grandeur). The temporary exhibits might not be what you'd expect (one recent show was about migrant farmworkers). ⏱ *45 min. 28 Broadway (Bowling Green).* ☎ *212/908-4100. www.financialhistory. org. Admission \$2. Tues–Sat 10am–4pm. Subway: 4/5 to Bowling Green; 2/3 to Wall St.*

The "Charging Bull" statue, symbol of Wall Street.

Literary Luminaries

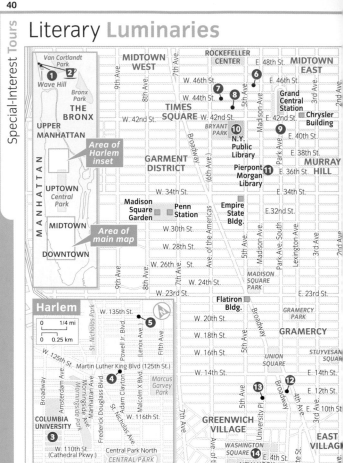

1. Wave Hill
2. Wave Hill Café
3. Columbia University
4. Theresa Towers
5. Schomburg Center for Research in Black Culture
6. Gotham Book Mart
7. The Algonquin
8. The New Yorker
9. Library Way
10. New York Public Library
11. Morgan Library
12. The Strand
13. Cedar Tavern
14. Washington Square Park
15. Housing Works Used Books Cafe

Long a city of writers, New York is a treasure trove of sites honoring authors, streets named for storytellers, and bookstores where you can find their works. Here are some of the most inspiring (and inspired) literary places. START: **Subway 1 or 9 to 231st Street and then bus Bx7 or Bx10 to 252nd Street.**

1 ★★ **Wave Hill.** New Yorkers know these gardens as a gorgeous botanical retreat, but Wave Hill also has a literary past. Writer and humorist Mark Twain lived in **Wave Hill House,** the property's fieldstone mansion, from 1901 to 1903, but it was the land that surrounded the house that inspired him. Twain particularly loved Wave Hill in winter, writing that its roaring blasts "sing their hoarse voices through the big tree-tops with a splendid energy that thrills me and stirs me and uplifts me and makes me want to live always." Today, Wave Hill encompasses 28 acres of gardens, grounds, and woodlands. My favorite is the **Aquatic Garden** with its water lilies, lotus, and other beautiful blooms. 🕐 *90 min. W. 249th St. & Independence Ave.* ☎ *718/549-3200. www. wavehill.org. Admission $5 adults (free in winter). Tues–Sun 9am–4:30pm (longer hours in summer).*

Subway: 1/9 to 231st St. & then Bx7 or Bx10 bus to 252nd St.

2 **Wave Hill Café.** In Wave Hill House, this cafe has a menu that's on the creative side (Thai beef salad, carrot-ginger soup), but you can also enjoy tea or coffee and a light snack. *Wave Hill House. No phone. $–$$.*

3 ★ **Columbia University.** Admittedly the **School of Journalism** isn't the prettiest building on campus (to be fair, it has an incredible amount of competition), but Columbia has long been the stomping grounds of literary lions. Hungarian-born editor and publisher Joseph Pulitzer founded the school in 1912, and today it attracts some very high-profile speakers, including *New Yorker* editor David Remnick and the legendary Bob Woodward; check the website for the calendar of public events. Another campus

The "Alma Mater" statue in front of Columbia's Low Memorial Library.

site of literary and architectural note is the **Low Memorial Library,** which was designed in 1897 by Charles McKim of McKim, Mead & White (the overall design of the campus was his brainchild as well). Also, the nondenominational **St. Paul's Chapel** hosts many artistic events. *116th St. & Broadway. www.jrn. columbia.edu.* ☎ *212/854-1754. Subway: B/C/1/9 to 116th St.*

④ Theresa Towers. During the Harlem Renaissance of the 1920s the former Theresa Hotel drew a glittering crowd, including many of the period's most famous writers, such as Zora Neale Hurston and Langston Hughes. Today it's an office building (you can step into the atrium but that's about it), but the structure's beauty and history make it a landmark. *125th St. & Adam Clayton Powell Blvd. Subway: 1/9/A/B/C/D to 125th St.*

⑤ ★★★ Schomburg Center for Research in Black Culture. The Manuscripts, Archives, and Rare Books Division houses the original manuscript of Richard Wright's *Native Son,* plus 3,900 other rare books and 15,000 pieces of sheet music and rare printed materials. *See p 69, bullet* **⑬.**

⑥ ★★ Gotham Book Mart. This bookstore contains a gallery and an estimated half-million volumes (both in and out of print) focusing on the

arts. The gallery features up-and-coming artists and photographers, but has also hung works by biggies like Andy Warhol. Fans of quirky author-illustrator Edward Gorey will find much to love here. The store (in its original 47th St. location) opened in 1920, and habitués have included W. H. Auden, Anaïs Nin, e. e. cummings, Marianne Moore, J. D. Salinger, Arthur Miller, Tennessee Williams, T. S. Eliot, Ezra Pound, and several cats. *16 E. 46th St. (btwn Madison & Fifth aves.).* ☎ *212/719-4448. Subway: B/D/F/V to 47th–50th St. Rockefeller Center.*

⑦ ★ The Algonquin. In the 1920s, this was where notable literati, including James Thurber and the acid-tongued Dorothy Parker, met to drink and trade bons mots at the so-called Round Table. The table still has a place of honor, but be warned: It's rectangular. The richly appointed lobby is an atmospheric spot for a drink or snack. *59 W. 44th St. (btwn Fifth & Sixth aves.).* ☎ *212/ 840-6800. www.algonquinhotel.com. Subway: B/D/F/V to 42nd St.*

⑧ *The New Yorker.* America's most celebrated literary magazine came into being at the Algonquin Round Table, just a block away from its former office space here. Over the decades it has featured writers such as E. B. White, James Thurber, John Cheever, John Updike, and Calvin

A Vicious Circle, a painting of the Round Table regulars by Natalie Ascencios.

Trillin, and you'll find their names and others on a plaque. (Today *The New Yorker* is in the Conde Nast building at 4 Times Square.) *25 W. 43rd St. (btwn Fifth & Sixth aves.). Subway: B/D/F/V to 42nd St.*

The Washington Square Arch.

⑨ ★ Library Way. Along 41st Street between Park and Fifth, you'll see bronze plaques embedded in the sidewalk. There are 96 in total, and all feature quotations from literature or poetry. Walking west along this street leads you to the New York Public Library. *41st St. (btwn Park & Fifth aves.). Subway: B/D/F/V to 42nd St.*

⑩ ★★★ New York Public Library. This magnificent Beaux Arts building houses the Humanities and Social Sciences Library. The collection is 15 million titles strong, and includes medieval manuscripts, ancient Japanese scrolls, modern novels, and even comic books. Exhibits on arts and literature are held here (check www.nypl.org), and there's a nice gift shop in the lobby. *See p 17, bullet ⑨.*

⑪ Morgan Library. Closed for a major renovation until early 2006, this mansion—once the private library of financier Pierpont Morgan—boasts one of the best collections of rare books and manuscripts in the world. I am always awed by the jewel-like tones and detailed illustrations of the medieval and Renaissance manuscripts. ⏱ *1 hr. 29 E. 36th St. (btwn Park & Madison aves.).* ☎ *212/685-0610. www.morganlibrary.org. For information on interim services and exhibits, call or check online. Subway: B/D/F/N/Q/R/V to 34th St.*

⑫ ★ The Strand. You can spend hours browsing the 18 miles of books crammed into the high, narrow shelves of this 1927 institution. *See p 93.*

⑬ Cedar Tavern. In its original location at 24 University Place (it moved up the street in 1963), this bar was frequented by Edna St. Vincent Millay, Theodore Dreiser, and Jack Kerouac and immortalized by satirist Dawn Powell in her novel *The Golden Spur.* Poke your head in to admire the dark, woody bar and the pressed tin ceiling. NYU students and locals outnumber literati these days. *82 University Place (at 11th St.).* ☎ *212/741-9754. Subway: 4/5/6/N/R/Q/W to 14th St./Union Sq.*

⑭ Washington Square Park. Novelist Henry James was born in 1843 in a house on the northern side of the park, and he described the neighborhood in his 1880 book *Washington Square.* The park's most visible landmark, the Washington Square Arch, was designed by Stanford White. *19–26 Washington Sq. N. (btwn Fifth Ave. & Macdougal St.). See also p 75, bullet ④. Subway: A/B/C/D/F/E/V to W. 4th St.*

⑮ Housing Works Used Books Cafe. This bookstore has food for thought *and* tummy, with 36,000 used and rare books, plus sandwiches, wraps, coffee, beer, and wine. All of the proceeds go to Housing Works, a nonprofit organization that provides help, healthcare, and housing to homeless New Yorkers living with AIDS/HIV. *126 Crosby St. (at Jersey St.).* ☎ *212/334-3324. www.housingworks.org/usedbookcafe/index.html. $–$$.*

Historic **New York**

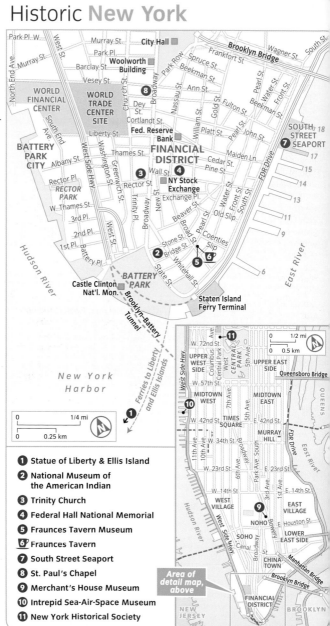

1 Statue of Liberty & Ellis Island

2 National Museum of the American Indian

3 Trinity Church

4 Federal Hall National Memorial

5 Fraunces Tavern Museum

6 Fraunces Tavern

7 South Street Seaport

8 St. Paul's Chapel

9 Merchant's House Museum

10 Intrepid Sea-Air-Space Museum

11 New York Historical Society

From 10,000 years of Native American heritage to the great immigration portal at Ellis Island, from the site of George Washington's inauguration to the USS *Intrepid*'s survey of military craft, a trip to New York opens a wide window onto American history. START: **Subway 4 or 5 to Bowling Green.**

1 ★★★ **kids** **Statue of Liberty & Ellis Island.** Annie Moore, an Irish teenager, celebrated her 15th birthday on January 1, 1892, as the first person to pass through Ellis Island, America's main point of entry for immigrants from 1892 to 1954. For Annie and the 12 million immigrants who subsequently entered the U.S. through Ellis Island, Lady Liberty was likely their first glimpse of America. The statue was slated to commemorate 100 years of American independence in 1876. But it wasn't until 1886 that the statue was finally dedicated on U.S. soil. On Liberty Island, you can explore the **Statue of Liberty Museum,** peer into the inner structure through a glass ceiling near the base of the statue, and enjoy views from the observation deck atop a 16-story pedestal. On Ellis Island, you can take self-guided or ranger tours of the immigration complex and view exhibits at the **Ellis Island Immigration**

Museum, in the main building. *See p 9, bullets* **11** *and* **12**.

2 ★★ **kids** **National Museum of the American Indian.** Long before European colonists arrived, the North and South American continents were the sole domain of Native Indian tribes and an abundant assortment of fauna. But once settlers arrived, the saga of the American Indian's rapid decline began. Guns and disease took their toll, but here in New York, it took a simple trade to ultimately displace the natives: In 1626, regional tribes sold Manhattan Island to the Dutch West India Company for 60 guilders. This museum's collection spans more than 10,000 years of North and South America's pre-European history. *See p 8, bullet* **8**.

3 ★★ **Trinity Church. Alexander Hamilton** is buried in the church's south cemetery. The original building was erected in 1698, but the

The Interior of Trinity Church.

present structure dates to 1846. *See p 8, bullet* ❻.

❹ ★ Federal Hall National Memorial.

This majestic structure is one of Wall Street's most recognizable monuments. It was on this site that the First Congress met and the Bill of Rights was written. It was where George Washington was inaugurated, on April 30, 1789. The capital moved to Philadelphia in 1790, and the original Federal Hall was torn down in 1812. The Memorial was built in 1842, and in 1883 the statue of George Washington was placed on the steps. It's directly across from the New York Stock Exchange. ⏱ *15 min. 26 Wall St. (btwn Nassau & William sts.).* ☎ *212/825-6888. www.nps.gov/feha. Free admission. Mon–Fri 9am–5pm. Subway: 2/3/4/5/6 to Wall St.*

❺ ★★ Fraunces Tavern Museum.

It was here that George Washington bade farewell to his officers at the end of the American Revolution, and his heartfelt words still inspire: "With a heart full of love and gratitude I now take leave of you. I most devoutly wish that your latter days may be as prosperous and happy as your former ones have been glorious and honorable." This 1907 building is an exact replica of the original 1717 tavern. The museum has period rooms, art and artifacts, and a series of temporary exhibits. ⏱ *45 min. 54 Pearl St. (near Broad St.).* ☎ *212/425-1778. www.frauncestavernmuseum.org. Admission $3 adults, $2 seniors & students, free for children under 6. Tues–Fri noon–5pm; Sat 10am–5pm. Subway: R/W to Whitehall St.; 4/5 to Bowling Green; 1/9 to South Ferry.*

❻ Fraunces Tavern.

Housed in the museum of the same name, Fraunces Tavern has changed since Washington dined here, but still offers a taste

of history. Enjoy soup, sandwiches, and salads. *54 Pearl St. (near Broad St.).* ☎ *212/425-1778. $–$$.*

❼ kids South Street Seaport.

Dating back to the 18th century, this landmark historic district on the East River encompasses 11 square blocks of buildings, a maritime museum, several piers, shops, and restaurants. Although today it's shamelessly commercial and touristy (the biggest draw is Pier 17, a barge converted into a mall with all the usual suspects—The Gap, Coach, Abercrombie & Fitch), visible reminders of the city's vibrant shipping past abound. The **South Street Seaport Museum** boasts paintings and prints, ship models, and temporary exhibitions; and several historic ships including the 1911 four-masted *Peking* are berthed at piers 15, 16, and 17. ⏱ *1½–2 hr. At Water & South sts.; museum visitor center is at 12 Fulton St.* ☎ *212/732-8257. www.southstseaport.org. Museum admission $5. Museum Apr–Sept Fri–Wed*

South Street Seaport's Historic District.

Intrepid *Sea-Air-Space Museum.*

10am–6pm, Thurs 10am–8pm; Oct–Mar Wed–Mon 10am–5pm. Subway: 2/3/4/5/J/Z/M to Fulton St.; A/ C to Broadway–Nassau.

⑧ ★ St. Paul's Chapel. This is Manhattan's only extant pre-revolutionary building. Historic figures who worshipped here include George Washington; Lord Cornwallis, who surrendered at the Battle of Yorktown in 1781; and Presidents Grover Cleveland and Benjamin Harrison. *See p 8, bullet* ⑤.

⑨ ★★ Merchant's House Museum. The merchant this Greek Revival house belonged to was Seabury Treadwell, who moved here in 1835. The architecture, original furniture, and personal possessions of the family make for an intriguing portrait of American life over the course of a century. The private walled garden at the back of the house is a serene delight. 🕐 *1 hr. 29 E. 4th St. (btwn Lafayette St. & Bowery).* ☎ *212/777-1089. www. merchantshouse.com. Admission $6 adults, $4 seniors & students. Thurs–Mon 1–5pm. Subway: 6 to Bleecker St.; N/R to 8th St.*

⑩ ★ kids Intrepid Sea-Air-Space Museum. The aircraft carrier known as the "Fighting I" suffered bomb attacks, kamikaze strikes, and a torpedo shot, but suc-

cessfully served the United States Navy for 31 years. Now a museum, its highlights include a wooden sub used during the American Revolution (you can crawl inside); the USS *Growler,* a nuclear missile submarine; and an extensive aircraft collection ranging from early wooden planes to modern supersonic jet fighters. Kids can enter the cockpit of an A–6 Intruder and manipulate the controls. *UPDATE: The Intrepid Sea-Air-Space Museum Complex is closed for renovation until Fall 2008. The Intrepid has been moved from Pier 86 to Bayonne, N.J., for refurbishing.*

⑪ ★ New York Historical Society. The New York Historical Society is a major repository of American history, culture, and art, with a special focus on New York and its broader cultural significance. The Henry Luce III Center for the Study of American Culture on the fourth floor, displays more than 40,000 objects, including Tiffany lamps, Audubon watercolors, life and death masks of prominent Americans, and even George Washington's camp bed. 🕐 *1½ hr. 2 W. 77th St. (at Central Park West).* ☎ *212/873-3400. www.nyhistory.org. Admission $8 adults, $5 seniors & students, free for children 12 & under. Tues–Sun 11am–6pm. Bus: M79. Subway: 1/9 to 79th St.*

Celluloid City: New York on Film & Television

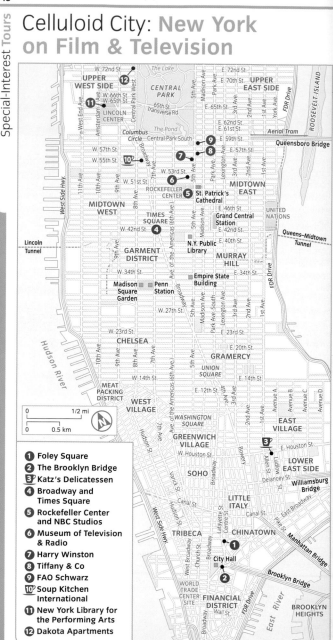

1. Foley Square
2. The Brooklyn Bridge
3. Katz's Delicatessen
4. Broadway and Times Square
5. Rockefeller Center and NBC Studios
6. Museum of Television & Radio
7. Harry Winston
8. Tiffany & Co
9. FAO Schwarz
10. Soup Kitchen International
11. New York Library for the Performing Arts
12. Dakota Apartments

From the Gothic towers of the Brooklyn Bridge to the gleaming windows of Tiffany & Co., images of New York are ubiquitous on film. Even if you've never visited the city, you may feel you know it already—but there's nothing like seeing the original. START: **Subway 4, 5, or 6 to Brooklyn Bridge/City Hall.**

❶ ★ **Foley Square.** Though not one of the most famous names in New York, Foley Square is nonetheless one of the most-filmed places in the five boroughs. The long-running TV series *Law & Order* beats a path up and down the courthouse steps here. *Bounded by Centre, Worth, & Lafayette sts. Subway: 4/5/6 to Brooklyn Bridge/City Hall.*

❷ **The Brooklyn Bridge.** One of the truly iconic sights in New York, its stunning Gothic-inspired towers and web of cables have been featured In movies like *Saturday Night Fever* and *Moonstruck*. See p 108.

Sarah Jessica Parker shoots a promo for Sex and the City *under the Brooklyn Bridge.*

Long-running hit Law & Order *filming in front of the courthouse.*

❸ ★★ **Katz's Delicatessen.** Although Katz's is one of the city's best Jewish delis, movie lovers may know it better as the site of Meg Ryan's, ahem, performance in *When Harry Met Sally.* It's an out-of-the-way stop, so make the most of it by grabbing a snack (or an early lunch) here. Served with New York attitude, Katz's offerings are first-rate: matzo ball and chicken noodle soups, potato knishes, cheese blintzes, egg creams, beef hot dogs, and more. *205 E. Houston St. (at Ludlow St.).* ☎ *212/254-2246. www.katzdeli.com. $–$$. Subway: 6 to Bleecker St.; F to Second Ave.*

❹ **Broadway and Times Square.** New Yorkers bemoan the Disneyfication of Times Square, but the neon nexus is much more visitor-friendly than it used to be. The Robert DeNiro–Jodie Foster film *Taxi Driver* was shot here, capturing the sad, seedy world of this neighborhood in the 1970s. Some things haven't changed, though: It's still unpleasantly packed with people, and the surging lights and blinking billboards can be migraine inducing. The only time you'll see Times Square quiet is in the eerie scene from *Vanilla Sky* when Tom Cruise dashes frantically about. *Subway: F/V to 42nd St./Bryant Park; 1/2/3/ 7/9/A/C/E/N/R/Q/W to 42nd St./Times Square.*

⑤ ★ Rockefeller Center and NBC Studios. This 1930s Art Deco wonder is a vision from the outside, but the tour of NBC studios will give you an up-close perspective on some of the shows filmed within. Starting at the NBC History Theater—which covers the network's early radio days—the tour takes you to the studio where *Saturday Night Live* has been filmed since 1975, as well as to the studio homes of *Late Night With Conan O'Brien, Dateline,* and *NBC Sports.* As you listen to the NBC page conducting your tour, keep in mind that Regis Philbin, Ted Koppel, and Kate Jackson all started out as pages here. If you get here on a weekday between 7 and 10am, you can join the big outdoor party that watches the taping of the *Today* show. (For more information on joining the studio audience of your favorite talk or news show, call the **NYCVB** at ☎ 212/484-1222.) ⏱ *70 min. Tour reservations recommended. 30 Rockefeller Plaza (at 49th St.). ☎ 212/664-7174. http://nbcstore.shopnbc.com. Adults $18, seniors & children 6–16 $15.50 (no children under 6 admitted). Tours daily on the half-hour from 8:30am–5:30pm (9:30am–4:30pm Sun). Subway: B/D/F/V to 47th–50th sts./Rockefeller Center.*

The entrance to the Museum of Television & Radio.

⑥ ★ kids Museum of Television & Radio. You can see performances by great personalities past and present—from Milton Berle to Jerry Seinfeld—at this interactive museum. Do your own computer search of the museum's 75,000 choices for shows you half-remember from childhood, personal favorites, or great moments like the tearing down of the Berlin Wall. Then settle down in the comfy chairs for your own private screening. ⏱ *1–3 hr., depending on the shows you pick. Call in advance to make a reservation. 25 W. 52nd St. (btwn Fifth & Sixth aves.). ☎ 212/621-6600. www.mtr.org. Admission $10 adults, $8 seniors & students, $5 children under 13. Tues–Sun noon–6pm (Thurs until 8pm, Fri theater programs until 9pm). Subway: B/D/F/V to 47th–50th sts.*

⑦ ★ Harry Winston. This ultra-glamorous shop has bejeweled countless celebs walking the red carpet, but its best appearance on film may have been in Woody Allen's *Everyone Says I Love You. 718 Fifth Ave. (at 56th St.).* ☎ *212/245-2000. Subway: E/V to Fifth Ave./53rd St.*

⑧ ★★ Tiffany & Co. Who can forget the image of the sublime Audrey Hepburn ogling jewels in *Breakfast at Tiffany's? 727 Fifth Ave. (btwn 56th & 57th sts.).* ☎ *212/755-8000. Subway: E/V to Fifth Ave./53rd St.*

⑨ ★ FAO Schwarz. Remember Tom Hanks dancing on the piano in *Big?* This legendary toy store looks different than it did in the film (thanks to a 10-month renovation in 2004), but you, too, can "play" the musical mat resembling a keyboard (it's on the second floor; expect a wait on weekends). If you're in town on a Sunday morning, CBS's *NFL Today* show is filmed in the plaza outside the store. (Across Fifth Ave. is the legendary **Plaza**—Eloise was the hotel's first famous "resident," and naturally, *Eloise at the Plaza* was filmed here). *767 Fifth Ave. (at 59th St.).* ☎ *212/ 644-9400.* www.fao.com. *Subway: N/R/W to Fifth Ave. & 59th St.*

⑩ ★ Soup Kitchen International. Just don't call him the Soup Nazi. Al Yeganeh, the curmudgeonly soup master made famous on *Seinfeld,* still ladles his product from a modest storefront, but only when it suits him (roughly Nov–Apr). Yes, the drill is regimented: You stand in a long, solemn line that snakes around the block; you place your money on the counter (*not* in Al's hand) and move swiftly to the left. No gaiety, no mirth. Definitely no questions about the soup. Why go through such humiliating paces? Two words: seafood bisque. *259-a W. 55th St. (btwn Broadway & Eighth Ave.). No phone.* www.soupkitchenintl.com. *Mon–Sat noon–6pm. $–$$.*

⑪ ★★ New York Library for the Performing Arts. A 3-year, $37-million renovation has transformed this into a peerless performing arts research collection. Of particular interest are the Rodgers and Hammerstein Archives of Recorded Sound, and the Billy Rose Theatre Collection, both of which have a strong film history component. You can browse sections of the collections, view temporary exhibits, and listen to free lectures. ⏱ *1 hr. 40 Lincoln Center Plaza (Broadway & 64th sts.).* ☎ *212/870-1643.* www.nypl.org. *Tues–Wed noon–8pm; Thurs–Fri noon–6pm; Sat 10am–6pm. Subway: 1/9 to Lincoln Center.*

⑫ Dakota Apartments. This 1884 apartment house with its dramatic gables, dormers, and oriel windows was the setting for the psychological horror film *Rosemary's Baby. 1 W. 72nd St. (at Central Park West). Bus: M7 to 72nd St. & Amsterdam Ave. Subway: 1/2/3/9 to 72nd St.*

Mia Farrow played a pregnant wife living in the Dakota in Rosemary's Baby.

Offbeat New York

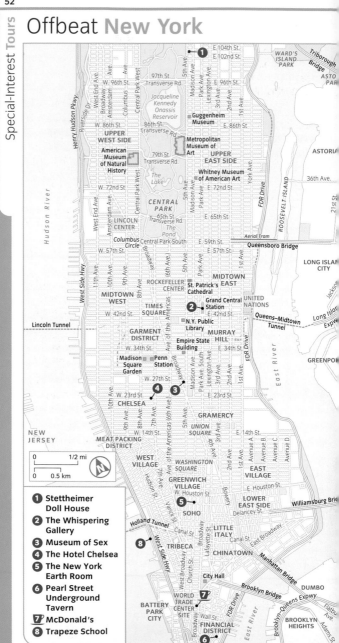

1. **Stettheimer Doll House**
2. **The Whispering Gallery**
3. **Museum of Sex**
4. **The Hotel Chelsea**
5. **The New York Earth Room**
6. **Pearl Street Underground Tavern**
7. **McDonald's**
8. **Trapeze School**

Seeing the unusual in New York is often just a matter of turning a corner. I've watched "ballet aerialists" dangling from the Stock Exchange, brass bands wailing in Chinatown street funerals, and wall-to-wall dachshunds preening during Dachshund Day in Washington Square Park. Here I give you more of the curious finds unique to this city. START: **Subway 6 to 103rd Street.**

1 ★★★ Stettheimer Doll House. This rare, remarkable dollhouse was the creation of Carrie Walter Stettheimer, a theater set designer who, with her two equally talented sisters, entertained the city's avant-garde artist community in the 1920s. Among the exquisite furnishings are period wallpaper, paper lampshades—and perhaps most remarkable—an art gallery featuring original miniatures of such famous works as Marcel Duchamp's *Nude Descending A Staircase* and an alabaster *Venus* by Gaston Lachaise. ⏱ *15 min. Museum of the City of New York, 120 Fifth Ave. (103rd St.).* ☎ *212/534-1672. www. mcny.org. Tues–Sun 10am–5pm. $7 adults; $5 students & seniors. Subway: 6 to 103rd St.*

2 The Whispering Gallery. Not only is the tiled Gustavino ceiling outside the Grand Central Oyster Bar beautiful, but it creates an acoustical phenomenon. Stand facing one of the pillars with your companion facing the one directly opposite—and whisper. You'll be able to hear one another—and no one else can listen in. *Grand Central Station, 42nd St. & Park Ave.* ☎ *212/340-2210. www.grandcentral terminal.com. Subway: 4/5/6 to 42nd St./Grand Central.*

3 ★ Museum of Sex. When this museum opened, it managed to cause a stir even among hard-bitten New Yorkers. Among the collections are early sex films, artifacts from burlesque theaters, S&M displays, painted nudes, and even blow-up dolls. ⏱ *1 hr. 233 Fifth Ave. (at 27th St.).* ☎ *866/MOSEX-NYC. www. museumofsex.com. Admission $15 adults, $14 students & seniors. No one under 18 admitted. Mon–Tues & Thurs–Fri 11am–6:30pm. Subway: N/R to 28th St.*

The Stettheimer Doll House at the Museum of the City of New York.

④ The Hotel Chelsea.

As Janis Joplin once said, "A lot of funky things happen at the Chelsea." Billed as "a rest stop for rare individuals," this legendary 12-story brick building maintains a distinct boho flair, from its lobby of abstract expressionist art (by

What not to do at the Museum of Sex.

artists who lived here in the 1950s and '60s) to its colorful history as a haven for creative, offbeat, even extremist, types. Built in 1884, the Chelsea became a hotel in 1905, one where artists and writers were encouraged to stay indefinitely. Among them: Thomas Wolfe, Dylan Thomas, O. Henry, Arthur Miller, and Bob Dylan. Radical activists gathered here in the 1930s, and the Warhol clan camped out in the '60s. Artists are still the main residents, but you can stay too, in one of the hotel rooms—and no two are alike. If you're staying elsewhere, feel free to stop in the lobby for a look around. *222 W. 23rd St. (btwn Seventh & Eighth aves.)* ☎ *212/243-3700. www. hotelchelsea.com. Subway: 1/9/A/C to 23rd St.*

⑤ The New York Earth Room.

Why would someone fill a perfectly clean, neat room with 250 cubic yards of dirt? Well, if it's SoHo, it's art, baby! Walter De Maria's "sculpture" weighs about 280,000 pounds. 🕑 *15 min. 141 Wooster St. (at Prince St.)* ☎ *212/989-5566. Free admission. Wed–Sun noon–6pm (closed 3–3:30pm). Subway: N/R to Prince St.*

⑥ Pearl Street Underground Tavern.

Little is left of 17th-century

New York, but an excavation in 1979 led to the discovery of the foundation of Lovelace's Tavern, built in 1670. In an ingenious move, the underground excavation was left in place—as was an early-18th-century cistern—and the street above it was replaced with glass, so that anyone walking by can look down and see the old foundation and artifacts. *Pearl St. at Coenties Alley. Subway: R/W to Whitehall St.; 4/5 to Bowling Green, 1/9 to South Ferry.*

⑦ McDonald's.

Why am I recommending the Golden Arches? This branch of the mega-chain is like no other. Just across the street from the NASDAQ building near Wall Street, this is a five-star fast-food setting, with fresh flowers on the tables, live piano music, and a doorman. Alas,

The Hotel Chelsea.

Swinging at the Trapeze School.

the food is just the same. *160 Broadway (btwn Maiden Lane & Liberty St.).* ☎ *212/385-2063. $.*

⑧ Trapeze School. One of the city's top head-turning sights these days is the high-wire trapeze sandwiched between the busy West Side Highway and the Hudson River. Between late April through October,

you can fly high in the air with the sparkling river spread out before you by taking one of the 2 hour classes at the New York Trapeze School here— no matter your skill level. *West St./ Hudson River Park (btwn Piers 34 & 26).* ☎ *917/797-1872. www.trapeze school.com. $45–$65/lesson. Bus: M20/21or 22; subway: 1/9/A/C/E to Canal St.*

Quirky New York Tours

Want to see more of New York's quirky side? Try one of these unconventional tours.

Soundwalk (www.soundwalk.com): Soundwalk's audio tours offer insider's peeks at Chinatown, the Lower East Side, Times Square, the Bronx, and the Meat-Packing District.

Radical Walking Tours (☎ **718/492-0069;** www.he.net/~radtours): These tours provide unconventional looks at conventional tourist sights. The Non–Jerry Seinfeld Upper West Side Tour stops at the former home of Fidel Castro and the site of the shootout with Black Panther H. Rap Brown and police.

Hidden Jazz Haunts (☎ **718/606-8442;** www.bigapplejazz.com): Tours hosted by New York Jazz expert Gordon Polatnick are the real deal for jazz buffs. Polatnick's tours are small (2 to 10 people) and are tailor-made to the jazz interests of his clients.

Adventures on a Shoestring (☎ **212/265-2663**): These inexpensive tours, which go behind the scenes of neighborhoods, range from a variety of Greenwich Village walks—haunted, picturesque, historic—to Historic Roosevelt Island.

New York's **Greatest Buildings**

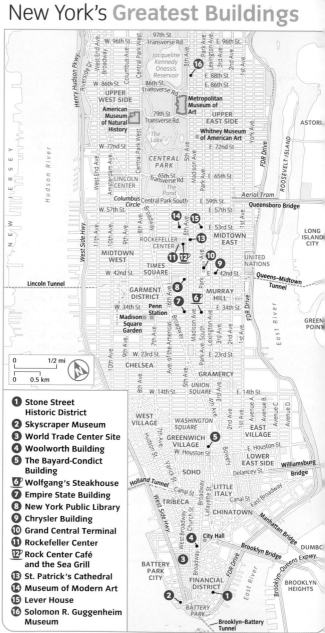

1. Stone Street Historic District
2. Skyscraper Museum
3. World Trade Center Site
4. Woolworth Building
5. The Bayard-Condict Building
6. Wolfgang's Steakhouse
7. Empire State Building
8. New York Public Library
9. Chrysler Building
10. Grand Central Terminal
11. Rockefeller Center
12. Rock Center Café and the Sea Grill
13. St. Patrick's Cathedral
14. Museum of Modern Art
15. Lever House
16. Solomon R. Guggenheim Museum

Manhattan's muscular, steel-and-concrete skyline is many things: a wonderfully eclectic architectural landscape; a visual metaphor for the always-in-flux dynamism of America's largest city; and a stunning, three-dimensional historical record of how the Big Apple has grown—and grown up—over the years. START: **Subway 2 or 3 to Wall Street.**

① ★ Stone Street Historic District. This narrow, winding street is a real find, dating back to the Dutch West India Company in the 1640s. The 15 existing brick structures lying in the shadow of Wall Street's canyons were built soon after the Great Fire of 1835 leveled the heavily commercial neighborhood. The Dutch-style facades trace the old cobblestone street, now home to attractive little restaurants and cafes/bars. *Bounded by Pearl St., Hanover Square, S. William St., & Coenties Alley. Subway: 2/3 to Wall St.*

② ★ Skyscraper Museum. Wowed by New York's sheer verticality? Learn more about the technology, culture, and muscle behind it all at this small museum. Housed in the same building as Ritz-Carlton Battery Park, it contains two galleries: one dedicated to the evolution of Manhattan's skyline, the other to changing shows. ⏱ *1 hr. 2 West St. (museum entrance faces Battery Place).* ☎ *212/968-1961. www.skyscraper.org. Admission $5 adults, $2.50 seniors & students. Wed–Sun noon–6pm. Subway: 1/9 to Rector St; 4/5 to Bowling Green.*

③ ★ World Trade Center Site. The enormity of the tragedy of September 11 is driven home by the sight of the massive "bathtub" that once held the twin towers, and literally kept the Hudson River at bay. *See p 7, bullet* **④**.

④ Woolworth Building. The irony, of course, is that this masterpiece was built with the profits of a nickel-and-dime empire. Architect Cass Gilbert designed it in 1913, and the neo-Gothic facade set a new standard for architectural grandeur. What made F. W. Woolworth proudest? The fact that he paid cash for the project. *See p 7, bullet* **②**.

⑤ The Bayard-Condict Building. Renowned Chicago architect Louis Sullivan was Frank Lloyd Wright's boss and, some say, mentor, and the only building he designed in New York is hidden away on a nondescript street downtown. It's a beaut, nonetheless: Constructed from 1897 to 1899, the 13-story building is a confection of a skyscraper, with fanciful terra cotta decoration and ornamental friezes. *65 Bleecker St. (btwn Broadway & Lafayette St.). Subway: 6 to Bleecker St.*

The Woolworth Building.

6 Wolfgang's Steakhouse.
Come here for a meal as bold as the architecture you're viewing. In a stunning historic space on the first floor of the old Vanderbilt Hotel, a 40-year waitstaff veteran of Peter Luger's storied steakhouse opened his own meat palace in 2004. The great Raphael Gustavino tiled the vaulted ceilings around 1910. *4 Park Ave. (at 33rd St.).* ☎ *212/889-3369. $$$$.*

7 ★★ Empire State Building.
It has 103 stories, 6,500 windows, 73 elevators, 70 miles of water pipes, and—if you were intrepid enough to walk it—1,860 steps from bottom to top. Completed in 1931, the limestone-and-stainless-steel Art Deco dazzler remains a visual touchstone for many New Yorkers. The lobby alone is worth the trip, with its shimmering metal-relief sculptures and rosy marble floors. The Empire State Building glows every night, bathed in colored floodlights to commemorate holidays or significant events—red, white, and blue for Independence Day; green for St. Patrick's Day; red, black, and green for Martin Luther King Day; blue and white for Hanukkah; even lavender and white for Gay Pride Day. ⏱ *1 hr. 350 Fifth Ave. (at 34th St.).* ☎ *212/736-3100. www.esbnyc.com. Observatory admission $10 adults, $9 seniors & children 12–17, $5 children 6–11, free for children under 6. Buy & print tickets in advance online to avoid lines. Mon–Fri 10am–midnight; Sat–Sun 9:30am–midnight; tickets sold until 11:25pm. Subway: 6 to 33rd St.; B/D/F/V to 34th St.*

8 ★ New York Public Library.
This monumental Beaux Arts structure is glorious inside and out—and it's a model of utility to boot, with almost two million cardholders. The **Main Reading Room,** restored in 1998, is all soaring space and burnished oak. The sculpted lions out front are festooned with garlands during the Christmas season. Out back is one of Manhattan's prettiest green spaces, **Bryant Park,** a great warm-weather spot to eat a bag lunch. *Fifth Ave. (btwn 42nd & 40th sts.).* ☎ *212/661-7220. www.nypl. org. Open Tues–Wed & Sat 11am–6pm; Thurs–Fri 10am–6pm; Sun 1–5pm. Subway: B/D/F/V to 42nd St.*

9 ★ Chrysler Building. This 1930 Art Deco masterpiece was

The Main Reading Room at the library gleams after a 1998 renovation.

Don't miss the Chrysler Building's Art Deco lobby.

designed to be the world's tallest building, and it was, if only for a year. In the race against other New York architects to build the tallest building of the era, William Van Alen secretly added a stainless-steel spire inside the fire shaft, hoisting it into place only after his competitors thought his building was completed. *405 Lexington Ave. (at 42nd St.). Subway: 4/5/6 to Grand Central.*

⓾ ★ Grand Central Terminal. This magnificent public space is also an engineering wonder. The "elevated circumferential plaza," as it was called in 1913, leads Park Avenue around the building. The network of trains—subway and commuter—that passes through here is vast, but even more impressive is the "bridge" over the tracks, designed to support a cluster of skyscrapers. The main concourse was restored to its original glory in 1998; the **sky ceiling** depicts the constellations of the winter sky above New York. They're lit with 59 stars surrounded by dazzling 24-karat gold and emit light fed through fiber-optic cables, their intensities roughly replicating the magnitude of the actual

stars as seen from Earth. Look carefully and you'll see a patch near one corner left unrestored as a reminder of the neglect this splendid masterpiece once endured. *42nd St. & Park Ave. ☎ 212/340-2210. www.grand centralterminal.com. Subway: 4/5/6/ 7/S to 42nd St.*

⓫ ★ Rockefeller Center. Rock Center was erected mainly in the 1930s, when the city was mired in the Depression and in thrall to Art Deco—the latter expressed both in the building's architecture and in the art commissioned to decorate it. The focal point is the 1933 **GE Building** at 30 Rockefeller Plaza, one of the city's most impressive buildings. The entrance sculpture, *Wisdom, Light and Sound,* by Lee Lawrie, is an Art Deco masterpiece, as is the artist's *Atlas,* at the entrance court of the International Building. The sunken plaza in front of 30 Rock is overseen by the gilded statue of *Prometheus,* by Paul Manship. *Bounded by 48th & 51st sts. & Fifth & Sixth aves. Subway: B/D/F/V to 47th-50th sts./Rockefeller Center.*

You won't go hungry in Rockefeller Center. In the **⓬ dining and shopping concourse** ($) downstairs at 30 Rock, you can pick up light meals of soup, salads, and sandwiches. If you prefer a nice sit-down lunch (and don't mind spending more), the pleasant dining rooms in the **Rock Center Café** (20 W. 50th St., btwn Fifth & Sixth aves.; ☎ 212/ 332-7620; $$) and the **Sea Grill** 19 W. 49th, btwn 5th & 6th aves.; same phone; $$) both face the famed skating rink.

⓭ ★★ St. Patrick's Cathedral. Hundreds of visitors and worshippers stream in and out of this massive Gothic cathedral daily.

The Guggenheim's architecture is as intriguing as its art.

Dedicated in 1879, the 2,200-seat structure has stained-glass windows made by artisans from Chartres, France. For those interested in visiting when the Archbishop of New York conducts services, Cardinal Egan usually presides over Mass at 10am on Sundays and on holidays. *See p 16, bullet* **7**.

14 ★★ **Museum of Modern Art.** The MoMA boasts the world's greatest collection of painting and sculpture from the late 19th century to the present, but its newly renovated home—transformed under the guidance of Japanese architect Yoshio Taniguchi—now encompasses 630,000 square feet, spread over six floors. Its highlight is a 110-foot-high tall atrium, which diffuses natural light throughout. ⏱ *2 hr. 11 W. 53rd St. (btwn Fifth & Sixth aves.).* ☎ *212/708-9400. www. moma.org. Admission $20 adults, $16 seniors, $12 students, free for kids 16 & under when accompanied by an adult. Sat–Mon & Wed–Thurs 10:30am–5:30pm; Fri 10:30am–8pm. Subway: E/V to Fifth Ave./53rd St.; B/D/F to 47th-50th sts.*

15 ★ **Lever House.** Built in 1952, this High Modern hymn to glass has undergone a spiffy renovation that has restored its original sparkle. The clean-lined, relatively small skyscraper was the first in New York to employ the "curtain wall" design philosophy, with a brilliant blue-green glass facade. The bottom level is a public space. *400 Park Ave. (btwn 53rd & 54th sts.). Subway: 6 to Lexington Ave.*

16 ★ **Solomon R. Guggenheim Museum.** Frank Lloyd Wright's only New York edifice—built in 1959—is a brilliant work of architecture. The Babylonian-style "inverted ziggurat" has been compared to a wedding cake or a nautilus shell, but it is full of life and movement. Just forget your fantasies about roller-skating down the ramp of the rotunda! ⏱ *1 hr. 1071 Fifth Ave. (at 89th St.).* ☎ *212/423-3500. www. guggenheim.org. Admission $15 adults, $10 seniors & students, free for children under 12. Sat–Wed 10am–5:45pm; Fri 10am–8pm. Subway: 4/5/6 to 86th St. Bus: M1/ 2/3/4.* ●

The Best
Neighborhood Walks

Belmont, the Bronx's Little Ital

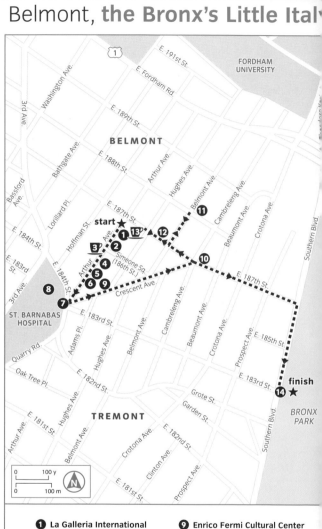

1. La Galleria International
2. Teitel Bros Grocery
3. Enzo's Café
4. Madonia Bros Bakery
5. Arthur Avenue Retail Market
6. Calandra Cheese Co.
7. D'Auria Murphy Triangle
8. St. Barnabas Hospital
9. Enrico Fermi Cultural Center
10. Terranova Bakery
11. Doo Wop Corner
12. Church of Our Lady of Mount Carmel
13. De Lillo Pastry Shop
14. Bronx Zoo

Manhattan's Little Italy has been downsized, but the Italian community of Belmont around Arthur Avenue in the Bronx is thriving. Home to countless small retailers, this neighborhood is a gourmand's dream. Don't try this tour on a Sunday, when most of the businesses, including the Arthur Avenue Retail Market, are closed. START: **Subway D to Fordham Road, then eastbound bus BX 12 to Arthur Avenue. (The walk from the Fordham Road station takes about 20 min.)**

❶ La Galleria International.
This homey shop is filled with porcelain dolls, silver, and lace. Many items were handcrafted in Italy; the most exquisite are the music boxes. *2376 Arthur Ave.* ☎ *718/329-2753. Subway: D to Fordham Rd., then eastbound BX 12 bus to Arthur Ave.*

❷ ★ Teitel Bros Grocery. The Teitel brothers established their business in 1915, and it's still going strong. The small space is crowded with imported Italian goods ranging from cheese to chocolate, and is almost always busy. *2372 Arthur Ave. (at corner of 186th St.).* ☎ *718/733-9400. www.teitelbros.com.*

❸ Enzo's Café. Many of the businesses around here sell great food, but Enzo's also sells great espresso and cappuccino, and there's usually plenty of seating. You can sample some of their cakes or Perugina candies at the same time. *2339 Arthur Ave. (btwn Frank Simeon Sq. & Crescent Ave.).* ☎ *718/733-4455. $.*

❹ ★★ Madonia Bros Bakery.
Family-owned since its founding in 1918, this bakery is famous for specialty breads like jalapeño-cheddar. Happily, there are always free samples on hand. *2348 Arthur Ave. (btwn Frank Simeon Sq. & Crescent Ave.).* ☎ *718/295-5573.*

❺ ★★★ kids Arthur Avenue Retail Market. Founded in 1940 (a plaque from Mayor Fiorella LaGuardia commemorates the event), this varied collection of vendors is a must-see and a must-taste. The market features fresh fruits and vegetables, meats and cheeses,

Warm, fresh loaves of bread are sold at bakeries along Arthur Avenue.

breads and cakes, and plenty of imported edibles. Even if you're not in a buying mood, many of the retailers will make sure you're sated with samples. There are also vendors selling cookware, books, and gift items. One of the most interesting outposts is **La Casa Grande Cigar Co.,** where you can watch cigars being hand-rolled. *2344 Arthur Ave. (btwn Frank Simeon Sq. & Crescent Ave.). No phone. www. arthuravenuebronx.com. Mon–Sat 7am–6pm.*

⑥ Calandra Cheese Co. Newer than most of its neighbors—it opened a mere 5 decades ago—this shop has a wide selection of cheeses. Prepare to be plied with samples. *2314 Arthur Ave. (btwn Frank Simeon Sq. & Crescent Ave.).* ☎ *718/365-7572.*

⑦ D'Auria Murphy Triangle. Named for two local boys who died in WWI, this tiny parkette has ample seating if you want to rest. Even if you don't, check out the marble bust of **Christopher Columbus,** created by Italian-American sculptor Attilio Piccirilli (1866–1945) in 1925. *183rd St. at Crescent Ave. (called Adams Place).*

⑧ St. Barnabas Hospital. Originally this grand building (dating to the mid-1800s) was the home of industrialist Jacob Lorillard, who called his massive mansion Belmont. *Third Ave. & 183rd St.*

⑨ ★ kids Enrico Fermi Cultural Center. Inside the Belmont branch of the New York Public Library is this cultural center with displays on the Italian-American experience, as well as Italian

Pete and Mike have been serving customers on Arthur Avenue since 1966.

newspapers, books, and videos. ⏲ *30 min. 610 E. 186th St. (at Hughes Ave.).* ☎ *718/933-6410. www.nypl.org. Mon & Fri 1–6pm; Tues noon–8pm; Wed 11am–6pm; Thurs 10am–6pm; Sat 10am–5pm.*

⑩ ★ Terranova Bakery. Considered one of the best traditional bakers in the neighborhood, Terranova produces excellent breads and rolls from its brick oven that sell for a fraction of what you'd pay in Manhattan. *691 E. 187th St. (at Beaumont Ave.).* ☎ *718/ 733-3827.*

⑪ Doo Wop Corner. Remember Dion and the Belmonts? They took their name from this street where they first started to harmonize. The corner of Belmont Avenue and 188th Street has a tribute to Dion Demucci. *Belmont Ave. & 188th St.*

Madre Italia by Bruno Luchese at the Enrico Fermi Cultural Center.

⑫ ★★★ Church of Our Lady of Mount Carmel. This stunner with its elaborate stained-glass windows and Italian-marble Corinthian columns is not only a showpiece, it's also a very active parish church. It began as a basement church in 1907; the main body was built in 1917. The glorious stained-glass windows actually predate the church by decades: They were a gift from France's "Citizen King" Louis Philippe to the original St. Patrick's Cathedral in lower Manhattan in the 1840s. Unfortunately for St. Pat's, the windows didn't fit, and they eventually ended up in the Bronx. *E. 187 St. (btwn Belmont & Hughes aves.).* ☎ *718/295-3770. Open daily 9am–5pm.*

Church of Our Lady of Mount Carmel.

⑬ ★ kids De Lillo Pastry Shop. You've been eating almost nonstop for the past couple of hours, but surely you can fit in one more cannoli before you head back. This bakery has a great selection of cakes and pastries, and a cafe area where you can sit and enjoy them. *606 E. 187th St. (btwn Arthur & Hughes aves.).* ☎ *718/367-8198. $.*

Visiting the Bronx Zoo ★★★

Getting to the Bronx from Manhattan takes a fair bit of time, so it's a smart idea to spend a full day once you're here. One great way to do this is to add on a visit to the **Bronx Zoo** kids (Fordham Rd. and Bronx River Pkwy; ☎ **718/652-8400;** www.bronxzoo.com). The zoo is a 10-minute walk from Belmont (interestingly, it was the construction of the zoo that originally brought many Italian laborers and artisans to Belmont). Walk along 187th Street and you'll see the zoo dead ahead after you pass Cambreleng Avenue. When you get to Southern Boulevard, there's a service-only gate to the left. Walk 4 blocks south to 183rd Street and Southern Boulevard. This entrance brings you in close to the wild horses and to the birds of prey, though you're not far from the amazing Congo Gorilla Forest, either. After your visit, exit via the Asia gate, which is 2½ blocks from the East Tremont subway stop at 180th Street. From here, you can take a 2 or 5 train back to Manhattan. Admission to the zoo costs $8 adults, $6 seniors, and $6 children 2 to 12. Hours are daily 10am to 4:30pm, with extended holiday and summer hours.

Historic **Harlem**

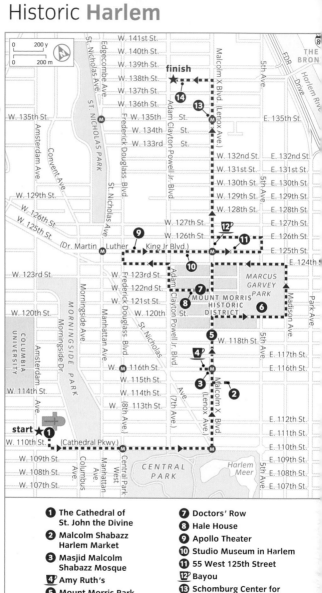

1. The Cathedral of St. John the Divine
2. Malcolm Shabazz Harlem Market
3. Masjid Malcolm Shabazz Mosque
4. Amy Ruth's
5. Mount Morris Park Historic District
6. Marcus Garvey Park
7. Doctors' Row
8. Hale House
9. Apollo Theater
10. Studio Museum in Harlem
11. 55 West 125th Street
12. Bayou
13. Schomburg Center for Research in Black Culture
14. Abyssinian Baptist Church

It wasn't until the mid–19th century that Nieuw Amsterdam and Nieuw Harlem—the two towns the Dutch founded on the island of Manhattan—became one. Largely shaped by African Americans who came north in large numbers after the Civil War and again after the end of World War I, Harlem has retained its own distinct character. START: **Subway 1 or 9 to 110th Street.**

1 ★★★ **The Cathedral of St. John the Divine.** Although it's in Morningside Heights, this not-to-be-missed work-in-progress makes a good jumping off point for your walk. Its sheer size is breathtaking—when completed, it will be the largest Gothic-style cathedral in the world—and you can walk around studying the elaborate stained-glass windows for hours. The land was purchased in 1887, the cornerstone was laid in 1892, and the choir was finally put in place in 1911. Work stopped with the advent of World War II, then resumed in 1979. St. John the Divine houses fantastic art treasures in its thematic chapels (dedicated to sports, poetry, patriotism, law, medicine, and firefighting, among others). Hanging above the

Stained-glass window at St. John the Divine.

choir are the 17th–century Barberini Tapestries, which depict scenes from the life of Christ. The tremendous rose window is composed of 10,000 pieces of colored glass. ⏱ *90 min. 1047 Amsterdam Ave. (btwn 111th & 112th sts.).* ☎ *212/316-7540. www.stjohndivine.org. Admission $2. Mon–Sat 7:30am–6pm; Sun 7:30am–7pm. Subway: 1/9 to 110th St.*

2 ★ **Malcolm Shabazz Harlem Market.** At this colorful outdoor bazaar, tiny shops and stalls hawk West African crafts and local souvenirs. There are also hair-braiding booths and African-style clothing. *52 W. 115th St. (btwn Lenox & Fifth aves.).* ☎ *212/987-8131. Daily 10am–7pm. Bus: M4. Subway: 2/3 to 115th St.*

3 **Masjid Malcolm Shabazz Mosque.** In a former life this was the Lenox Casino. In 1965 it was reborn as a mosque (originally called Mohammed Temple of Islam); the building was thoroughly renovated to incorporate aspects of Middle Eastern architecture and was topped off with an aluminum dome. *102 W. 116th St. (Lenox Ave.).* ☎ *212/662-2200. Open daily 9am–5pm.*

4 ★★ **Amy Ruth's.** This cozy restaurant serves fine Southern soul food. *113 W. 116th St. (btwn Lenox Ave. & Adam Clayton Powell Blvd.).* ☎ *212/280-8779. www.amyruths restaurant.com. $–$$.*

Stately brownstones in the Mount Morris Park Historic District.

⑤ ★★ Mount Morris Park Historic District. Mount Morris' impressive collection of 19th- and 20th-century row houses was built for wealthy white merchants. The homes come in various styles, from Romanesque Revival to Queen Anne, and many have been restored to their former glory. *Bounded by 119th St., 124th St., Lenox Ave. & Mount Morris Park West.*

⑥ ★ Marcus Garvey Park. This rocky outcropping was simply too tough to develop. It's one of the highest natural points on Manhattan, making it a perfect lookout spot (firefighters built an iron watchtower here in 1865, which you can still climb for a fantastic view). The park was renamed in 1973 in honor of famous black nationalist leader Marcus Garvey. *120th St. & Mount Morris Park West.*

⑦ ★★★ Doctors' Row. This lovely stretch of row houses (though a few brownstones are boarded up) dates from the late 1800s. My favorites are nos. 133 through 143, which were built by architect Francis H. Kimball; these are the most beautiful surviving Queen Anne–style houses in the entire city. *122nd St. & Lenox Ave.*

⑧ Hale House. Established in 1969 by Mother Clara Hale to aid drug-addicted (and now also HIV-infected) infants and their mothers. Hale died in 1992; 4 years later, sculptor Robert Berks memorialized her in a sculpture surrounded by etched bronze plaques of children. *152 W. 122nd St. (btwn Seventh Ave. & Malcolm X Blvd.).* ☎ 212/663-0700.

⑨ ★★★ Apollo Theater. This legendary theater has featured them all—Bessie Smith, Count Basie, Billie Holiday, Louis Armstrong, Dizzy Gillespie, Duke Ellington, Charlie

The Apollo Theater dates from 1914.

"Bird" Parker, Nat "King" Cole, Marvin Gaye, Gladys Knight, Aretha Franklin, Stevie Wonder, B. B. King, and more. Amateur Night at the Apollo started the careers of Ella Fitzgerald, James Brown, Lauryn Hill, and the Jackson 5. Unfortunately, tours are available only to groups of 20 or more and must be booked well in advance. *253 W. 125th St. (Frederick Douglass Blvd.).* ☎ *212/531-5300. www.apollotheater.com.*

⑩ ★ Studio Museum in Harlem. Since 1968 the SMH has been devoted to collecting, preserving, and promoting 19th- and 20th-century African-American art as well as traditional African art and artifacts. ⏱ *90 min. 144 W. 125th St. (btwn Lenox Ave. & Adam Clayton Powell, Jr., Blvd.).* ☎ *212/864-4500. www.studiomuseum.org. Admission $7 adults, $3 seniors & students, free for children under 12. Sun & Wed–Fri noon–6pm; Sat 10am–6pm. Subway: 2/3/A/B/C/D to 125th St.*

⑪ 55 W. 125th St. This office building gained instant fame in 2001 when former president Bill Clinton moved in.

⑫ ★★ Bayou. Turtle soup and fried oysters are two of the specialties at this Creole restaurant. *308 Lenox Ave. (btwn 125th & 126th sts.).* ☎ *212/426-3800. $–$$.*

⑬ ★★★ Schomburg Center for Research in Black Culture. This national research library has more than five million items documenting the experiences of people of African descent around the world. The collections include manuscripts and rare books, moving image and recorded sound, art and artifacts, and photographs and prints. Entry is free and much of the collection is open to anyone.

⏱ *45 min. 515 Malcolm X Blvd. (btwn 135th & 136th sts.).* ☎ *212/491-2200. www.nypl.org. Free admission. Tues–Wed noon–8pm; Thurs–Fri noon–6pm; Sat 10am–6pm.*

⑭ Abyssinian Baptist Church. This Baptist church is Harlem's most famous. Its congregation first gathered downtown in 1808, when a group of African Americans and Ethiopians withdrew from the First Baptist Church to protest its segregated seating policy. The congregation built here in 1922 under the leadership of Adam Clayton Powell Sr. (his son was the preacher, activist, and congressman for whom the nearby boulevard was named). You can join the crowds that gather for Abyssinian's Sunday services at 9am and 11am. ⏱ *20 min. 132 W. 138th St. (btwn Malcolm X Blvd. & Adam Clayton Powell Jr. Blvd.).* ☎ *212/862-7474. www.abyssinian.org.*

Visitors to the Schomburg Center.

Chelsea's **Masterpieces**

1 Flatiron Building
2 Hotel Chelsea
3 PaceWildenstein
4 Barbara Gladstone Gallery
5 Gagosian Gallery
6 DIA: Chelsea
7 Wild Lily Tea Room
8 Max Protetch Gallery
9 Church of the Guardian Angel
10 Cushman Row
11 Chelsea Market
12 Rubin Museum of Art

In the '80s, New York's art scene was all about SoHo and the East Village, but for several years now my favorite place to visit small commercial galleries has been the Chelsea Art District, located in the rough-hewn western edges of the neighborhood among industrial lofts, garages, and repair shops. This is the perfect area for an art fix. START: **Subway N or R to 23rd Street.**

1 ★ Flatiron Building. The Flatiron's triangular shape wasn't chosen for artsy reasons—it was simply the only way to fill the intersections of Fifth Avenue, 23rd Street, and Broadway. That happy accident in 1902 created one of the city's most recognizable buildings, and one of the first skyscrapers. There's no observation deck, so what you see from the street is what you get. *175 Fifth Ave. (Broadway). Subway: N/R to 23rd St.*

2 Hotel Chelsea. Want some local flavor? Step into the lobby of the Chelsea, which is both a hotel and residential apartments. The hotel prides itself on the colorful coterie that passes through its doors. Over the years that has included artists like Claes Oldenburg, Jackson Pollack, and Jim Dine. Plaques at the entrance honor the many writers

Paintings in the lobby of the Hotel Chelsea.

Flatiron Building.

who also lived here: Mark Twain, O. Henry, Dylan Thomas, Thomas Wolfe, and more. Note the delicate wrought-iron balconies extending along the facade of this 12-story brick building. *See p 54, bullet* **4**.

3 PaceWildenstein. The massive space is deliberately shorn of decoration so as not to detract from the dramatic paintings and sculptures. It's one of the neighborhood's best-known galleries, so expect to see major artists like Alexander Calder (1898–1976) and Mark Rothko (1903–1970) represented. *534 W. 25th St. (btwn Tenth & Eleventh aves.).* ☎ *212/929-7000. www.pacewildenstein.com. Tues–Sat 10am–6pm.*

4 ★★ Barbara Gladstone Gallery. Gladstone's sizable roster of American and European artists includes famous names like Matthew

Barney (creator of the *Cremaster* cycle) and German artist Rosemarie Trockel. *515 W. 24th St. (btwn Tenth & Eleventh aves.).* ☎ *212/206-9300. www.gladstonegallery.com. Tues–Sat 10am–6pm.*

5 ★★ **Gagosian Gallery.** This is a must-see. Most of Chelsea's galleries aren't large enough to hold more than one major exhibit at a time, but the Gagosian is an exception. Past shows have included works by neo-expressionist Julian Schnabel and controversial British artist Damien Hirst, he of the tanks of pigs in formaldehyde. *555 W. 24th St. (btwn. Tenth & Eleventh aves.).* ☎ *212/741-1111. www.gagosian. com. Tues–Sat 10am–6pm.*

6 ★ **DIA: Chelsea.** This famous nonprofit gallery is closed for renovations until 2006. However, its renowned "Artists on Artists" lecture series will remain open. The series explores the works of contemporary artists from the point of view of their peers. All lectures start at 6:30pm; the schedule is on the website. *548 W. 22nd St. (btwn Tenth & Eleventh aves.).* ☎ *212/989-5566. www.diacenter. org. Tickets $6 adults, $3 seniors & students.*

7 ★ **Wild Lily Tea Room.** This Taiwainese-inspired oasis is a perfect place for a pot of tea or light fare such as steamed dumplings, scones, and pastries. The tearoom displays paintings and ceramics by local artists. *511 W. 22nd St. (at Tenth Ave.).* ☎ *212/691-2258. www.wildlilytearoom.com. $.*

8 ★ **Max Protetch Gallery.** Adjacent to Wild Lily, this gallery specializes in drawings. Previous exhibits have included works by architects like Rem Koolhaas, Michael Graves, and the legendary Frank Lloyd Wright. *511 W. 22nd St. (at Tenth Ave.).* ☎ *212/633-6999. www.maxprotetch.com. Tues–Sat 10am–6pm.*

9 **Church of the Guardian Angel.** This lovely brick-and-limestone example of Romanesque architecture was built in 1931. At that time it was known as the Shine Church of the Sea because of its proximity to the Chelsea piers (the real ones, not the entertainment center). Be sure to admire the ornate entrance. *193 Tenth Ave. (btwn 21st & 22nd sts.).* ☎ *212/929-5966. Mass Sat 5pm, Sun 9am & noon.*

Max Protetch Gallery.

The Sports Center at Chelsea Pier has two sundecks.

10 ★ Cushman Row. In the late 1830s, much of Chelsea's real estate was developed by a merchant named Don Alonzo Cushman. His little empire included the stunning Greek Revival houses on West 20th Street between Ninth and Tenth avenues. The houses from no. 406 to no. 418 are better known as Cushman Row (there's a little plaque at no. 412 in tribute). *20th St. (btwn Ninth & Tenth aves.).*

11 Chelsea Market. Fast food doesn't get any better than that served in this ingeniously restored biscuit factory. Here you have your choice of delicious quick stops, with food ranging from sweet (Fat Witch Bakery) to savory (Cleaver Company). *75 Ninth Ave. (btwn 15th & 16th sts.). www.chelseamarket.com. $–$$.*

12 ★★ Rubin Museum of Art. You've checked out some contemporary galleries; now it's time to enjoy some historic masterpieces. This non-commercial gallery of Himalayan art was added to the Chelsea art scene in 2004. *See p 18, bullet* **15**.

Visiting Chelsea Piers

All this art and history got your blood going? It may be time to hit the links. Yes, at the massive Chelsea Piers sports complex, you can drive golf balls out over the Hudson River (caught by a giant net, of course) to your heart's content. The views aren't bad either. The complex also has a bowling alley, batting cages, two sundecks, and basketball courts. *23rd St. & Hudson River.* ☎ *212/336-6400. $20: 80 balls (peak), 118 balls (off-peak); club rentals $4. Oct–March 6:30am–11pm; April–Sept 6am–midnight. Bus: M23; subway: C/E to 23rd St.*

Greenwich **Village**

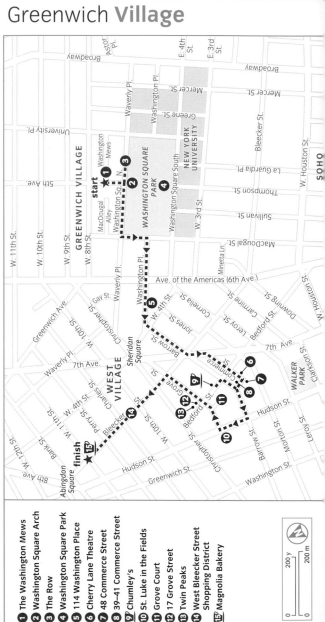

1 The Washington Mews
2 Washington Square Arch
3 The Row
4 Washington Square Park
5 114 Washington Place
6 Cherry Lane Theatre
7 48 Commerce Street
8 39–41 Commerce Street
9 Chumley's
10 St. Luke in the Fields
11 Grove Court
12 17 Grove Street
13 Twin Peaks
14 West Bleecker Street Shopping District
15 Magnolia Bakery

200 y
200 m

This storied neighborhood has been home to writers, painters, and entertainers for decades. It's also one of Manhattan's most picturesque and historic districts, whose small scale and dearth of skyscrapers and industrial space give it a real neighborhood feel. START: **Subway N or R to 8th Street.**

❶ ★ The Washington Mews. Visitors who stumble upon this cobbled alleyway discover a living slice of old New York. The north side of the mews is comprised of original 19th-century stables that were converted into stuccoed houses painted in pastels and whimsically decorated—even the stable doors are integrated into the designs. The south side was built in 1939 to mirror the north, but lacks the offbeat grace notes of the original. *Enter either at University Place or Fifth Ave. btwn 8th St. & Waverly Place.*

❷ ★ Washington Square Arch. This impressive Roman-style arch, designed by Stanford White, was first built of wood in 1889 to commemorate the centennial anniversary of George Washington's inauguration; the current version was completed in 1891 in white marble. The arch is one of the most important landmarks in lower New York. Over the years it has come to be a symbol of the neighborhood's spirit of freedom and individuality. After a painstaking year-long restoration in 2004, the ivory arch practically gleams. *Fifth Ave. & Waverly Place.*

❸ ★★ The Row. These are some of Manhattan's most celebrated town houses, built in elegant Greek Revival style for society's blue bloods from 1832 to 1833 and looking much as they did in the days of early-19th-century New York. Henry James' heroine in *Washington Square* lived here, as did many memorable characters in Edith Wharton's novels. Head west, and

you can see more survivors from that era at 19–26 Washington Square North. *1–13 Washington Square North (btwn Fifth Ave. & University Place).*

❹ Washington Square Park. This relatively small park gets plenty of use (some say overuse) from local residents, New York University students, long-in-the-tooth guitarists, dog-walkers, and assorted riff-raff. The land on which it was built in the 1820s was once a cemetery for victims of yellow fever, and the site of public hangings (from a centuries-old elm that still stands in the northwest corner of the park). These days, a roguish quality remains, with hucksters performing comedy and magic acts on a regular basis. A multimillion-dollar renovation is in the works, however, so it may be quite a

Lion sculptures guard buildings on Washington Square North.

different park by the time you visit. *Bordered by University & Waverly places & W. 4th & Macdougal sts.*

⑤ 114 Washington Place.
Note the fancy boot scrapers on the wrought-iron stair railings from the days when transportation was largely on horseback and the streets were filled with horse manure. As you stroll, you'll spot boot scrapers of all designs all over the Village.

⑥ Cherry Lane Theatre.
Writer/poet Edna St. Vincent Millay and her artist peers converted an 1817 box factory into the Cherry Lane Playhouse in 1924. In 1929, legendary acting teacher Lee Strasberg directed F. Scott Fitzgerald's only published full-length play, *The Vegetable,* here. (It closed after 13 performances.) It's still a working theater; call to see what's playing during your visit. *38 Commerce St. (at Bedford St.).* ☎ *212/989-2020. www.cherrylanetheatre.com.*

⑦ 48 Commerce St. Note the working gas lamp in front of the 1844 home of a wealthy merchant. The New York Gas Light Company began laying gas pipes in 1823, and gas lamps—many with an ornamental post design—continued to shine into the 20th century.

⑧ ★★ 39–41 Commerce St.
These three-story twin houses are among the most striking examples of early-19th-century architecture in the Village—and the fact that they neatly mirror one another adds to the visual appeal. Topped with elegant mansard roofs and linked by a courtyard, nos. 39 and 41 were built in 1831 and 1832, respectively.

⑨ ★★ Chumley's. One of the last original speak-easies in the city, Chumley's has no signage, no indication of what's inside. Its entrance on 86 Bedford St. was originally the

back door, where customers were told to "86 it" whenever cops made a raid during Prohibition. Another entrance is around the corner through a courtyard at 58 Barrow St. Either one will bring you into the warmth of a historic Village tavern, complete with blazing fireplace, good grub, a handful of lounging dogs, and a vintage jukebox. Opened in 1928, Chumley's was a prime watering hole for literary types in the 1930s, and book jackets from some of the 20th-century's most celebrated writers line the wooden walls. *86 Bedford St. or 58 Barrow St.* ☎ *212/675-4449. $–$$.*

⑩ ★ St. Luke in the Fields. This charming little church is a reconstruction of the original, which was built in 1822 and badly damaged in a fire in 1981. The site on Hudson Street was

A private entrance at Grove Court.

It's hard to resist Magnolia's delicious cupcakes.

donated by Trinity Church, and, from 1891 to 1876, St. Luke was part of Trinity Parish. One of the church's founding wardens was Clement Clarke Moore, a gentleman scholar who is perhaps best known as the author of *'Twas the Night Before Christmas.* You're welcome to stroll about the interior and linger in the pretty church gardens (open Tues–Sun 8:30am–dusk). Sunday services at at 8, 9:15, and 11:15am. *487 Hudson St. (at Grove St.).*

⑪ ★ **Grove Court.** This lovely gated mews set back from the street was once considered a slum; it was built for workingmen around 1853 and known at the time as "Mixed Ale Alley." Today, the genteel Greek Revival structures enjoy a rarity in a city where space is at a premium: a large open courtyard. *10–12 Grove St. (btwn Hudson & Bedford sts.).*

⑫ **17 Grove St.** This 1822 house is one of the last remaining wood-framed houses in the Village. Note the little 1823 cottage in back (behind the slatted fence), at 100 Bedford St., which was the workshop of the former owner, a sashmaker.

⑬ **Twin Peaks.** This 1830 house was given a fanciful Tudoresque renovation in 1925. It stands out among the straightforward 19th-century architecture that dominates the neighborhood. *102 Bedford St. (at Grove St.).*

⑭ ★ **West Bleecker Street Shopping District.** West Bleecker Street, from Christopher Street to Bank Street, became a trendy boutique alley almost overnight. Small-scale and pleasant to stroll, you'll find **Intermix** (no. 365; ☎ 212/929-7180), **Ralph Lauren** (nos. 380–381; ☎ 212/645-5513), **Marc Jacobs** (nos. 385 and 403–405; ☎ 212/924-6126), **Lulu Guinness** (no. 394; ☎ 212/367-2120), and more. *West Bleecker St. (btwn Christopher & Bank sts.).*

⑮ ★ **Magnolia Bakery.** What draws the crowds to this dessert shop? Cupcakes, hundreds of 'em—but only a dozen per customer, please. It's quite a scene, with lines around the block and constant tour-bus activity. In addition to the color-ful, buttercream-frosted cupcakes, Magnolia has plenty of other first-rate desserts, like banana pudding and pecan pie. *401 Bleecker St. (at 11th St.).* ☎ *212/462-2572. $.*

Prospect Park **& Park Slope**

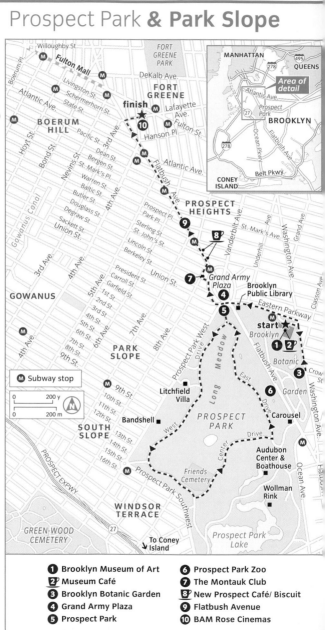

1. Brooklyn Museum of Art
2. Museum Café
3. Brooklyn Botanic Garden
4. Grand Army Plaza
5. Prospect Park
6. Prospect Park Zoo
7. The Montauk Club
8. New Prospect Café/ Biscuit
9. Flatbush Avenue
10. BAM Rose Cinemas

The attractions in and around Prospect Park are well worth the 25-minute subway ride from midtown. Expect gorgeous parkland, the city's second largest art museum, plus lovely 19th-century brownstones and hip clothing boutiques. START: **Subway 2 or 3 to Eastern Parkway.**

❶ ★★★ **kids** **Brooklyn Museum of Art.** In any other city, this spectacular museum would be a star attraction, but in New York it's often overlooked because of its location outside Manhattan. The collection in New York's second-largest museum is well worth a trip, however. Highlights include the **Ancient Egyptian collection,** the **Asian art collection** (which specializes in both classic and contemporary works from Japan), and the **Luce Center for American Art** (an "open storage" annex holding 9,000 works, from Tiffany lamps to 19th-century furniture by local artisans). Designed by architects McKim, Mead & White in 1897, the museum received a new front entrance and a dramatic plaza complete with fountains in 2004. ⏱ *2–3 hr. 200 Eastern Pkwy. (at Washington Ave.).* ☎ *718/638-5000. www.brooklynmuseum.org. Admission $8 adults, $4 seniors & students, free for children under 12. Wed–Fri 10am–5pm; Sat–Sun 11am–5:45pm. Subway: 2/3 to Eastern Pkwy.*

❷ The ground-floor **Museum Café** ($) at the Brooklyn Museum of Art is a good place to refuel before you continue, but if it's nice out, wait until you get to the Botanic Garden (bullet ❸) and eat at the casual outdoor **café** ($).

❸ ★★★ **Brooklyn Botanic Garden.** This tranquil, elegant retreat is my favorite garden in the city. It encompasses the **Cranford Rose Garden,** a **Children's Garden,** the **Osborne Garden** (3 acres of formal gardens), the **Fragrance Garden** (designed for the visually impaired but appreciated by all), and the **Japanese Hill-and-Pond Garden.** In colder weather you can investigate one of the world's largest collections of bonsai in the **C. V. Starr Bonsai Museum,** and indoor plants (everything from cacti to orchids) in the **Steinhardt Conservatory.** If you come in April or May, seek out the lush carpet of bluebells and check the website for the timing of the **Cherry Blossom Festival.** ⏱ *1–2 hr. 1000 Washington Ave. (at Eastern Pkwy.).* ☎ *718/623 7200. www.bbg.org Admission $5 adults, $3 seniors & students, free for children under 16. Apr–Sept Tues–Fri 8am–6pm, Sat–Sun 10am–6pm; Oct–Mar Tues–Fri 8am–4:30pm, Sat–Sun 10am–4:30pm.*

❹ **Grand Army Plaza.** This multi-lane traffic circle and the tremendous **Soldiers' and Sailors' Memorial Arch** presiding over it are reminiscent of Paris' Place Charles de Gaulle and the Arc de Triomphe. The arch was built in 1892 to honor Union

Late Shang Dynasty Ritual Wine Vessel from the Brooklyn Museum of Art.

Look for the bas-reliefs of Lincoln and Grant within Soldiers' and Sailors' Memorial Arch.

soldiers who died in the Civil War. *Within Plaza St. at the intersection of Flatbush Ave., Prospect Park W., Eastern Pkwy., and Vanderbilt Ave.*

5 ★★★ kids **Prospect Park.** Central Park designers Frederick Law Olmstead and Calvert Vaux considered Prospect Park to be their masterpiece. The park has 562 acres of woodland, including Brooklyn's last remaining virgin forest, plus meadows, bluffs, and ponds. For the best views, enter at Grand Army Plaza and walk to your right either on the park's ring road (called West Drive here) or on the parallel pedestrian path to Meadowport Arch, and proceed to **Long Meadow.** Overlooking

Prospect Park's boathouse.

Long Meadow is **Litchfield Villa,** an 1857 mansion that became the headquarters for the New York Parks system. Eventually West Drive turns into Center Drive, which will take you past the **Friends' Cemetery** Quaker burial ground. Center Drive leads to East Drive, which on its way back to Grand Army Plaza, passes the 1906 Beaux Arts **boathouse,** the 1912 **carousel,** the zoo, and **Lefferts Homestead Children's Historic House Museum** (☎ 718/789-2822), a 1783 Dutch farmhouse with a museum of period furniture and exhibits. *Bounded by Prospect Park W., Parkside Ave. & Flatbush Ave.* ☎ *718/965-8951. www.prospectpark.org.*

6 ★ kids **Prospect Park Zoo.** If you've got kids in tow, you won't want to miss the zoo at the eastern end of the park. Children in particular take delight in encountering many animals up close, including wallabies and prairie dogs. ⏱ *1 hr.* ☎ *718/399-7339. Admission $5 adults, $1.25 seniors, $1 children 3–12. Mon–Fri 10am–5pm; Sat–Sun 10am–5:30pm.*

7 ★ **The Montauk Club.** The northwestern side of Prospect Park is home to the upscale neighborhood of Park Slope, and wandering its tree-lined streets is a great way to spend an afternoon. I'm a longtime admirer of the late-19th-century brownstones, many of which have been lovingly restored (walk along Montgomery Place between Eighth Ave. and Prospect Park West to see what I mean). If there were an award for most stunning building, it would go to the **Montauk Club,** which was designed in 1891 by architect Francis H. Kimball to resemble a Venetian palace. It's a private club, but hosts many public events throughout the year. *25 Eighth Ave. (at Lincoln Place).* ☎ *718/638-0800.*

8 At tiny **New Prospect Café** (393 Flatbush Ave.; ☎ 718/638-2148; $–$$), you can enjoy soups, salads, sandwiches, and more elaborate meals. Pulled-meat sandwiches and fried chicken are the specialties at **Biscuit** (367 Flatbush Ave.; ☎ 718/398-2227, $).

9 ★ **Flatbush Avenue.** Shops on Flatbush range from fast-food dives to high-fashion boutiques with prices significantly lower than Manhattan's. **Hooti Couture** at no. 321 (corner of Seventh Ave.; ☎ 718/857-1977) sells high-quality vintage clothing and accessories, and is one of my favorite places to

A detail from the Montauk Club.

Park Slope's brownstones.

shop. **Nouveau Décor** at no. 333 (btwn Sterling Ave. & Park Place; ☎ 718/230-0310) sells elegant furnishings with an exotic twist; most of the pieces are American-made. Both international and local clothing designers are on show at **Redberi** at no. 339 (btwn Sterling Ave. & Park Place; ☎ 718/622-1964), making it a great spot to find unique pieces.

10 **BAM Rose Cinemas.** When this movie theater opened in 1998 near Fort Green, its art house movies brought a much-needed cultural boost to the neighborhood. Bam-Cafe on the second floor has big, squashy chairs and huge windows. It's a great place to enjoy a drink or a light meal before or after your movie and it also has a regular roster of live musical acts. Both local talent and bigger names perform jazz, R&B, and more. You can catch the 2/3/4/5/B/D/N/R/Q subway lines back to Manhattan at the Atlantic Avenue station, a couple blocks south of BAM on Flatbush Avenue. *30 Lafayette Ave. (btwn Ashland Place & St. Felix St.).* ☎ *718/636-4100. $$.*

Chinatown **& Lower East Side**

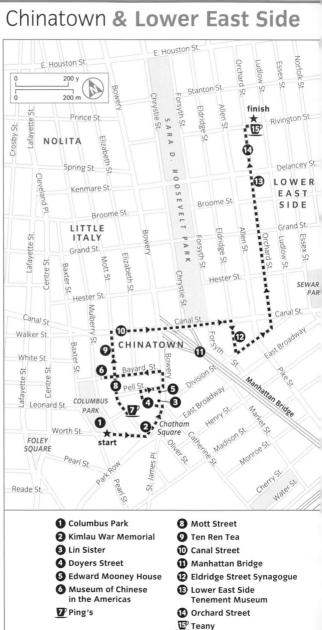

1 Columbus Park
2 Kimlau War Memorial
3 Lin Sister
4 Doyers Street
5 Edward Mooney House
6 Museum of Chinese
   in the Americas
7 Ping's
8 Mott Street
9 Ten Ren Tea
10 Canal Street
11 Manhattan Bridge
12 Eldridge Street Synagogue
13 Lower East Side
   Tenement Museum
14 Orchard Street
15 Teany

Long known for its vibrant street life, the Lower East Side was also home to notorious slums (including Five Points) where Irish, Italian, Jewish, and Chinese immigrants crowded into tenements. Although much survives from that era—including a number of tenement buildings—today the neighborhood hums with the energy of cutting-edge restaurants, bars, and live-music clubs. START: Subway 4, 5, or 6 to Brooklyn Bridge/City Hall.

❶ ★ **Columbus Park.** This park lies where New York's worst slum, known as Mulberry Bend, once stood surrounded by tenements with names like Bone Alley, Kerosene Row, and Bandits' Roost. Most of the houses were torn down in the early 20th century. The exception was the Chinatown section, which was left alone out of racist fears that the Chinese would move into other neighborhoods. *Bounded by Mosco, Mulberry, Bayard, and Baxter sts. Subway: 4/5/6 to Brooklyn Bridge/City Hall.*

❷ **Kimlau War Memorial.** This memorial arch in Chatham Square was erected in 1962 to honor the Chinese Americans who gave their lives fighting in World War II. The square also contains an imposing statue of Lao-Tse, the Chinese philosopher and founder of Taoism. *Chatham Square.*

❸ ★ **Lin Sister.** This three-story apothecary is a marvel. A wall of wooden drawers, each containing medicinal herbs, dominates the first floor. On the upper levels reflexology massage and acupuncture treatments are offered, and a homeopathic doctor is available for consultations. *4 Bowery. (at Division St.). ☎ 212/962-5417. www.linsisterherb.com.*

❹ **Doyers Street.** As you walk along Bowery, keep an eye out for Doyers Street, a small alleyway. This area was once notorious for activity by gangs known as *tongs* (the "activity" was mainly of the violent sort and often involved hatchets, which gave rise to the term "hatchet man"). Doyers Street has a sharp bend in it—locals call it an elbow—which made it impossible to see who was around the corner.

❺ **Edward Mooney House.** This Georgian brick structure, painted red with eggshell trim, is the oldest row house in the city, dating from George Washington's New York days. Wealthy merchant Edward Mooney had the house built in 1785 on property abandoned by a Tory during the American Revolution. *18 Bowery (at Pell St.).*

❻ ★★ **kids** **Museum of Chinese in the Americas.** It is difficult to comprehend the cruel hardships that the first generations of Chinese suffered in New York. This museum, founded in 1980, documents the history and culture of the Chinese in America from the early

A display at the Museum of Chinese in the Americas.

A woman ladles out tea in Ten Ren Tea.

1800s to the present. ⏲ *45 min. 70 Mulberry St., 2nd floor (at Bayard St.).* ☎ *212/619-4785. www.moca-nyc.org. Tues–Thurs & Sat–Sun noon–6pm; Fri noon–7pm. Adults $3, under 12 free; free Fri. Subway: N/R/Q/W/J/M/Z/6 to Canal St.*

7 ★★ **Dim sum.** Chinatown is famous for its dim sum palaces, where servers offer choice little delicacies from carts they wheel around the restaurant floor. Great for sharing (and a smart economical choice),

these offerings often include *har gow* (shrimp dumplings), pork buns, even chicken feet. One of my favorites is **Ping's** (22 Mott St.; ☎ 212/602-9988; $), which has exceptional dim sum noodles and fresh seafood.

8 ★ **Mott Street.** This is the heart of old Chinatown, and the epicenter of the boisterous Chinese New Year celebrations that begin with the first full moon after January 21st. But at any time of year it's a great place to wander and shop. Some addresses to note (all are between Canal and Pell sts.): **Fashion Beauty New York** at no. 81 for cheap-chic Asian clothing and accessories; **Good Field Trading** at no. 74, for imported stationery, toys, and electronics; **Bok Lei Po Trading** at no. 63, the best martial-arts supply store; and **Fung Wong Bakery** at no. 41, for fresh-baked egg tarts.

9 ★ **Ten Ren Tea.** The famous Taiwanese tea maker Ten Ren has a particularly charming outpost on Mott Street. Some of the teapots on

Cooked ducks hang in a Chinatown restaurant window.

Special

Peking Duck

HLF $ 12⁰⁰
WHL $ 18⁵⁰

Eldridge Street Synagogue.

display are museum-worthy, and the selection of teas is impossible to beat. *75 Mott St. (btwn Canal & Bayard sts.).* ☎ *212/349-2286. www.tenrenusa.com.*

🔟 **Canal Street.** From West Broadway to the Manhattan Bridge, this is one of the city's liveliest and most congested thoroughfares. Stalls hawk everything from "designer" handbags to electronics. One of my favorite spots is **Kam Man** at no. 200, which has a supermarket upstairs (great for made-in-Japan candy) and a massive collection of ceramics downstairs. Other good bets are **Pearl Paint** (p 98), and **195 Dragon Jewelry** at no. 195 for beautifully carved jade.

⓫ ★ **Manhattan Bridge.** This 1905 suspension bridge may not be as artistically inspired as the Brooklyn Bridge, but the monumental Beaux Arts colonnade and arch at its entrance are quite arresting. *Canal St. & Bowery.*

⓬ ★ **Eldridge Street Synagogue.** When it was built (1886–1888) by Eastern European Jews, it was the most magnificent synagogue on the Lower East Side. Its congregation included such luminaries as Eddie Cantor, Jonas Salk, and Edward G. Robinson. Over the years, however, membership declined and the structure fell into disrepair. The rickety interior sanctuary was cordoned off in the 1950s, where it remained empty for more than 25 years, suffering such indignities as termite infestation, staircase collapses, and near-total deterioration of the roof. A grassroots renovation project is now underway to restore the synagogue to its former glory. Designed by the Herter Brothers, specialists in tenements, the landmark structure has been largely encroached by Chinatown, but its terra-cotta-and-brick Moorish facade is still beguiling, and the interior decor includes delicate stained-glass rose windows. One way to appreciate the structure is to attend an evening concert; see the website for a schedule. ⏱ *20 min. 12 Eldridge St. (btwn Canal & Division sts.).* ☎ *212/219-0888. www.eldridgestreet.org. Guided tours available Tues, Thurs & Sun; call in advance for details. Tour tickets $5 adults, $3 seniors & children; $1 self-guided tour (Sun only). Sun 11am–4pm; other days by appointment. Subway: B/D to Grand St.; 6/N/R to Canal St.*

⓭ ★★★ **kids Lower East Side Tenement Museum.** Conceived as a monument to the experience of "urban pioneers" in America, this don't-miss museum documents the lives of immigrant residents in a six-story tenement built in 1863 at 97 Orchard St. (accessible only via the highly recommended guided tours). The tenement rooms are eerily authentic, and for good reason: 97 Orchard was essentially boarded up from 1935 to 1987; when it was finally opened, everything was exactly as it had been left in 1935, a virtual time capsule of tenement life. Artifacts found range from the mundane (medicine tins and Russian cigarettes) to the personal (a 1922

Orchard Street is usually jammed with shoppers every day but Saturday.

Ouija board and an infant's button-up shoe). Among several tours to choose from, "Getting By" is an account of the backbreaking, hard-scrabble life that many immigrants faced in the late 19th and early 20th centuries. Another, "Piecing It Together," explains how crucial the garment trade was to many new arrivals. Book your visit online at least a week in advance—this is one of New York's most popular museums. ⏱ *1–1½ hr. Visitors' Center at 90 Orchard St. (Delancey St.).* ☎ *212/431-0233. www.tenement. org. Tours $9 adults, $7 seniors & students. Tues–Fri 1–4pm; Sat–Sun 11am–4:45pm. Subway: B/D to Grand St.; F to Delancey.*

🄯 **Orchard Street.** In the 19th century, this street was a vast out-door marketplace lined with rows of pushcarts. Today, stores have replaced the pushcarts, but in the spirit of tradition, many shop owners are willing to haggle over prices. On Sundays the street is closed to vehicular traffic between Delancey

and Houston streets. Keep in mind that many of the shops are closed Friday afternoon and Saturday for the Jewish Sabbath. Check out stores between Rivington and Grand streets like: **Harry Zarin** (318 Grand; ☎ 212/925-6112; www.harryzarin. com), for great fabrics and trims; **Frock** (148 Orchard St.; ☎ 212/594-5380), for vintage designer clothing; **Pippin** (p 97), for well-priced vintage jewelry; and Guss Pickles (85 Orchard St.; ☎ 800/252-GUSS), where you'll smell the sharp, briny aroma of the last purveyor of pickles on the Lower East Side halfway down the street. These barrels have been here since 1910; options include sours, half sours, and hots.

🄯 For vegetarian sandwiches, snacks, and tea, head to musician Moby's **Teany** (90 Rivington St. btwn Ludlow & Orchard sts.; ☎ 212/475-9190; $). Or, if it's getting on toward cocktail hour, enjoy a glass of wine at one of my favorite bars, **Punch & Judy** (p 132). ●

Shopping **Best Bets**

Best **Designer Clothing Discounts**
★★★ Century 21, *22 Cortlandt St. (p 93)*

Most **Luscious Foods**
★★ Dean & DeLuca, *560 Broadway (p 96)*

Best **Place to Deck Out Your Dream House**
★★★ ABC Carpet & Home, *881 & 888 Broadway (p 96)*

Most **Beautiful Store Design**
★★ Prada, *575 Broadway (p 95)*

Best **Footwear**
★★ Manolo Blahnik, *31 W. 54th St. (p 97);* and ★ Otto Tootsi Plohound, *137 Fifth Ave. (p 98)*

Best **Antique Furnishings**
★ Chelsea Antiques Building, *110 W. 25th St. (p 92);* and ★★ Sinotique, *19A Mott St. (p 92)*

Best **All-Around Department Store**
★★ Bloomingdale's, *1000 Third Ave. (p 93)*

Best **Browsing**
★★ Takashimaya, *693 Fifth Ave. (p 94)*

The Chelsea Antiques Building has 12 floors and over 100 dealers.

Best **for Kids**
★★ Maxilla & Mandible, *451 Columbus Ave. (p 96)*

Best **Men's Designer Clothes**
★ Jeffrey New York, *449 W. 14th St. (p 95);* and ★ Scoop, *873 Washington St. (p 95)*

Best **Women's Designer Clothes**
★ Scoop, *873 Washington St. (p 95);* and ★ Intermix, *125 Fifth Ave. (p 95)*

Best **Rare CDs & Vinyl**
★ Bleecker St. Records, *239 Bleecker St. (p 97);* and Jazz Record Center, *236 W. 26th St. (p. 97)*

Best **Vintage Jewelry**
★ Pippin, *72 Orchard St. (p 97)*

Best **Wine & Liquor**
★ Sherry-Lehmann, *679 Madison Ave. (p 97)*

Best **Deals on Electronics**
J&R Music & Computer World, *23 Park Row (p 94)*

Best **Stationery & Art Supply**
Kate's Paperie, *561 Broadway (p 98);* and ★ Pearl Paint, *308 Canal St. (p 98)*

Best **Lingerie**
★ Agent Provocateur, *133 Mercer St. (p 95);* and ★★ Henri Bendel, *712 Fifth Ave. (p 93)*

Best **Beauty Products**
★★ Face Stockholm, *110 Prince St. (p 92)*

Most **Original Jewelry**
★ Fragments, *116 Prince St. (p 97)*

Best **Modern Art Gallery**
★★ Barbara Gladstone Gallery, *515 W. 24th St. (p 71);* and ★ Max Protetch Gallery, *511 W. 22nd St. (p 72)*

Downtown **Shopping**

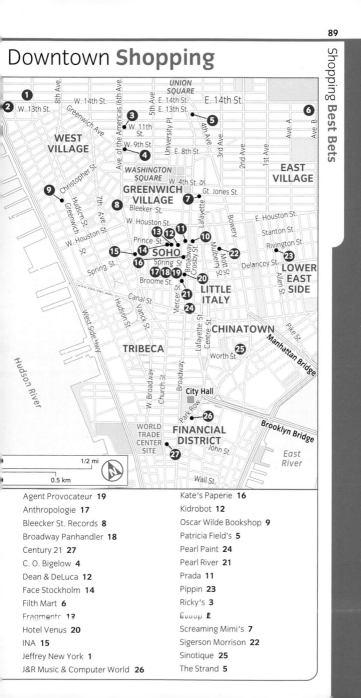

Agent Provocateur **19**
Anthropologie **17**
Bleecker St. Records **8**
Broadway Panhandler **18**
Century 21 **27**
C. O. Bigelow **4**
Dean & DeLuca **12**
Face Stockholm **14**
Filth Mart **6**
Fragments **13**
Hotel Venus **20**
INA **15**
Jeffrey New York **1**
J&R Music & Computer World **26**

Kate's Paperie **16**
Kidrobot **12**
Oscar Wilde Bookshop **9**
Patricia Field's **5**
Pearl Paint **24**
Pearl River **21**
Prada **11**
Pippin **23**
Ricky's **3**
Screaming Mimi's **7**
Sigerson Morrison **22**
Sinotique **25**
The Strand **5**

New York **Shopping, A to Z**

Antiques & Collectibles

★ Chelsea Antiques Building
CHELSEA This 12-floor building houses more than 100 dealers and is open daily. I dare you to leave without buying *something*. *110 W. 25th St. (btwn Sixth & Seventh aves.).* ☎ *212/929-0909. No credit cards. Subway: F to 23rd St. Map p 90.*

Fishs Eddy UNION SQUARE AREA
Come here for vintage and reproduction dishes, flatware, and glasses. *889 Broadway (at 19th St.).* ☎ *212/420-9020. www.fishseddy.com. AE, MC, V. Subway: L/N/R/4/5/6 to 14th St./Union Sq. Map p 90.*

★★ Sinotique CHINATOWN
Stunning and exotic furniture, wall coverings, carvings, and statues, all imported from Asia, and all antique originals. *19A Mott St. (btwn Mosco St. & Bowery).* ☎ *212/587-2393. www.sinotique.com. MC, V. Subway: J/M/Z/6 to Canal St. Map p 89.*

Beauty

★ C. O. Bigelow GREENWICH
VILLAGE This 162-year-old apothecary carries an eclectic collection of personal care products, including Weleda, Neal's Yard, and its own excellent house label. Quality is high but the prices are reasonable. *414 Sixth Ave. (btwn 8th & 9th sts.).* ☎ *212/533-2700. www.bigelow chemists.com. AE, DISC, MC, V. Subway: A/C/E/F/V to W. 4th St. Map p 89.*

★★ Face Stockholm SOHO
Their in-house makeup line is one of the best. *110 Prince St. (Greene St.).* ☎ *212/966-9110. AE, MC, V. Subway: N/R to Prince St. Map p 89.*

Ricky's GREENWICH VILLAGE
A haven for tweens, teens, and the young at heart with multicolored wigs, rainbow-colored lipstick, and glitter galore. *466 Sixth Ave. (at 11th St.).* ☎ *212/924-3401. AE, DISC, MC, V. Subway: A/C/E/B/D/F to W. 4th St. Map p 89.*

Books

★★ Barnes & Noble UNION
SQUARE This is one of the chain's biggest and best stores for browsing. *33 E. 17th St. (Broadway).* ☎ *212/253-0810. www.bn.com. AE, DC, DISC, MC, V. Subway: 4/5/6 to Union Sq. Map p 90.*

★★ Borders COLUMBUS CIRCLE
This well-organized shop is a joy to spend time in. *10 Columbus Circle*

Ricky's eclectic offerings include wigs and T-shirts as well as drugstore basics.

(at W. 59th St. and Central Park West). ☎ 212/823-9775. www. bordersstores.com. AE, DC, DISC, MC, V. Subway: 1/2/3/9/A/B/C/D to 59 St./Columbus Circle. Map p 90.

★★ **Coliseum Books** MIDTOWN WEST This sizable independent store has a knowledgeable staff. 11 W. 42nd St. (btwn Fifth & Sixth aves.). ☎ 212/803-5890. www. coliseumbooks.com. AE, DC, DISC, MC, V. Subway: B/D/F/V to 42nd St. Map p 90.

★★ **Oscar Wilde Bookshop** GREENWICH VILLAGE I think this is the best gay and lesbian bookstore in New York. Although it's relatively small, Oscar Wilde is atmospheric and intimate, with a solid collection and a fine selection of first editions. 15 Christopher St. (btwn Sixth & Seventh aves.). ☎ 212/255-8097. www.oscarwildebooks.com. AE, MC, V. Subway: 1/9 to Christopher St. Map p 89.

★★ **Rizzoli** MIDTOWN WEST This clubby Italian bookstore is the place to browse visual art and design books, plus quality fiction and gourmet cookbooks. 31 W. 57th St. (btwn Fifth & Sixth aves.). ☎ 212/759-2424. AE, MC, V. Subway: N/R to Fifth Ave. Map p 90.

★★ **The Strand** UNION SQUARE AREA A local legend, it's worth a visit for its staggering "18 miles of books" and bargain titles at up to 85% off list price. 828 Broadway (at 12th St.). ☎ 212/473-1452. www.strand books.com. AE, DC, DISC, MC, V. Subway: L/N/R/4/5/6 to Union Sq. Map p 89.

Department Stores
Barneys New York MIDTOWN EAST The Madison Avenue shop is all about high style and attitude; **Barneys Co-Op** is friendlier and hipper. 660 Madison Ave. (at 61st St.). ☎ 212/826-8900.

The men's department is usually more sedate than the women's at Century 21.

www.barneys.com. Subway: N/R to Fifth Ave. Barneys Co-Op: 236 W. 18th St. (btwn Seventh & Eighth aves.). ☎ 212/593-7800. AE, DC, DISC, MC, V. Subway: 1/9 to 18th St. Map p 90.

★ **Bergdorf Goodman** MIDTOWN The place for ladies who lunch and anyone who reveres couture. 754 Fifth Ave. (at 57th St.). ☎ 212/753-7300. www.bergdorfgoodman.com. AE, DC, MC, V. Subway: E/F to Fifth Ave. Map p 90.

★★ **Bloomingdale's** MIDTOWN EAST More accessible and affordable than Barneys, Bergdorf, or Saks, this is a sentimental favorite. 1000 Third Ave. (Lexington Ave. at 59th St.). ☎ 212/705-2000. www. bloomingdales.com. AE, MC, V. Subway: 4/5/6 to 59th St. Map p 90.

★★★ **Century 21** FINANCIAL DISTRICT An hour is all it takes to get addicted to the seriously discounted designer clothes and housewares. 22 Cortlandt St. (btwn Broadway & Church St.). ☎ 212/227-9092. www. c21stores.com. AE, MC, V. Subway: 1/2/3/4/5/M to Fulton St.; A/C to Broadway/Nassau St.; E to Chambers St. Map p 89.

★★ **Henri Bendel** MIDTOWN A superstylish emporium for grown-up girls who love the funky and the

Bendel's window displays.

frilly. The lingerie department is the best in the city. *712 Fifth Ave. (btwn 55th & 56th sts.).* ☎ *212/247-1100. AE, DC, DISC, MC, V. Subway: N/R to Fifth Ave. Map p 90.*

Macy's HERALD SQUARE The size is unmanageable, the service is dreadful, but they do sell everything. At least walk by the charming window displays. *At Herald Square, W. 34th St. & Broadway.* ☎ *212/695-4400. www.macys.com. AE, MC, V. Subway: B/D/F/N/Q/R/1/2/3/9 to 34th St. Map p 90.*

The prices can be high, but this location of Saks is a good size for browsing.

★ Saks Fifth Avenue MIDTOWN
This legendary flagship store is a classic. It stocks big-name designers in fashion, accessories, and housewares, all with price tags to match. *611 Fifth Ave. (btwn 49th & 50th sts.).* ☎ *212/753-4000. www.saks fifthavenue.com. AE, DC, DISC, MC, V. Subway: B/D/F/Q to 47th-50th sts./ Rockefeller Center; E/F to Fifth Ave. Map p 90.*

★★ Takashimaya MIDTOWN
This petite outpost of Japan's most famous department store chain is a charmer. *693 Fifth Ave. (btwn 54th & 55th sts.).* ☎ *212/350-0100. AE, DC, MC, V. Subway: E/F to Fifth Ave. Map p 90.*

Electronics
B&H Photo & Video GARMENT DISTRICT This camera superstore has everything from lenses to darkroom equipment. *420 Ninth Ave. (at 34th St.).* ☎ *800/606-6969. www.bh photovideo.com. AE, DISC, MC, V. Subway: A/C/E to 34th St. Map p 90.*

J&R Music & Computer World
FINANCIAL DISTRICT This is the city's top computer, electronics, small appliance, and office equipment retailer. *23 Park Row (at Ann St., opposite City Hall Park).* ☎ *800/426-6027 or 212/238-9000. www. jandr.com. AE, DISC, MC, V. Subway: 2/3 to Park Place; 4/5/6 to Brooklyn Bridge/City Hall. Map p 89.*

Fashion (Men & Women)
★ Donna Karan New York
UPPER EAST SIDE You gotta love the concept: Beautiful clothes displayed around the garden in the store's center.

819 Madison Ave. (btwn 68th & 69th sts.). ☎ *212/249-4100. AE, DC, MC, V. Subway: N/R/W to Fifth Ave./53rd St. Map p 90.*

★ **H&M** MIDTOWN The Swedish super-discounter has *très* chic men's and women's clothing, and the prices are low, low, low. *640 Fifth Ave. (at 51st St.).* ☎ *212/489-0390. www.hm.com. AE, MC, V. Subway: E/F to Fifth Ave. Map p 90.*

★ **Jeffrey New York** MEATPACKING DISTRICT This outpost of the famed Atlanta mega-boutique is accessible and user-friendly. Its great accessories and shoes galore make it a worthy schlep for style hounds. *449 W. 14th St. (Tenth Ave.).* ☎ *212/206-1272. AE, MC, V. Subway: A/C/E/L to 14th St. Map p 89.*

★★ **Loehmann's** CHELSEA Clothing may be crammed together and the third-floor changing room lacks privacy, but the deals are usually worth it. *101 Seventh Ave. (16th St.).* ☎ *212/352-0856. MC, V. Subway: 1/2/3/9 to 14th St. Map p 90.*

Patricia Field's Hotel Venus SOHO Downtown cool from the clothing designer for *Sex and the City. 382 W. Broadway (btwn Spring & Broome sts.).* ☎ *212/966-4066. www.patriciafield.com. AE, DISC, MC, V. Subway: 6 to Spring St. Map p 89.*

★ **Prada** SOHO The sleek, chic Italian trendsetter occupies a spectacular space designed by architect Rem Koolhaas. *575 Broadway (Prince St.).* ☎ *212/334-8888. AE, DISC, MC, V. Subway: N/R to Prince St. Map p 89.*

★ **Scoop** MEATPACKING DISTRICT Ever wonder what a fashion editor's closet looks like? This is it: a collection of pieces from a variety of designers with everything fashion-forward and edgy, but not so cutting edge as to be unwearable. *873 Washington St. (btwn 13th & 14th sts.).* ☎ *212/929-1244. AE, DC, DISC, MC, V. Subway: A/C/E to 14th St. Map p 89.*

Fashion (Women)

★ **Agent Provocateur** SOHO This outpost of the British fantasy lingerie emporium is a must-see. The line runs the gamut from the PVC-and-steel "Dita" playsuit to the sophisticated and romantic "Yasmine" undies. *133 Mercer St. (btwn Prince & Spring sts.).* ☎ *212/965-0229. www.agentprovocateur.com. AE, MC, V. Subway: R/W to Prince St. Map p 89.*

Anthropologie SOHO This chain sells funky, slightly exotic, and affordable clothing and accessories. *375 W. Broadway (btwn Spring & Broome sts.).* ☎ *212/343-7070. www.anthropologie.com. AE, MC, V. Subway: C/E to Spring St. Map p 89.*

★ **Intermix** FLATIRON DISTRICT Sharp but generally affordable clothing and accessories. *125 Fifth Ave. (btwn 19th & 20th sts.).* ☎ *212/533-9720. AE, DISC, MC, V. Subway: N/R to 23rd St. Also at 210 Columbus Ave. (btwn 69th & 70th sts.).* ☎ *212/769-9116. AE, DISC, MC, V. Subway: C to 72nd St. Map p 90.*

Prada's coolly elegant mannequins.

Gifts

★★ kids Maxilla & Mandible
UPPER WEST SIDE Stop by for unusual rocks and shells, luminescent butterflies in display boxes, and real fossils. *451 Columbus Ave. (btwn 81st & 82nd sts.).* ☎ *212/724-6173. www.maxillaandmandible. com. AE, DISC, MC, V. Subway: B/C to 81st St. Map p 90.*

Metropolitan Museum of Art Store
Great for reproduction jewelry, china, books, toys, textiles, and objets d'art from the Met's collection. *Rockefeller Center, 15 W. 49th St.* ☎ *212/332-1360. www.metmuseum. org/store. AE, DISC, MC, V. Subway: B/D/F/V to 47th-50th sts./Rockefeller Center. Map p 90.*

★ Pearl River
SOHO Asian clothing, housewares, foods, and gifts are cheaper in Chinatown, but this is one-stop shopping. *477 Broadway (Grand St.).* ☎ *212/431-4770. www.pearlriver.com. AE, DISC, MC, V. Subway: N/R to Canal St. Map p 89.*

Home Design & Housewares

★★★ ABC Carpet & Home
UNION SQUARE AREA This two-building emporium is legendary, and it deserves to be: It's the ultimate home fashions and furnishings store. *881 & 888 Broadway (at 19th St.).* ☎ *212/473-3000. http://abchome. com. AE, DISC, MC, V. Subway: L/N/R/4/5/6 to 14th St./Union Sq. Map p 90.*

★ Broadway Panhandler
SOHO Cooks will love browsing for professional-quality cookware. *477 Broome St. (btwn Greene & Wooster sts.).* ☎ *212/966-3434. AE, MC, V. Subway: C/E to Spring St. Map p 89.*

Terence Conran Shop
MIDTOWN EAST Sleek contemporary lines, lightweight materials (chrome, blond woods, colorful plastic), and fun twists on standard household goods. *407 E. 59th St. (at First Ave.).* ☎ *212/755-9079. www.conran.com. AE, DC, MC, V. Subway: 4/5/6 to 59th St. Map p 90.*

Gourmet Food

★★ Dean & DeLuca
SOHO Excellent cheese, meat, fish, and dessert counters (check out the stunning cakes). *560 Broadway (at Prince St.).* ☎ *212/226-6800. www.deandeluca.com. AE, DISC, MC, V. Subway: N/R to Prince St. Map p 89.*

★ Fauchon
MIDTOWN EAST This Parisian boutique flies in sweet treats daily and its tea salon is delightful. *442 Park Ave. (at 56th St.).* ☎ *212/308-5919. www.fauchon. com. AE, DC, MC, V. Subway: 4/5/6 to 59th St. Map p 90.*

Silky kimonos hanging at Pearl River.

By all means gaze at the diamonds inside, but Tiffany's window displays are also worth a look.

★ **Sherry-Lehmann** UPPER EAST SIDE   One of the city's best selections of wine. *679 Madison Ave. (btwn 61st & 62nd sts.).* ☎ *212/838-7500. www.sherry-lehmann.com. AE, MC, V. Subway: N/R to Lexington Ave.; 4/5/6 to 59th St. Map p 90.*

Jewelry & Precious Stones
The Diamond District MIDTOWN
This is the heart of the city's diamond trade, though many of the merchants deal in semi-precious stones, too. If you know your four C's, it's a great place to get a deal on diamonds; if you don't, stick with window-shopping. Most shops are open Monday to Friday only. *47th St. (btwn Fifth & Sixth aves.). Subway: B/D/F/V to Rockefeller Center. Map p 90.*

★ **Fragments** SOHO   Looking for original pieces? Fragments sells work by more than 100 artists working in various mediums. Prices vary dramatically, starting at $50 and going above $20,000. *116 Prince St. (btwn Greene & Wooster sts.).* ☎ *212/334-9588. AE, DC, DISC, MC, V. Subway: C/E to Spring St. Map p 89.*

★ **Pippin** LOWER EAST SIDE   From stately pearls to funky Bakelite jewelry, this gem of a shop carries it all. Both men's and women's accessories are sold. *72 Orchard St. (btwn Grand and Broome sts.).* ☎ *212/505-5159. AE, MC, V. Subway: F to Delancey St. Map p 89.*

★★ **Tiffany & Co.** MIDTOWN
Deservedly famous, this iconic multi-level store carries jewelry, watches, tableware and stemware, and a variety of gift items. Love the silver yo-yo! *727 Fifth Ave. (57th St.).* ☎ *212/755-8000. www.tiffany.com. AE, DC, DISC,*

MC, V. Subway: N/R to Fifth Ave. Map p 90.

Music & Video
★ **Bleecker St. Records** GREENWICH VILLAGE   The well-organized CD and LP collections include rock, jazz, folk, blues, and punk. *239 Bleecker St. (Carmine St.).* ☎ *212/255-7899. AE, MC, V. Subway: A/C/E/F/V to W. 4th St. Map p 89.*

Colony Music Center TIMES SQUARE   This nostalgia emporium is filled with a pricey but excellent collection of vintage vinyl and new CDs (sheet music and theater posters, too). *1619 Broadway (49th St.).* ☎ *212/265-2050. www.colonymusic. com. AE, DISC, MC, V. Subway: N/R to 49th St.; 1/9 to 50th St. Map p 90.*

Jazz Record Center CHELSEA
The place to find rare and out-of-print jazz records. *236 W. 26th St. (btwn Seventh & Eighth aves., 8th floor).* ☎ *212/675-4480. www.jazz recordcenter.com. AE, MC, V. Subway: 1/9 to 28th St. Map p 90.*

Virgin Megastore   Always busy, this complex has an extensive singles department, countless listening posts, and a huge video section. *1540 Broadway (at 45th St.).* ☎ *212/921-1020. www.virginmega.com. AE, DC, DISC, MC, V. Subway: N/R/1/2/3/7/9 to Times Sq./42nd St. Also at 52 E. 14th St. (at Broadway).* ☎ *212/598-4666. AE, DC, DISC, MC, V. Subway: 4/5/6/N/R/L to 14th St./Union Sq. Map p 90.*

Shoes & Handbags
★★ **Manolo Blahnik** MIDTOWN WEST   These wildly sexy women's shoes could turn anyone into a foot

An "urban vinyl action figure" at Kidrobot.

fetishist. *31 W. 54th St. (btwn Fifth & Sixth aves.).* ☎ *212/582-3007. AE, MC, V. Subway: E/F to Fifth Ave. Map p 90.*

★ **Otto Tootsi Plohound** FLATIRON DISTRICT   A silly name for a smart place selling discounted designer shoes. *137 Fifth Ave. (20th St.).* ☎ *212/460-8650. AE, DC, DISC, MC, V. Subway: N/R to 23rd St. Map p 90.*

★ **Sigerson Morrison** NOLITA Very modern shoes with clever retro detailing. *28 Prince St. (btwn Mott & Elizabeth sts.).* ☎ *212/219-3893. www.sigersonmorrison.com. AE, MC, V. Subway: B/D/F/Q to Broadway/ Lafayette St.; N/R to Prince St.; 6 to Spring St. Map p 89.*

Stationery & Art Supplies
Kate's Paperie SOHO   It's fun just to browse the exquisite and high-priced paper products at Kate's. *561 Broadway (btwn Prince & Spring sts.).* ☎ *212/941-9816. www.katespaperie. com. AE, DISC, MC, V. Subway: N/R to Prince St. Map p 89.*

★ **Pearl Paint** CHINATOWN   All the cool art school students shop here. This is hands-down New York's best discount art-supply store. *308 Canal St. (btwn Broadway & Mercer sts.).* ☎ *212/431-7932. www.pearl paint.com. AE, DISC, MC, V. Subway: N/R to Canal St. Map p 89.*

Toys
kids Kidrobot SOHO   The "urban vinyl action figures" and remote-controlled cars are pure fun—and not just for kids. *126 Prince St. (Wooster St.).* ☎ *212/966-6688. www.kidrobot.com. AE, MC, V. Subway: N/R to Prince St. Map p 89.*

kids Toys "R" Us TIMES SQUARE Check out the T-Rex on the second floor and take a spin on the Ferris wheel if you can tear your kids away from the lavish toy displays. *1514 Broadway (44th St.).* ☎ *800/869-7787. AE, DISC, MC, V. Subway: 1/2/3/7/9/A/C/E/N/Q/R/S to 42nd St. Map p 90.*

Vintage & Consignment
Filth Mart EAST VILLAGE   Rocker heaven! Classic '60s to '80s concert T-shirts, denim, and leather. *531 E. 13th St. (btwn aves. A & B).* ☎ *212/ 387-0650. AE, DC, DISC, MC, V. Subway: N/Q/R/W/4/5/6 to Union Sq. Map p 89.*

★★ **INA** SOHO   Resale couture clothing at down-to-earth prices. *101 Thompson St. (btwn Prince & Spring sts.).* ☎ *212/941-4757. AE, MC, V. Subway: C/E to Spring St. Map p 89.*

★ **Screaming Mimi's** NOHO The clothing is well organized and well priced, and there are vintage housewares, too. *382 Lafayette St. (btwn E. 4th & Great Jones sts.).* ☎ *212/677-6464. www.screaming mimis.com. AE, DISC, MC, V. Subway: 6 to Astor Place. Map p 89.* ●

Central **Park**

1. Harlem Meer
2. Conservatory Garden
3. The Reservoir
4. The Obelisk
5. The Great Lawn
6. The Ramble
7. The Lake
8. The Boathouse Restaurant
9. Bethesda Fountain
10. The Mall
11. The Carousel
12. Wollman Rink
13. Delacorte Clock
14. The Arsenal
15. Central Park Wildlife Conservation Center

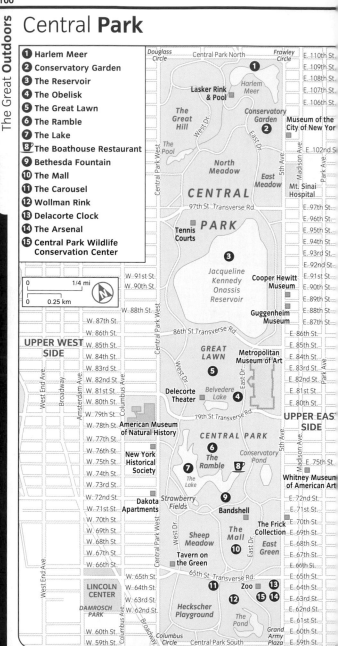

Often referred to as Manhattan's backyard, Central Park is far more than that. It's a vibrant masterpiece that was carved out of a muddy swamp and squatters' camp in the 1850s by landscape architects Frederick Law Olmstead and Calvert Vaux. Today it's enjoyed by thousands of city residents and visitors who flock here to stroll, run, bike, relax, picnic, and play. START: **Subway 2 or 3 to Central Park North.**

1 Harlem Meer. This 11-acre "meer" (the Dutch word for lake) wasn't part of the original Central Park. Added in 1863, it has a natural, rugged shoreline complemented by swans a-swimming. The Charles A. Dana Discovery Center (📞 212/860-1370) on the northern shore hosts Central Park Conservancy seasonal exhibits, community programs, and holiday celebrations in its Great Hall and contains a year-round visitor center. *East side from 106th to 110th sts.*

2 ★★ Conservatory Garden. This formal garden was commissioned by the WPA (Work Projects Administration) in 1936. Its showpieces are many: an elegant Italian garden built around a classical fountain, a lovely mazelike English garden, a bronze statue of the children from the novel *The Secret Garden* standing in a reflecting pool. In summer, water lilies float in the pool and flowering plants and shrubs fill the garden. From here walk south through the park, or, to save a mile of walking, take any bus down Fifth Avenue and get off at 86th Street, re-entering the park at this point. *Fifth Ave. & 105th St.*

3 The Reservoir. Created in 1862 as a part of the Croton Water System, the reservoir was in use till 1994. Occupying 106 acres and extending the width of the park, it is surrounded by bridle and jogging paths. The reservoir holds a billion gallons of water, is 40 feet at its greatest depth, and now serves only as an emergency backup water supply. The 1½-mile-long upper path overlooks the reservoir and has great skyline views. Walk along the path behind the Metropolitan Museum of Art to reach the Obelisk. *85th to 96th sts.*

4 The Obelisk. *See p 12, bullet 4.*

5 ★ The Great Lawn. Active types can enjoy a game of softball, volleyball, or soccer, but this is also a great spot for a picnic, especially on those warm summer nights when the New York Philharmonic or Metropolitan Opera performs for free. Find the schedule at www.centralpark nyc.org and bring along picnic fare from nearby gourmet grocery Zabar's (Broadway and 80th St.). At the southern end, **Belvedere Castle ★** (see p 12, bullet 5) and its surrounding duck pond are particularly picturesque. *Mid-Park from 79th to 85th sts.*

The Conservatory Garden's Burnett Fountain portrays characters from The Secret Garden, *a children's classic.*

6 ★ The Ramble. It looks wild—especially in comparison with the rest of the park—but it was actually *designed* to mirror untamed nature. Olmstead called it his "wild garden," and it takes up 38 of the park's acres. The Ramble has a bad reputation after dark (I wouldn't set foot in it after sunset), but during the day it's wonderful to explore. The curving paths that lead through the wooded area are not only inviting to walk; they offer some of the best scouting ground for bird-watchers in the city—some 230 species have been spotted here so far. A statue of a panther overlooks the east drive between 77th and 76th streets. *Mid-Park from 73rd to 79th sts.*

7 ★★ The Lake. It's not quite as large as the Reservoir, but it's by far the most beautiful body of water in the park. Who would guess that idyllic lake was once a swamp? Everyone appreciates the serenity of this part of the park, but I love the fact that you can actually see skyscrapers reflected in the water. *Mid-Park from 71st to 78th sts.*

8 The Boathouse Restaurant. At the eastern end of the Lake is the Boathouse Restaurant, open from April 15 through November, offering alfresco lakeside seating on a wooden deck under a white canopy. The menu is contemporary American, but not surprisingly, the setting is more compelling than the food. The Boathouse also has an **outdoor grill/bar** that is very popular in the warm months (Apr–Nov 11am–11pm daily) and an **express cafe** serving breakfast and light fare

Bethesda Terrace is a great people-watching spot in summer.

(year-round 8am–6pm daily; to 4:30 in winter). *East side btwn 74th and 75th sts.* ☎ 212/517-2233. $–$$$.

9 ★★ Bethesda Terrace. Meet *Bethesda, the Angel of the Waters,* the only sculpture commissioned as part of the park's original design. Olmstead and Vaux were both determined to put nature first, second, and third (as Vaux was once quoted saying), but they acknowledged the need for a central meeting place in the park. The surrounding two-tiered terrace was part of the original design as well, though what you see now was rebuilt in the 1980s (the stone and carvings match the original). *Mid-Park at 72nd St.*

10 ★ The Mall. This grand, shaded promenade—designed with a Versailles spirit—is roughly ¼ mile long. It's bordered by rows of stately American elms, whose branches form a cathedral-like arch overhead. At the south end are statues of Columbus, Shakespeare, and other historic and literary figures. *Mid-park from 66th to 72nd sts.*

11 kids The Carousel. Legend has it that this charming merry-go-round was originally turned by a blind mule and a horse. Its colorful steeds are among the largest carousel ponies in the world. The original carousel was built in 1871; fires destroyed it and a successor. The current carousel was built in 1951. *Mid-Park at 64th St.* ☎ 212/879-0244.

12 kids Wollman Rink. This relative newcomer was built into the northern bay of The Pond in 1951. In winter it's for ice skates, and for the rest of the year it's home to a series of special attractions, such as the Victoria Gardens Amusement Park, which has great rides for

Skaters on Wollman Rink.

young children. *East side btwn 62nd & 63rd sts.*

⓭ kids Delacorte Clock. With six dancing animals designed by Italian sculptor Andrea Spadini, this clock has been captivating park visitors since the '60s. The performances on the hour are the best (the half-hour ones are shorter but still sweet). *East side & 65th St. (in the Zoo).*

⓮ The Arsenal. This Gothic Revival building actually predates the park itself. It looks like the fortress it briefly was, housing troops during the Civil War. It later served as the original home of the American Museum of Natural History. It was even home to some of P. T. Barnum's circus animals, from a black bear to white swans. Today it houses the park headquarters and a third-floor art gallery, which features a series of ever-changing exhibits focusing on the natural environment. *64th St. & Fifth Ave.* ☎ *311 in New York City or 212/NEW-YORK. www.nycgovparks.org. Mon–Fri 9am–5pm.*

⓯ ★★ kids Central Park Wildlife Center and the Tisch Children's Zoo. Better known as the Central Park Zoo, the Wildlife Center dates back to the mid–19th century, when caged animals on loan from circuses and other outlets were put on display near the Arsenal, over Olmstead's and Vaux's protests. The landscape designers feared losing natural scenery to gaudy attractions. The current zoo was built in 1988 to replace a 1934 WPA-built structure that had become cramped and outdated. Today the zoo's 5½ acres houses about 450 animals. My favorites are the sea lions playing in the Central Garden pool, the brightly colored toucan, the Japanese snow monkeys, and the always irresistible penguins. In the small Tisch Children's Zoo kids can feed and pet tame farm animals. ⏱ *75 minutes. East side btwn 63rd & 66th sts.* ☎ *212/ 861-6030. www.centralparkzoo. com. Admission $6 adults, $1.25 seniors, $1 children 3–12, under 3 free. Daily 10am–5:30pm.*

Green-Wood **Cemetery**

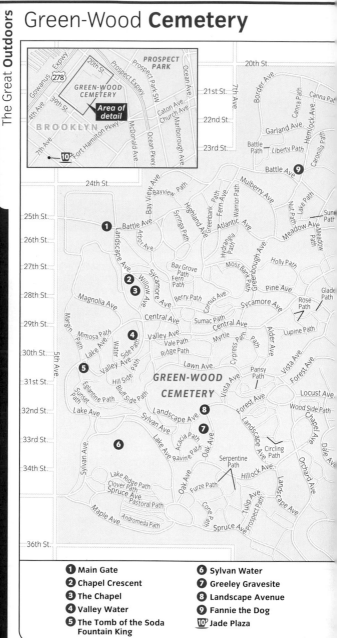

1. Main Gate
2. Chapel Crescent
3. The Chapel
4. Valley Water
5. The Tomb of the Soda Fountain King
6. Sylvan Water
7. Greeley Gravesite
8. Landscape Avenue
9. Fannie the Dog
10. Jade Plaza

In 1866 the *New York Times* said: "It is the ambition of the New Yorker to live upon Fifth Avenue, to take his airings in the Park, and to sleep with his fathers in Green-Wood." Today Brooklyn's Green-Wood Cemetery is one of the best places in the city to enjoy the outdoors. This 1838 necropolis is anything but gloomy. It has stunning scenery, a breathtaking chapel, and ornate mausoleums. START: **Subway N or R to 25th Street in Brooklyn.**

① ★★ Main Gate. Green-Wood has five entrances, but this Gothic gate with spires that stretch church-like into the sky is by far the most spectacular. A New York City Historic Landmark, it was built from 1861 to 1865 by architect Richard M. Upjohn. At the information booth inside you can pick up a free map of the grounds that lists the many famous (and infamous) residents—some 600,000 in all. These include Samuel Morse, Henry Ward Beecher, Leonard Bernstein, Boss Tweed, Nathaniel Currier and James Ives, and hundreds of Civil War soldiers. Self-guided walking tour booklets are also available for a fee. You will see "No Photography" signs, but that rule isn't generally enforced unless you try to take pictures of mourners. 🕑 *2 hr. 500 25th St. (Fifth Ave.), Brooklyn.* ☎ *718/768-7300. www.green-wood. com. Daily 8am–4pm (extended hours in summer). Subway: N/R to 25th St. in Brooklyn.*

② ★ Chapel Crescent. Green-Wood's grand chapel (bullet **③**), is surrounded by some stunning tombs. Two of my favorites are the B. Stephens tomb, which is shaped like a small Egyptian pyramid, and the Chambettaz tomb, with its angel statue overlooking the crescent. The Chambettaz tomb also has symbols from the secret society of the Freemasons—look for them on the pedestals on either side of the angel.

③ ★★★ The Chapel. A few minutes' walk from the main gates is Green-Wood's crowning glory. The chapel is a relatively recent arrival, having been built in 1911 by Warren & Wetmore. Its design was inspired by Tom Tower at Oxford's Christ Church college, which was designed by Christopher Wren in the 17th century. The multi-domed structure is built entirely of Indiana limestone. The interior is surprisingly small given its overall size, but frequently hosts

Green-Wood's elaborate main gate is also a building.

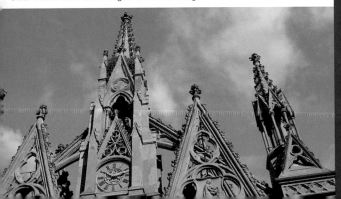

Weddings sometimes take place at Green-Wood's chapel.

readings and special exhibits that explore funerary art. Call or check the website for a schedule. ☎ *718/768-7300. www.green-wood.com.*

4 Valley Water. Some of Green-Wood's ponds have been filled in to create new burial plots, but this one is surrounded by evergreens. The avenue that curves around Valley Water is a treasure trove of 19th-century sculpture. Many of the monuments are partially draped by a carved "cloth." This popular Victorian Resurrectionist style reflected a belief that the body in the grave would rise on Judgment Day, when the cloth would fall away as if pulled back by the hand of God.

5 ★ The Tomb of the Soda Fountain King. This towering work of sculpture is really just one giant tombstone: In 1870, it won the Mortuary Monument of the Year award (didn't know there was such a thing, did you?). This is the resting place of John Matthews, the man who invented the soda fountain—and that information is about the only thing not carved into it. Gargoyles, members of the Matthews family, a personification of grief, and Matthews himself are all here.

6 Sylvan Water. This is the largest body of water in Green-Wood. It's surrounded by a series of tombs, some of which look large enough to house a (living) family.

7 ★ Greeley Gravesite. Horace Greeley was an anti-slavery advocate who founded the *New York Tribune* and was a national figure ("Go West, young man" is one of his famous aphorisms). He and many members of his family are buried in this plot on one of Green-Wood's hills. The views from here are lovely.

Valley Water.

Fannie the Dog's touching headstone.

8 **Landscape Avenue.** Green-Wood has many paved roads and footpaths, all of them named. "Landscape Avenue" is particularly apt as it offers memorable vistas and some great statuary. It winds and twists, but eventually leads back past the chapel to the Main Gates.

9 **Fannie the Dog.** Anyone who has ever loved a pet will find the words engraved on Fannie's simple headstone moving. " . . . Frosts of winter nor heat of summer/Could make her fail if my footsteps led/And memory holds in its treasure casket/The name of my darling who lies dead."

Eating Near Green-Wood

You could spend all day discovering Green-Wood Cemetery, but there are few restaurants close by and you can't bring food in. One option is to start or end your tour in Sunset Park, home to one of New York's largest Chinese communities (take the N train to 62nd St. in Brooklyn). Along Eighth Avenue between 60th and 50th streets, you'll find dozens of bakeries, restaurants, and dim sum palaces. You can enjoy lunch or a snack at any of these, but I recommend arriving hungry any time between 8am and 4pm for dim sum at **Jade Plaza,** 6022 Eighth Ave between 60th and 61 streets (☎ **718/492-6888**), a hectic, authentic, delicious experience. As the waiters wheel their carts by, just indicate which dishes interest you. Keep an eye out for large balls of sticky rice rolled in banana leaves and studded with roast pork; plump dumplings stuffed with pork, chicken, or seafood; or any of the rice noodle dishes.

The Brooklyn **Bridge**

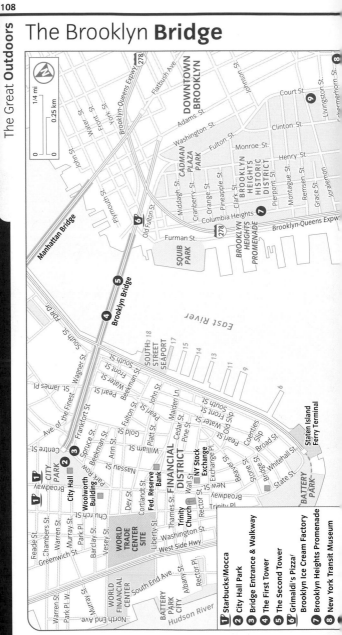

1. Starbucks/Mocca
2. City Hall Park
3. Bridge Entrance & Walkway
4. The First Tower
5. The Second Tower
6. Grimaldi's Pizza/ Brooklyn Ice Cream Factory
7. Brooklyn Heights Promenade
8. New York Transit Museum

Of New York's many bridges, none is as famous as the Brooklyn Bridge. This neo-Gothic icon is as awe-inspiring now as when it opened in 1883. Walking across will take 20 to 40 minutes, so you should have time at the end to spend in Brooklyn. START: **Subway 4, 5, or 6 to Brooklyn Bridge/City Hall.**

1 Breakfast on the Bridge. The food options around City Hall are mainly of the fast variety, but they'll do for a drink or snack to take on the bridge. Try **Starbucks** (291 Broadway at Reade St; ☎ 212/406-5310; $) or **Mocca** (78 Reade St. btwn Church St. & Broadway; ☎ 212/233-7570; $). *Subway: 4/5/6 to Brooklyn Bridge/City Hall.*

2 City Hall Park. As you head toward the bridge, walk around the park's perimeter to admire **City Hall** and the **Municipal Building**, which is built over the street. Across Broadway is the **Woolworth Building**, whose Gothic detailing makes it one of the city's loveliest skyscrapers. *See p 7, bullet* **2**.

3 Bridge Entrance & Walkway. There's a sidewalk entrance to the bridge on Park Row, which leads to the pedestrian walkway above the traffic. While the bridge is usually busy with traffic, the walk can be amazingly tranquil (by New York standards). Stay to the right while you walk; cyclists use the left lane. As you head toward the first of the bridge's two towers, you'll find a bench on your right—a perfect spot to relax, sip some coffee, and take in the view of Manhattan.

4 ★★ The First Tower. The tower seems to loom larger, the closer you got. As the path widens, you'll find plaques describing the construction of the bridge. One of them focuses on cable spinning, which is more interesting than it sounds—at least when you're

standing high above the East River, realizing that those cables are all that's holding you up. Others illustrate buildings in Manhattan's skyline to help you identify them. My favorite view is of Governor's Island to the south, which has served as a sheep farm, a racetrack, a quarantine station, and most recently, a Coast Guard station.

5 The Second Tower. The views of New York Harbor get more inspiring as you approach Brooklyn. On a clear day, it's easy to spot the Statue of Liberty and Ellis Island (back when the bridge was built, you could easily see the Hudson River and the New Jersey shore, too). The second tower is a virtual clone of the first, even down to the plaques that surround its expanded pedestrian area.

Enjoy a snack on the bridge while you sit and admire the view.

Sunset views are particularly stunning from the Promenade.

6 Brooklyn's food is something to brag about. Depending on what you're in the mood for, **Grimaldi's Pizza** (19 Old Fulton St.; ☎ 718/858-4300; $) and the **Brooklyn Ice Cream Factory** (Fulton Ferry Landing; ☎ 718/246-3963; $) are both great places to stop.

7 ★★★ **Brooklyn Heights Promenade.** This is one of my favorite places to walk in New York. On your left is the stunning Manhattan skyline; on your right are lovingly preserved historic homes where zillionaires live.

8 ★ **kids** **New York Transit Museum.** In a decommissioned 1930s subway station, the museum tells the history of New York's subway from 1900 to the present. There are more than 150,000 photographs of subway construction in the museum's collection, as well as tile mosaics from abandoned stations

and miniature models. There are plenty of interactive displays for kids; my favorite thing is seeing the classic subway cars up close. ⏱ *1 hr. Boerum Place & Schermerhorn St., Brooklyn.* ☎ *718/694-5100. www.mta.nyc.ny.us/mta/museum. Admission $5 adults, $3 seniors & children 3–17. Tues–Fri 10am–4pm; Sat–Sun noon–5pm. Subway: 2/3/4/5 to Borough Hall.*

9 ★ **Borough Hall**. When Brooklyn was an independent city, this was its City Hall. It's a gorgeous example of Greek Revival architecture that was built in 1848. If you visit on a weekday, you can visit the Community Room Gallery, which features works by local artists. From here, you can catch the 2, 3, 4, or 5 subway back to Manhattan. ⏱ *15 min. 209 Joralemon St. (btwn Court & Adams sts.).* ☎ *718/802-3700. www.brooklyn-usa.org. Free admission. Mon–Fri 9am–5pm. Subway: 2/3/4/5 to Borough Hall.* ●

6 The Best **Dining**

Dining Best Bets

Best for a **Red Meat Fix**
★★★ Blue Smoke $$ *116 E. 27th St. (p 117)*; and ★★★ Peter Luger $$$ *178 Broadway (Brooklyn) (p 121)*

Best **Vegetarian**
★★★ Pure Food and Wine $$ *54 Irving Place (p 121)*

Best **French** (Classic or Modern)
★★ Daniel $$$$ *60 E. 65th St. (p 118)*; and ★★★ Tocqueville $$–$$$ *15 E. 15th St. (p 124)*

Best **Meal for Under $25**
★ Nyonya $ *194 Grand St. (p 121)*; and ★ Snack $ *105 Thompson St. (p 122)*

Best **Upscale Mexican**
★ Pampano $$$ *209 E. 49th St. (p 121)*; and ★ Rosa Mexicano $$ *61 Columbus Ave. (p 122)*

Best **Chinese**
★★ Grand Sichuan International $ *229 Ninth Ave. (p 119)*; and ★★ Joe's Shanghai $$ *9 Pell St. (p 120)*

Best **Alfresco Dining**
★★ Cafe St. Bart's $$$ *109 E. 50th St. (p 117)*; and ★★ Home $$ *20 Cornelia St. (p 119)*

Best **Vietnamese**
★ Nha Trang $ *87 Baxter St. (p 120)*

Best **Spanish**
★★ Suba $$ *109 Ludlow St. (p 123)*

Blue Smoke's ribs are a great hit with kids.

Best **Desserts**
★★★ davidburke & donatella $$$ *133 E. 61st St. (p 118)*

Best **Pizza**
★ Grimaldi's Pizza $$ *19 Old Fulton St. (p 110)*

Best **Seafood**
★★★ Aquavit $$$ *65 E. 55th St. (p 116)*; and ★★★ Le Bernardin $$$$ *55 W. 51st St. (p 120)*

Most **Romantic**
★★★ One if by Land, Two if by Sea $$$$ *17 Barrow St. (p 121)*

Best **Brunch**
★★ Sylvia's $ *328 Lenox Ave. (p 123)*

Best **Splurge**
★★ Alain Ducasse at the Essex House $$$$ *158 W. 58th St. (p 116)*; and ★★★ Jean-Georges $$$$ *1 Central Park West (p 119)*

Best **Sushi**
★★★ Nobu/Next Door Nobu $$$ *105 Hudson St. (p 120)*; and ★ Riingo $$$ *205 E. 45th St. (p 122)*

Best **Indian**
★★ Tamarind $$ *41–43 E. 22nd St. (p 123)*

Best **for Families**
★★ Carmine's $$ *2450 Broadway (p 117)*

Best **Greek**
★ Snack $ *105 Thompson St. (p 122)*; and ★★ Thalassa $$–$$$ *197 Franklin St. (p 123)*

Best **Thai**
★ Pam Real Thai $ *404 W. 49th St. (p 121)*

Best **Italian**
★★ Babbo $$$ *110 Waverly Place (p 116)*

Downtown **Dining**

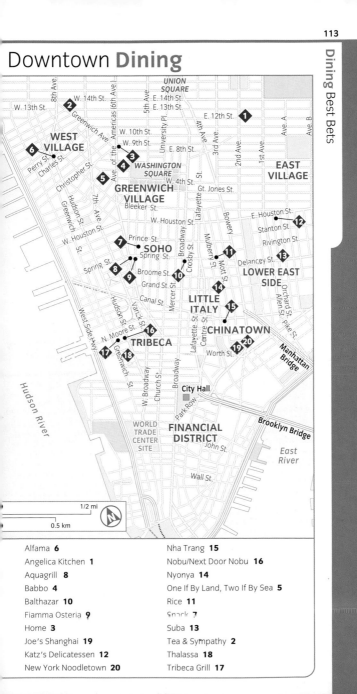

Alfama **6**	Nha Trang **15**
Angelica Kitchen **1**	Nobu/Next Door Nobu **16**
Aquagrill **8**	Nyonya **14**
Babbo **4**	One If By Land, Two If By Sea **5**
Balthazar **10**	Rice **11**
Fiamma Osteria **9**	Snack **7**
Home **3**	Suba **13**
Joe's Shanghai **19**	Tea & Sympathy **2**
Katz's Delicatessen **12**	Thalassa **18**
New York Noodletown **20**	Tribeca Grill **17**

Midtown & Uptown **Dining**

Alain Ducasse
at the Essex House **4**

Aquavit **21**

Blue Smoke **15**

Café des Artistes **1**

Cafe St. Bart's **19**

Carmine's **8**

Daniel **23**

davidburke & donatella **22**

db Bistro Moderne **16**

Dos Caminos **14**

EJ's **24**

Eleven Madison Park **13**

Grand Sichuan
International **9**

Jean-Georges **3**

Le Bernardin **5**

Pampano **18**

Pam Real Thai **7**

Pure Food and Wine **11**

Riingo **17**

Rosa Mexicano **2**

Ruby Foo's **1 & 6**

Tamarind **12**

Tocqueville **10**

21 Club **20**

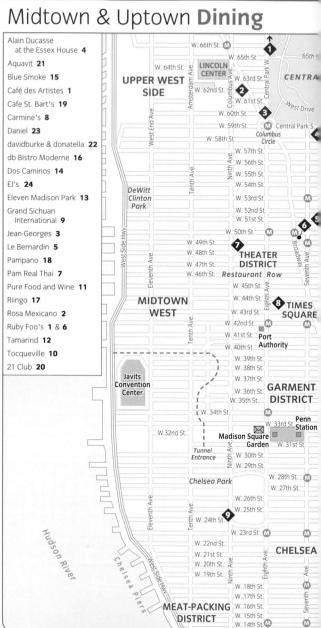

New York **Restaurants, A to Z**

★★ **Alain Ducasse at the Essex House** MIDTOWN WEST *CLASSIC FRENCH*   My husband hates dressing up for dinner, but even he thinks this place is worth it. Europe's most famous Michelin three-star chef has elevated special-occasion dining to a new level. *158 W. 58th St. (btwn Sixth & Seventh aves.).* ☎ *212/265-7300. www.alain-ducasse.com. 3-course lunch $65; 3- to 4-course dinner $165–$185; tasting menus $185–$280. AE, DC, DISC, MC, V. Dinner Tues–Sat, lunch Thurs–Fri. Subway: N/R/W to 57th St. Map p 114.*

★ **Alfama** WEST VILLAGE *PORTUGUESE*   Everything from the warm welcome to the homey cooking makes this spot feel like a little corner of Portugal. The *Pasteis de Belem* cream pastries are the closest to the real thing I've had outside of Lisbon. *551 Hudson St. (Perry St.).* ☎ *212/645-2500. Main courses $15–$28. AE, MC, V. Lunch & dinner daily. Subway: 1/9 to Christopher St. Map p 113.*

Angelica Kitchen EAST VILLAGE *VEGAN*   There's often a line in front of this cheerful restaurant that prepares everything fresh daily (95% of all ingredients are organic). But while it's good for you, it's also tasty, especially the Dragon Bowls, which blend rice, beans, tofu, and veggies. *300 E. 12th St. (Second Ave.).* ☎ *212/228-2909. Main courses $6–$15. No credit cards. Lunch & dinner daily. Subway: L/N/R/4/5/6 to 14th St./Union Sq. Map p 113.*

★★ **Aquagrill** SOHO *SEAFOOD* The raw bar flies in oysters from around the world daily, and the menu features some of the best fish in the city. Many preparations are simple and designed to showcase the flavor of the fish, but ambitious creations like Atlantic salmon with falafel crust are the real showstoppers. *210 Spring St. (Sixth Ave.).* ☎ *212/274-0505. Main courses $15–$26 at dinner. AE, MC, V. Lunch & dinner daily. Subway: C/E to Spring St. Map p 113.*

★★★ **Aquavit** MIDTOWN WEST *SCANDINAVIAN*   The interior won't impress anyone familiar with the indoor waterfall at the original location, but the food is as spectacular as ever. The herring, salmon, and gravlax are simply irresistible. *65 E. 55th St. (btwn Madison & Park aves.).* ☎ *212/307-7311. www.aquavit.org. Main courses $20–$32. AE, DC, MC, V. Lunch Sun–Fri, dinner Mon–Sat. Subway: 4/5/6/N/R/W to 59th St. Map p 114.*

★★ **Babbo** WASHINGTON SQUARE AREA *ITALIAN*   This is the centerpiece of celebrity chef "Molto"

Dill Curried Gravlax at Aquavit.

Balthazar is a great spot for late-night dining.

Mario Batali's edible empire. He has no equal when it comes to creative pastas. *110 Waverly Place (Sixth Ave.).* ☎ *212/777-0303. www. zbabbonyc.com. Main courses $17–$29; 7-course tasting menus $59–$65. AE, MC, V. Dinner Mon–Sun. Subway: A/C/E/F/B/D to 4th St. Map p 113*

Balthazar SOHO *BISTRO* With terrific food (think steak frites, perfectly seared fish, and a warm goat cheese tart with caramelized onions), tightly packed tables, and a noise level that forbids quiet conversation, Balthazar feels like an authentic Parisian brasserie. *80 Spring St. (btwn Crosby & Broadway).* ☎ *212/965-1785. Main courses $12–$32. AE, MC, V. Breakfast, lunch & dinner daily. Subway: 6 to Spring St.; N/R to Prince St. Map p 113.*

★★★ **kids Blue Smoke** GRAMERCY/MURRAY HILL *BARBECUE/ SOUTHERN* Restaurateur Danny Meyer reproduces the barbecue flavors of his St. Louis childhood. It's hard to go wrong with the tender ribs, collard greens, and house ale. *116 E. 27th St. (btwn Park & Lexington aves.).* ☎ *212/447-7733. www.blue smoke.com. Main courses $10–$22. AE, DC, DISC, MC, V. Lunch & dinner daily. Subway: 6 to 28th St. Map p 114.*

★ **Café des Artistes** UPPER WEST SIDE *CLASSIC FRENCH* This was established in 1917 as a haven for artists, many of whom lived in the upstairs hotel. Today's scene is more bourgeois than bohemian, but the excellent cuisine (hearty pot-au-feu, Dover sole in brown butter) is more than enough of a draw. *1 W. 67th St. (Central Park West).* ☎ *212/877-3500. www.cafenyc. com. Main courses $29–$42. AE, DC, DISC, MC, V. Lunch & dinner daily. Subway: 1/9 to 66th St. Map p 114.*

★★ **Cafe St. Bart's** MIDTOWN EAST *REGIONAL AMERICAN* The church's west-facing terrace overlooks Park Avenue, making for a great alfresco setting (in winter there's a well-heated tent). The menu runs the gamut from penne salad with Maine lobster to horse-radish-crusted salmon. *109 E. 50th St. (btwn Park & Lexington aves.).* ☎ *212/935-8434. Main courses $15–$28. AE, MC, V. Breakfast & lunch Mon–Fri, dinner Mon–Sat. Subway: 6 to 51st St. Map p 114.*

★★ **kids Carmine's** MIDTOWN WEST *ITALIAN* Think big: vast dining room; massive family-style portions of hearty (not haute) pastas and crowd-pleasers like fried calamari, garlic bread, and Caesar salad;

and a huge fun quotient. *200 W. 44th St. (btwn Seventh & Eighth aves.).* ☎ *212/221-3800. www.carminesnyc. com. Main courses $15–$49. AE, DC, DISC, MC, V. Lunch & dinner daily. Subway: 1/2/3/7/9/A/C/E/S to 42nd St./ Times Sq. Map p 114.*

★★ **Daniel** UPPER EAST SIDE *FRENCH COUNTRY* The eye-popping neoclassical setting pairs well with Daniel Boulud's refined cooking. The menu changes frequently but highlights have included venison with a chestnut crust and sweet-potato puree. *60 E. 65th St. (btwn Madison & Park aves.).* ☎ *212/288-0033. www. danielnyc.com. Main courses $34–$38. AE, MC, V. Dinner Mon–Sat. Subway: 6 to 68th St. Map p 114.*

★★★ **davidburke & donatella** UPPER EAST SIDE *CONTEMPORARY AMERICAN* One of my new favorites, this elegant spot offers superlative food that doesn't take itself seriously—and the playful presentations are breathtaking. Everything is whimsical and delicious (try the Lollypop Tree for dessert). *133 E. 61st St. (btwn Park & Lexington aves.).* ☎ *212/813-2121. www.dbdrestaurant. com. Main courses $26–$42. AE, DC, MC, V. Lunch & dinner Mon–Fri. Subway: 4/5/6 to 59th St. Map p 114.*

Cheesecake lollypops with bubblegum whipped cream at davidburke & donatella.

★ **db Bistro Moderne** MIDTOWN WEST *BISTRO* Daniel Boulud's "casual" restaurant (you wear Miu Miu here instead of Prada) is most famous for its $50 burger with fresh shaved black truffles, but you can also order classics like rosemary-braised lamb shank. *55 W. 44th St. (btwn Fifth & Sixth aves.).* ☎ *212/ 391-2400. Main courses $27–$31. AE, DC, MC, V. Lunch Mon–Sat, dinner daily. Subway: B/D/F/Q to 42nd St. Map p 114.*

Dos Caminos GRAMERCY/ MURRAY HILL *MEXICAN/FUSION* It's impossibly crowded and noisy, but the fish tacos, ceviches, and guacamole prepared tableside are still reason enough to visit. Skip the overrated prickly pear margaritas. *373 Park Ave. S. (btwn 26th & 27th sts.).* ☎ *212/294-1000. Appetizers $8–$12; entrees $17–$24. AE, DISC, MC, V. Lunch & dinner Tues–Sun. Subway: 6 to 28th St. Map p 114.*

kids EJ's Luncheonette GREEN-WICH VILLAGE *AMERICAN* This retro diner chain serves up American fare in a 1950s setting. *1271 3rd Ave. (at 73rd St.).* ☎ *212/473-0600. Main courses $4–$12. Breakfast, lunch & dinner daily. Subway: 6 to 68th St. Map p 114.*

★ **Eleven Madison Park** FLAT-IRON DISTRICT *FRENCH COUNTRY/ AMERICAN* This is another gem from restaurateur Danny Meyer. The cooking emphasizes hearty fare, including organ meats. The two-story windows have spectacular views of the park at night. *11 Madison Ave. (at 24th St.).* ☎ *212/889-0905. A la carte lunch $15–$24, 3-course prix-fixe lunch $25; dinner main courses $23–$31; tasting menu (5–7 courses) $60–$80. AE, DC, DISC, MC, V. Lunch Mon–Sat, dinner daily. Subway: N/R/6 to 23rd St. Map p 114.*

Pasta at Fiamma Osteria.

★ **Fiamma Osteria** SOHO *ITALIAN*
The stunning Northern Italian decor
is surpassed only by the sumptuous,
modern Italian food, including the
pan-roasted cod with shrimp and
broccolini. Dinner is raucous so
don't expect quiet conversation.
*206 Spring St. (btwn Sixth Ave. &
Sullivan St.).* ☎ *212/653-0100. Main
courses $21–$32. AE, DISC, MC, V.
Lunch Mon–Sat, dinner daily. Subway: C/E to Spring St. Map p 113.*

★★ **Grand Sichuan International** CHELSEA *CHINESE* Come
here for complex, strong flavors, in
plates like Chairman Mao's pork
with chestnuts. *229 Ninth Ave.
(at 24th St.).* ☎ *212/620-5200.
Main courses $3–$14. AE, DC, MC, V.
Lunch & dinner daily. Subway: C/E to
23rd St. Map p 114.*

★★ **Home** GREENWICH VILLAGE
AMERICAN Chef David Page and
co-owner Barbara Shinn have made
home-style cooking something to cel-
ebrate at this cozy restaurant. Blue
cheese fondue with rosemary toast is
a signature dish. Dine year-round in
the heated garden. *20 Cornelia St.
(btwn Bleecker & W. 4th sts.).*
☎ *212/243-9579. Main courses
$14–$18. AE, DISC, MC, V. Breakfast
Mon–Fri, lunch & dinner daily, brunch*
*Sat–Sun. Subway: A/C/E/F/B/D to W.
4th St. Map p 113.*

★★★ **Jean-Georges** COLUMBUS
CIRCLE *FRENCH* A meal here
underscores why chef/owner Jean-
Georges Vongerichten is universally
loved by foodies. Asian flavors heat
up the French menu. *In the Trump
International Hotel & Tower, 1 Central Park West (at 60th St./Columbus
Circle).* ☎ *212/299-3900. www.jean-
georges.com. Main courses $26–$42;
3- or 7-course fixed-price dinner
$85–$115. AE, DC, MC, V. Lunch
Mon–Fri, dinner Mon–Sat. Subway:
A/B/C/D/1/9 to 59th St./Columbus
Circle. Map p 114.*

Jean-Georges serves caviar in an eggshell.

★★ Joe's Shanghai CHINATOWN *SHANGHAI/CHINESE* This is more upscale than many of its neighbors, and it's my favorite Chinatown eatery. The stars of the huge menu are the signature soup dumplings, quivering steamed pockets filled with hot broth and your choice of pork or crab. *9 Pell St. (btwn Bowery & Mott sts.).* ☎ *212/233-8888. Main courses $4–$17. No credit cards. Lunch & dinner daily. Subway: N/R/ Q/W/6 to Canal St.; F to Delancey St. Map p 113.*

★★ Katz's Delicatessen LOWER EAST SIDE *DELI* Founded in 1888, it's arguably the city's best Jewish deli. The hot dogs, overstuffed sandwiches, and giant knishes are all excellent—and very filling. *205 E. Houston St. (Ludlow St.).* ☎ *212/254-2246. Sandwiches $2.15–$10; other items $5–$18. AE, MC, V. Breakfast, lunch & dinner daily. Subway: F to Second Ave. Map p 113.*

★★★ Le Bernardin MIDTOWN WEST *FRENCH/SEAFOOD* Seafood doesn't get better than the seared rare yellowtail here. The formal service is impeccable, as is the pricey wine list. *55 W. 51st St. (btwn Sixth & Seventh aves.).* ☎ *212/489-1515.*

www.le-bernardin.com. Fixed-price dinner $87; tasting menus $100– $135. AE, DC, DISC, MC, V. Lunch Mon–Fri, dinner Mon–Sat. Subway: N/R to 49th St.; 1/9 to 50th St. Map p 114.

New York Noodletown CHINA- TOWN *CHINESE/SEAFOOD* Not much ambience but fantastic food— try the salt-baked squid and the hacked roast duck in noodle soup— and a great late-night bet. Many of the appetizers are hearty enough for a whole meal. *28½ Bowery (at Bayard St.).* ☎ *212/349-0923. Main courses $4–$13. No credit cards. Breakfast, lunch & dinner daily. Sub- way: N/R/6 to Canal St. Map p 113.*

★ Nha Trang CHINATOWN *VIET- NAMESE* When I was a penniless *Harper's* intern, I came here for the inexpensive menu. And I still come here because this friendly, bustling place serves up the best Vietnamese fare in Chinatown. *87 Baxter St. (btwn Canal & Bayard sts.).* ☎ *212/ 233-5948. Main courses $4–$13. No credit cards. Brunch & dinner daily. Subway: N/R/6 to Canal St. Map p 113.*

★★★ Nobu/Next Door Nobu TRIBECA *JAPANESE* Renowned chef Nobuyuki Matsuhisa's cooking

Step up to the crowded counter at Katz's to place your order.

Chef Nobuyuki Matsuhisa opened Nobu in partnership with Robert De Niro.

bursts with creative spirit. Can't get a reservation at Nobu? Take heart. **Next Door Nobu,** the slightly more casual version, has a no-reservations policy. *105 Hudson St. (at Franklin St.).* ☎ *212/219-0500 for Nobu;* ☎ *212/334-4445 for Next Door Nobu. www.myriadrestaurant group.com. Small plates and main courses $8–$32; sushi $3–$10 per piece. AE, DC, MC, V. Nobu Lunch & dinner Mon–Fri. Next Door Nobu dinner daily. Subway: 1/9 to Franklin St. Map p 113.*

★ **Nyonya** LITTLE ITALY *MALAYSIAN* Spacious and bustling, this restaurant looks like a South Asian tiki hut. Try the Malaysian national dish, *roti canai* (an Indian pancake with a curry chicken dipping sauce). *194 Grand St. (btwn Mulberry & Mott sts.).* ☎ *212/334-3669. Main courses $5–$16. No credit cards. Lunch & dinner daily. Subway: 6 to Spring St. Map p 113.*

★★★ **One if by Land, Two if by Sea** GREENWICH VILLAGE *AMERICAN* This candlelit, rose-filled 18th-century carriage house is a perennial favorite among romantics. The menu has added excellent dishes like Muscovy duck with figs,

but you can still order the traditional favorite, beef Wellington. *17 Barrow St. (btwn W. 4th St. & Seventh Ave. S.).* ☎ *212/255-8649. www.oneifby land.com. 3-course prix fixe $63; 7-course tasting menu $79. AE, DC, DISC, MC, V. Dinner daily. Subway: 1/9 to Christopher St.; A/E/C/F/B/D to 4th St. Map p 113.*

★ **Pampano** MIDTOWN EAST *MEXICAN/SEAFOOD* Elegant, upscale Mexican cuisine: There are tacos, but they're filled with lobster. The best way to start is with the tasting plate of several ceviches. It's a scene, but a festive one with a lively bar and a lovely upstairs dining area. *209 E. 49th St. (Third Ave.).* ☎ *212/751-4545. Main courses $21–$26. AE, DC, MC, V. Lunch Mon–Fri, dinner daily. Subway: E/V to 53rd St; 6 to 51st St. Map p 114.*

★ **kids Pam Real Thai** MIDTOWN WEST *THAI* Good Thai food is hard to find in New York, making this place a terrific find. The crispy duck yum is deliciously spicy. *404 W. 49th St. (Ninth Ave.).* ☎ *212/333-7500. Main courses $5–$12. AE, MC, V. Lunch & dinner daily. Subway: C/E to 50th St./Eighth Ave. Map p 114.*

★★★ **Peter Luger Steakhouse** BROOKLYN *STEAK* This Brooklyn institution is porterhouse heaven. *178 Broadway (Driggs Ave.), Williamsburg, Brooklyn.* ☎ *718/387-7400. www. peterluger.com. Main courses $20–$35 at dinner. No credit cards. Lunch & dinner daily. Subway: J/M/Z to Marcy Ave. (Or take a cab.)*

★★★ **Pure Food and Wine** GRAMERCY *VEGETARIAN* I considered the Raw Food movement bizarre until I ate here. Now I'm in love with the spicy Thai lettuce wraps and the tomato-zucchini lasagna. Nothing is cooked above 118°F (48°C), but the dishes are sublime. *54 Irving Place (17th St.).* ☎ *212/477-1010. Main courses*

$18–$23. AE, MC, V. Dinner daily. Subway: L/N/R/4/5/6 to 14th St./ Union Sq. Map p 114.

Rice NOLITA *ASIAN* This tiny spot has a very affordable seasonal menu built around different rices: Pick your grain from the seven options and pair it with any of 10 toppings. *227 Mott St. (btwn Prince & Spring sts.).* ☎ *212/226-5775. Main courses $6–$13. No credit cards. Lunch & dinner daily. Subway: 6 to Spring St. Map p 113.*

★ **Riingo** MIDTOWN EAST *FUSION* The meals tend to be experimental, like the rib-eye carpaccio with warm eel, but the risks generally pay off nicely. Great sushi, too. *205 E. 45th St. (Third Ave.).* ☎ *212/867-4200. Main courses $14–$42. AE, DISC, MC, V. Lunch Mon–Fri, dinner daily. Subway: 4/5/6/7S to 42nd St. Map p 114.*

★ **Rosa Mexicano** UPPER WEST SIDE *CONTEMPORARY MEXICAN* The 30-foot-high blue-tile waterfall competes for attention with the guacamole prepared tableside. The frozen pomegranate margarita is a must. *61 Columbus Ave. (62nd St.).*

☎ *212/977-7700. www.rosa mexicano.com. Main courses $13– $18 at lunch, $17–$25 at dinner. AE, DC, DISC, MC, V. Lunch & dinner daily. Subway: A/B/C/D/1/9 to 59th St. Map p 114.*

★ **Ruby Foo's** UPPER WEST SIDE *JAPANESE/ASIAN* Yes, it looks like a bordello and dinner—especially in the touristy Times Square branch— can be a mob scene, but I love the fresh, playful sushi rolls, the tangy noodle dishes, and the giant slabs of chocolate cake. *2182 Broadway (btwn 77th & 78th sts.).* ☎ *212/ 724-6700. Also at 1626 Broadway (49th St.).* ☎ *212/724-6700. www. brguestrestaurants.com. Dim sum and sushi rolls $5–$10; main courses $11–$25. AE, MC, V. Lunch & dinner daily. Subway: N/R to 49th St. Map p 114.*

★ **Snack** SOHO *GREEK* The menu is traditional Greek, and it's unusually well priced for the quality. The usual suspects, like *taramosalata* (carp roe dip) and *spanikopitakia* (spinach pastries), are nicely done. *105 Thompson St. (btwn Prince &*

The fresh guacamole at Rosa Mexicano.

A trio of marinated raw fish at Suba.

Spring sts.). ☎ 212/925-1040. *Main courses $6–$14. No credit cards Lunch & dinner daily; closes early Sun–Mon (8:30pm). Subway: C/E to Spring St. Map p 113.*

★★ **Suba** LOWER EAST SIDE *SPANISH* With its surrealist design and innovative Latin cuisine such as the chipotle-marinated yellowfin tuna, Suba is a sensualist's delight. *109 Ludlow St. (Delancey St.).* ☎ 212/982-5714. *Tapas $3–$12; main courses $18–$25. AE, DC, DISC, MC, V. Dinner daily. Subway: F to Delancey St. Map p 113.*

★★ **Sylvia's** HARLEM *SOUL FOOD* The lady has become an empire (canned food products, fragrances, etc.) but the Sunday gospel brunch at the original Harlem restaurant is still a delight. Think southern fried chicken, smothered chicken, collards, and barbecue ribs. Yum. *328 Lenox Ave. (btwn 126th & 127th sts.).* ☎ 212/996-0660. *Main courses $12–$17. www.sylviassoulfood.com. AE, DC, DISC, MC, V. Breakfast*

Mon–Fri, lunch & dinner daily. Subway: 2/3 to 125th St.

★★ **Tamarind** FLATIRON DISTRICT *INDIAN* Twists on old standards make this one of the city's top Indian restaurants. *41–43 E. 22nd St. (btwn Broadway & Park Ave.).* ☎ 212/674-7400. *Main courses $11–$30. AE, DC, MC, V. Lunch & dinner daily. Subway: N/R/6 to 23rd St. Map p 114.*

Tea & Sympathy GREENWICH VILLAGE *BRITISH* This British charmer features all the standards, from spaghetti on toast and bangers and mash to roast beef with Yorkshire pudding. The traditional afternoon tea ($22) is worth lingering over. *108 Greenwich Ave. (btwn 12th & 13th sts.).* ☎ 212/807-8329. *www. teaandsympathynewyork.com. Main courses $11–$17. MC, V. Lunch & dinner daily. Subway: 1/2/3/9/A/C/E to 14th St. Map p 113.*

★★ **Thalassa** TRIBECA *GREEK* Food snobs will tell you that good Greek food doesn't exist in New York

Prix-Fixe Dining

Everyone loves a deal, and Restaurant Week is one of New York's best. It started more than a decade ago when some of the city's best dining spots began to offer three courses for a fixed low price at lunch ($20) and dinner ($35). Now it's an institution—and lasts for several weeks. Some restaurants offer prix-fixe menus year-round or have discounted menus on certain days or times. For example, the **21 Club** (21 W 52nd St., btwn Fifth & Sixth aves; (☎ **212/ 582-7200**) has a $37 prix fixe if you're seated by 6:30pm. Check out **www.opentable.com** or **www.nycvisit.com** for more information on Restaurant Week and participating restaurants.

Once a speakeasy, the 21 Club has a legendary Prohibition-era wine cellar.

outside of Astoria, but this lovely spot is a great find. Dishes, like the pan-seared sole, are lightly treated with olive oil and lemon to enhance the natural flavors. *197 Franklin St. (btwn Greenwich & Hudson sts.).* ☎ *212/941-7661. Main courses $14–$29. AE, DC, DISC, MC, V. Lunch Mon–Thurs, dinner daily. Subway: 1/9 to Franklin St. Map p 113.*

★★★ **Tocqueville** UNION SQUARE AREA *AMERICAN/FRENCH* Another of my favorite places to dine, with truly inspired dishes like seared sea scallops with foie gras and the pork chop with clams and fingerling potatoes. There's a great pre-theater prix-fixe menu for $38. *15 E. 15th St. (btwn University & Fifth aves.).*

☎ *212/647-1515. Main courses $19– $31. AE, MC, V. Lunch Mon–Sat, dinner Mon–Sun. Subway: L/N/R/4/ 5/6 to 14th St./Union Sq. Map p 114.*

★ **Tribeca Grill** TRIBECA *AMERI-CAN/FRENCH* Aka the Miramax Cafeteria; if you want to stargaze, this downtown favorite is a solid bet. The food doesn't coast on the reputation; dishes like the roasted baby chicken with Niçoise potatoes are delightful. *375 Greenwich St. (Franklin St.).* ☎ *212/941-3900. www.myriadrestaurantgroup.com. Main courses $19–$29 at dinner. AE, DC, DISC, MC, V. Lunch Sun–Fri, dinner daily. Subway: 1/9 to Franklin St. Map p 113.* ●

The Best **Nightlife**

Nightlife Best Bets

Best **Champagne Bar**
★ Bubble Lounge, *228 W. Broadway (p 130)*

Best **Post-Theater Bar**
★★★ Kemia Bar, *630 Ninth Ave. (p 131)*

Best **Historic Club**
★★★ Cotton Club, *656 W. 125th St. (p 133)*

Best **Gay-or-Straight Lounge**
★★★ Hell, *59 Gansevoort St. (p 134)*

Best **Dive Bar**
★ Chumley's, *86 Bedford St. (p 130)*

Best **Choice of Single-Malt Scotches**
★★ dba, *41 First Ave. (p 130)*

Best **Place to Bowl & Have a Martini**
★★ Bowlmor/Pressure, *110 University Place (p 130)*

Best **Neighborhood Bar**
★★ The Ginger Man, *11 E. 36th St. (p 131)*

Best **Piano Bar**
★★ Brandy's Piano Bar, *235 E. 84th St. (p 134)*

Best **Hotel Bar**
★★ King Cole Bar, *2 E. 55th St. (p 131)*

Best **Museum Bar**
★★★ Great Hall Balcony Bar, *Metropolitan Museum of Art, 1000 Fifth Ave. (p 131)*

Best **Vodka Selection**
★★ Pravda, *281 Lafayette St. (p 132)*

Best **Retro Bar**
★ Lansky Lounge & Grill, *104 Norfolk St. (p 131)*

Best **Irish Pub**
★★ Tír Na Nóg, *5 Penn Plaza (p 132)*

Best **Views**
★ Rainbow Room, *30 Rockefeller Plaza (p 132)*

Best **Drag Queens**
★★★ SBNY, *50 W. 17th St. (p 134)*

Best **Sangria & Tapas**
★★ Ñ, *33 Crosby St. (p 132)*

Best **Real-Life Mermaid**
★★ Coral Room, *512 W. 29th St. (p 133)*

Best **DJs and Sound System**
★★★ crobar, *530 W. 28th St. (p 133)*

Lansky Lounge & Grill.

Downtown Nightlife

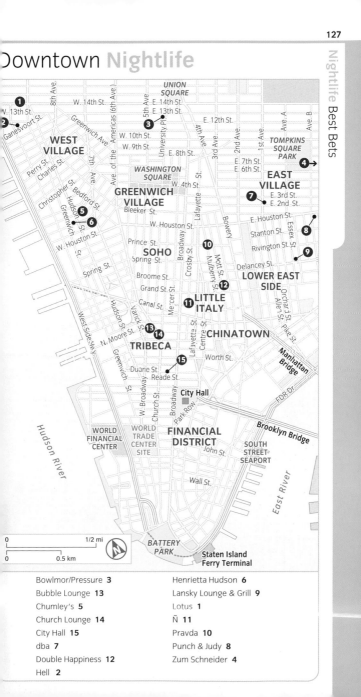

Bowlmor/Pressure **3**	Henrietta Hudson **6**
Bubble Lounge **13**	Lansky Lounge & Grill **9**
Chumley's **5**	Lotus **1**
Church Lounge **14**	Ñ **11**
City Hall **15**	Pravda **10**
dba **7**	Punch & Judy **8**
Double Happiness **12**	Zum Schneider **4**
Hell **2**	

Midtown & Uptown Nightlife

MANHATTAN

Area of
Harlem inset

UPTOWN

Area of
Uptown
inset

Central
Park

MIDTOWN

Area of
main map

DOWNTOWN

W. 66th St.
W. 65th St.
65th S
LINCOLN
CENTER
W. 63rd St.
CENTRA
W. 64th St.
UPPER WEST
SIDE
W. 62nd St.
Amsterdam Ave.
Columbus Ave.
Central Park W
West Drive
W. 61st St.
W. 60th St.
West End Ave.
W. 59th St. ⓂCentral Park S.
Columbus
Circle
W. 58th St.
W. 57th St.
W. 56th St.
W. 55th St.
W. 54th St.
Tenth Ave.
Ninth Ave.
W. 53rd St.
W. 52nd St.
MIDTOWN W. 51st St.
WEST W. 50th St. Ⓜ
W. 49th St.
THEATER
DISTRICT
W. 48th St.
W. 47th St.
Broadway
W. 46th St. Restaurant Row
W. 45th St.
TIMES
SQUAR
W. 44th St.
Eighth Ave.
Seventh Ave.
W. 43rd St.
W. 42nd St. Ⓜ
W. 41st St. Port
W. 40th St. Authority
W. 39th St.
W. 38th St.
W. 37th St.
Tenth Ave.
W. 36th St. GARMENT
W. 35th St. DISTRICT
Javits
Convention
Center
W. 34th St.
W. 33rd St. Penn
Statior
Madison Square
Garden W. 31st St.
W. 32nd St.
Tunnel
Entrance
W. 30th St.
Ninth Ave.
W. 29th St.
W. 28th St. Ⓜ
Chelsea Park W. 27th St.
W. 26th St.
W. 25th St.
Tenth Ave.
W. 24th St.
W. 23rd St. Ⓜ Ⓜ
W. 22nd St.
W. 21st St.
W. 20th St. CHELSEA
W. 19th St.
Eighth Ave.
Seventh Ave.
W. 18th St. Ⓜ
W. 17th St.
W. 16th St.
W. 15th St.
W. 14th St Ⓜ

Harlem

0   1/4 mi

W. 135th St.

W. 125th St
Martin Luther King Blvd (125th St.)
St. Nicholas Park
Powell Jr. Blvd. (Lenox Ave.)
Fifth Ave.
Morningside Ave.
Marcus
Garvey
Park
COLUMBIA
UNIVERSITY
Amsterdam Ave.
Broadway
Manhattan Ave.
Frederick Douglass Blvd.
Adam Clayton
Malcolm X Blvd
St. Nicholas Ave.
W. 116th St.
W. 110th St.
(Cathedral Pkwy.) Central Park North
CENTRAL PARK

Hudson
River

Uptown

0   1/2 mi

E. 96th St.
E. 93rd St.
Jacqueline
Kennedy
Onassis
Reservoir
UPPER EAST
SIDE
Park Ave.
Third Ave.
Second Ave.
E. 85th St.
CENTRAL
PARK
Metropolitan
Museum of Art
5th Ave.
Madison Ave.
Lexington Ave.
E. 79th St.
MEAT-
PACKING
DISTRICT

0   1/4 mi

0   0.25 km

UPPER EAST SIDE

E. 66th St.
E. 65th St.
E. 64th St.
E. 63rd St.
E. 62nd St.
E. 61st St.
Roosevelt Island Tram
E. 60th St.
E. 59th St.
E. 58th St.
E. 57th St.
E. 56th St.
E. 55th St.
E. 54th St.
E. 53rd St.
E. 52nd St.
E. 51st St.
E. 50th St.
E. 49th St.
E. 48th St
E. 47th St.
E. 46th St.
E. 45th St.
E. 44th St
E. 43rd St.
E. 42nd St.
E. 41st St.
E. 40th S
E. 39th S
E. 38th S
E. 37th St.
E. 36th St.
E. 35th St.
E. 34th St.
E. 33rd St.
E. 32nd St.
E. 31st St.
E. 30th St.
E. 29th St.
E. 28th St.
E. 27th St.
E. 26th St.
E. 25th St.
E. 24th St.
E. 23rd St.
E. 22nd St.
E. 21st St.
E. 20th St.
E. 19th St.
E. 18th St.
E. 17th St.
E. 16th St.
E. 15th St.

Transverse
East Drive

PARK

The Pond

St. Patrick's Cathedral

MIDTOWN EAST

ROCKEFELLER CENTER

Queensboro Bridge

East River

Queens-Midtown Tunnel

Mitchell Place

UNITED NATIONS

Grand Central Terminal

Bryant Park

New York Public Library

MURRAY HILL

Empire State Building

Madison Square Park

Flatiron Building

FLATIRON DISTRICT

Gramercy Park

GRAMERCY PARK

Union Sq.

Union Square

Sutton Pl.
Sutton Pl. South
Beekman Place
First Ave.
FDR Drive
Second Ave.
Third Ave.
Lexington Ave.
Park Ave.
Madison Ave.
Fifth Ave.
Vanderbilt Ave.
Sixth Ave. (Ave. of the Americas)
Broadway
Park Ave. S.
N.D. Perlman Pl.
Irving Pl.

Avalon **8**
Brandy's Piano Bar **14**
Club Shelter **10**
Copacabana **3**
Coral Room **6**
Cotton Club **15**
crobar **5**
The Ginger Man **9**
Great Hall Balcony Bar **13**
Kemia Bar **1**
King Cole Bar **12**
Rainbow Room **11**
Ruby Falls **4**
SBNY **7**
Tír Na Nóg **2**

New York Nightlife, A to Z

Bars & Cocktail Lounges

★★ Bowlmor/Pressure UNION
SQUARE The lanes at trendy Bowlmor aren't for bowling-league types: They'd hate the DJs, martinis, and flirtatious vibe. If pool's your pleasure, head upstairs to Pressure, a huge mod lounge that Austin Powers would feel at home in. *110 University Place (btwn 12th & 13th sts.).* ☎ *212/255-8188 (Bowlmor), or 212/352-1161 (Pressure). www.bowlmor. com or www.pressurenyc.com. Subway: 4/5/6/L/N/R to 14th St./ Union Sq. Map p 127.*

★ Bubble Lounge TRIBECA
More than 300 champagnes and sparkling wines are served in this upscale bar, decorated to resemble a diva's living room. No jeans, sneakers, or baseball caps. *228 W. Broadway (btwn Franklin & White sts.).* ☎ *212/431-3443. www.bubble lounge.com. Subway: 1/9 to Franklin St. Map p 127.*

★ Chumley's GREENWICH VILLAGE
My husband calls this one of New York's great dives, and that's a solid

You can also enter Chumley's through the courtyard at 58 Barrow Street.

description. This former speakeasy draws a young crowd with its heady selection of microbrews. *86 Bedford St. (at Barrow St.).* ☎ *212/675-4449. Subway: 1/9 to Christopher St. Map p 127.*

Church Lounge TRIBECA
Want to rub elbows with Hollywood types? Drop by around 11pm at this sprawling-but-stylish lobby bar at the Tribeca Grand Hotel (p ###). *2 Sixth Ave. (at White & Church sts.).* ☎ *212/519-6600. Subway: 1/9 to Franklin St.; A/C/E to Canal St. Map p 127.*

★★ City Hall DOWNTOWN
Debate all you like over a bottle of this bar's more than 800 wines. Set in a landmark 1863 building, the towering columns, cavernous ceiling, and elegant banquettes all proclaim its grandeur. Another plus is the service, which is helpful, knowledgeable, and warm. *131 Duane St. (Church St.).* ☎ *212/227-7777. Subway: A/C/1/2/3/9 to Chambers St. Map p 127.*

★★ dba EAST VILLAGE
Lounges dominate the city, but dba is a refreshing change of pace. It's an unpretentious neighborhood bar—a beer- or whiskey-lover's dream. The collection of single-malt scotches is phenomenal. *41 First Ave. (btwn 2nd & 3rd sts.).* ☎ *212/475-5097. www. drinkgoodstuff.com. Subway: F to Second Ave. Map p 127.*

Double Happiness CHINATOWN
The only street-level signage reads WATCH YOUR STEP, making this lounge feel like a local secret. Try the green tea martini, one of the house specials. *173 Mott St. (btwn Grand & Broome sts.).* ☎ *212/941-1282. Subway: 6 to Spring St. Map p 127.*

SINGLE MALT SCOTCH

[blackboard text, menu of whiskies]

dba's extensive drink offerings are written on blackboards.

★★ The Ginger Man MURRAY HILL

This is my favorite neighborhood pub: It's not exactly cozy, but the back room with the velvety couches is great if you can score a seat. Expect a huge local crowd, a welcoming feel, and 66 ales on tap. *11 E. 36th St. (btwn Fifth & Madison aves.).* ☎ *212/532-3740. Subway: 6 to 33rd St. Map p 128.*

★★★ Great Hall Balcony Bar

UPPER EAST SIDE   I promise, this bar is anything but touristy, despite its location in the Metropolitan Museum of Art. Every Friday and Saturday night from 4 to 8:30pm the lobby's mezzanine level transforms into a lounge with live classical music. *Metropolitan Museum of Art, 1000 Fifth Ave. (82nd St.).* ☎ *212/ 535-7710. www.metmuseum.org. Subway: 4/5/6 to 86th St. Map p 128.*

★★★ Kemia Bar MIDTOWN WEST

I'm reluctant to reveal this exotic-looking-yet-comfy bar, my current favorite. But I'm sharing it because the Moroccan-themed setting, vanilla- and sugarcane-infused martinis, and friendly waitstaff make it practically irresistible. Kemia's proximity to the Theater District makes it the perfect place to drop by after a show. Just don't tell anyone else! *630 Ninth Ave. (btwn 44th & 45th sts.).* ☎ *212/582-3200. Subway: A/C/E to 42nd St. Map p 128.*

★★ King Cole Bar MIDTOWN EAST

The Bloody Mary was born here, in the tony St. Regis Hotel. The Maxfield Parrish mural alone is worth the price of a classic cocktail (admittedly on the pricey side). Small as the bar is, it's a truly memorable spot. *2 E. 55th St. (Fifth Ave.).* ☎ *212/744-4300. Subway: F to Fifth Ave./53rd St. Map p 128.*

★ Lansky Lounge & Grill

LOWER EAST SIDE   This swanky spot has the retro vibe of a 1920s speakeasy. Shed your 21st-century inhibitions and order up one of the oversize vodka martinis. *104 Norfolk St. (btwn Rivington & Delancey sts.).* ☎ *212/677-9489. www.lansky lounge.com. Subway: F to Delancey St. Map p 127.*

The mural at the King Cole Bar.

Dancing at the Rainbow Room.

★★ **Ñ** SOHO This narrow, candlelit tapas bar is a gem. Ñ (pronounced like the Spanish letter, *eh*-nyeh) is the place to savor some fruity sangria, but there's also a full bar for non-Spanish tastes. You can order some of the city's best tapas, which come out of a very tiny kitchen in back. *33 Crosby St. (btwn Grand & Broome sts.).* ☎ *212/219-8856. Subway: N/R to Prince St.; 6 to Spring St. Map p 127.*

★★ **Pravda** SOHO Red may be dead now, but pre-Glasnost glamour reigns at this martini lounge, which serves up more than 70 types of vodka from 18 countries. The only street-level sign reads "281"; follow the stairwell down. *281 Lafayette St. (btwn Houston & Prince sts.).* ☎ *212/ 226-4944 or 212/334-5015. Subway: N to Prince St. Map p 127.*

★ **Punch & Judy** LOWER EAST SIDE I love this place because it succeeds at being both hip and cozy. The staff is friendly and the ever-changing wine list features a different region each month. *26 Clinton St. (btwn Houston & Stanton sts.).* ☎ *212/982-1116. www.punchand judy.com. Subway: F to Second Ave. Map p 127.*

★ **Rainbow Room** MIDTOWN WEST Cocktails are priced sky-high, but the view is incomparable. Combine that view with Art Deco elegance and live piano music, and you've got one great, romantic date. *30 Rockefeller Plaza (49th St.).* ☎ *212/632-5000. www.rainbow room.com. Subway: B/D/F/V to 47th–50th sts./Rockefeller Center. Map p 128.*

★★ **Tír Na Nóg** MIDTOWN WEST New York is packed with Irish pubs, but this standout makes you feel as if you're on a patch of the Emerald Isle. The friendly bartenders, Murphy's on tap, and lively music make for a perfect pub experience. *5 Penn Plaza (Eighth Ave., btwn 33rd & 34th sts.).* ☎ *212/630-0249. www.tirna nognyc.com. Subway: A/C/E to 34th St./Penn Station. Map p 128.*

Zum Schneider EAST VILLAGE Just what Alphabet City needed: an authentic indoor Bavarian beer garden. With its long tables and bench seating, this is a *sehr gut* place to go with a group. *107 Ave. C (7th St.).* ☎ *212/598-1098. www.zum schneider.com. Subway: F to Second Ave.; L to First Ave. Map p 127.*

Dance Clubs

Avalon CHELSEA   New Yorkers still go to church—though some of them have turned into nightclubs. This former church is the most famous. I love the catwalks and balconies within; the small rooms off the dance floor are another nice touch. *660 Sixth Ave. (20th St.). ☎ 212/807-7780. $15–$25 cover. Subway: F to 23rd St. Map p 128.*

★ **Club Shelter** MIDTOWN WEST   The big draw is the "Saturday Night Shelter Party," where 1980s house music takes over. Yes, it's cheesy but it's also fabulous. *20 W. 39th St. (btwn Fifth & Sixth aves.). ☎ 212/719-9867. $15–$20 cover. Subway: B/D/F/Q/V/7 to 42nd St. Map p 128.*

Copacabana MIDTOWN WEST   This cavernous dance palace features house music and live bands playing hot Latin music. Follow the moves of the showgirls (and boys) if you dare. *560 W. 34th St. (btwn Tenth & Eleventh aves.). ☎ 212/239-2672. Up to $40 cover. Subway: A/C/E to 34th St./Penn Station. Map p 128.*

★★ **Coral Room** MIDTOWN WEST   Love that mermaid—she swims by every so often in the club's tank. (She's real—come see for yourself.) The aquatic theme reigns throughout, except where the pounding dance music is concerned. *512 W. 29th St. (Tenth Ave.). ☎ 212/244-1965. Cover free or up to $20. Subway: 1/9 to 28th St. Map p 128.*

★★★ **Cotton Club** HARLEM   The legendary Harlem hot spot is still a-sizzle. The house band—the 13-piece Cotton Club All-Stars—will have you kicking your heels in no time (visiting artists make appearances here,

Keep an eye out for the mermaid at the Coral Room.

too). *656 W. 125th St. (Martin Luther King Blvd.). ☎ 212/663-7980. $15–$32 cover. Subway: 1/9 to 125th St. Map p 128.*

★★★ **crobar** CHELSEA   The odds of getting past the velvet rope increase with the size of a space, making this a good bet (think dancing/wiggle room for 3,000). The sound system and international DJs are unbeatable. *530 W. 28th St. (btwn Tenth & Eleventh aves.). ☎ 212/629-9000. www.crobar.com. $20–$30 cover. Subway: C/E to 23rd St. Map p 128.*

★ **Lotus** MEATPACKING DISTRICT   This triple-decker space is still hot, hot, hot, even though it's not new anymore. It's also still a beauty, filled with models (well, the women are, at least), and the watermelon martinis are divine. *409 W. 14th St. (Ninth Ave.). ☎ 212/243-4420. $10–$20 cover. Subway: A/C/E to 14th St. Map p 127.*

The Cotton Club was New York's most famous nightclub in the 1920s and 1930s.

The Gay & Lesbian Scene

★★ Brandy's Piano Bar UPPER EAST SIDE   The crowd is a mix of gay and straight, men and women, at this intimate piano bar. It's friendly and relaxed—so much so that the talented waitstaff who do most of the singing don't mind when patrons join in. *235 E. 84th St. (btwn Second & Third aves.).* ☎ *212/650-1944. Subway: 4/5/6 to 86th St. Map p 128.*

★★★ Hell MEATPACKING DISTRICT Who knew going to Hell would be this much fun? This sexy lounge serves up excellent mixed drinks to an interesting crowd (gay men and the straight women who love them). *59 Gansevoort St. (btwn Washington & Greenwich sts.).* ☎ *212/727-1666. Subway: A/C/E to 14th St. Map p 127.*

★ Henrietta Hudson WEST VILLAGE   This very popular ladies' lounge has been calling out to lipstick lesbians since 1991. The theme nights (Mamacita Sundays feature Latin music, Grind Tuesdays are all about soul), pack the house. *438 Hudson St. (Morton St.).* ☎ *212/924-3347. www.henriettahudsons. com. Subway: 1/9 to Houston St. Map p 127.*

Henrietta Hudson has a sidewalk cafe and a pool table.

★★★ SBNY CHELSEA   Welcome to gay heaven: This is a world of beautiful bartenders, mirrors everywhere the eye can see, and New York's best drag queens. No theme night anywhere is more successful than Musical Mondays: These singalongs draw a mixed gay/straight crowd and stars like Nathan Lane. *50 W. 17th St. (btwn Fifth & Sixth aves.).* ☎ *212/691-0073. www. splashbar.com. Subway: F/V to 14th St.; 4/5/6/N/R/L/Q/W to 14th St./ Union Sq. Map p 128.* ●

Breaking In

Getting beyond the velvet rope is an art form in New York. It's not for the faint of heart—and frankly, I'd advise against having your heart set on getting into the latest celebrity hot spot (unless you're a celebrity, of course). But if you're determined, here are some tips to increase your chances of making the cut. Dress up, show-pony: You'd better be stylin'. Standing out by looking fabulous will open doors. Get there early: True, the scene doesn't really start till after 11pm, but getting in at that point is a long shot. Arriving at 9pm isn't cool, but who cares if it gets you in the door? Park the attitude: Be nice to the doorman, no matter how mean he seems to you. Don't name-drop: Saying you're a friend of the owner will get you a one-way ticket to Palookaville. These are New Yorkers—they've heard it all already!

Arts & Entertainment
Best Bets

Most **Unusual Venue**
★ Bargemusic, Fulton Ferry Landing, *Brooklyn (p 141)*

Best **Free Music**
★★★ Juilliard School, Lincoln Center, *Broadway at 65th St. (p 141)*

Best **World Music**
★★ S.O.B.'s, *204 Varick St. (p 146)*

Best **Historic Venue**
★★★ Apollo Theater, *253 W. 125th St. (p 142)*

Best **Food** at a Club
★★ Jazz Standard, *116 E. 27th St. (p 145)*

Best **Classical Dance Troupe**
★★★ New York City Ballet, *Lincoln Center, Broadway and 64th St. (p 141)*

Best **Modern Dance Troupe**
★★ Alvin Ailey American Dance Theater, Joan Weill Center for Dance, *405 W. 55th St. (p 141)*

Best **Author Readings**
★ 92nd Street Y Tisch Center for the Arts, *1395 Lexington Ave. (p 143)*

Best **Repertory Theater Group**
★ New York Gilbert and Sullivan Players, *Symphony Space, Broadway and 95th St. (p 146)*

Best **New Comedians**
★ Gotham Comedy Club, *34 W. 22nd St. (p 147)*

Best **Rock-'n'-Roll Bar**
★★ Mercury Lounge, *217 E. Houston St. (p 145)*

Most **Unforgettable Visual Spectacle**
★★★ Metropolitan Opera, Lincoln Center, *Broadway and 64th St. (p 146)*

Best **Jazz Club**
★★ Birdland, *315 W. 44th St. (p 144)*; and ★★ Lenox Lounge, *288 Malcolm X Blvd. (p 144)*

Most **Avant-Garde Offerings**
★ The Knitting Factory, *74 Leonard St. (p 145)*

Best **Find**
★ Amato Opera Theatre, *319 Bowery (p 146)*; and ★★ St. Nick's Pub, *773 St. Nicholas Ave. (p 146)*

Most **Cutting-Edge Major Venue**
★★★ Brooklyn Academy of Music, *30 Lafayette Ave., Brooklyn (p 142)*

Best **Place to See Shakespeare**
★★ Public Theater, *425 Lafayette St. (p 143)*

Best **Church Concert Series**
★★ Church of the Transfiguration, *1 E. 29th St. (p 142)*

The fountains at Lincoln Center.

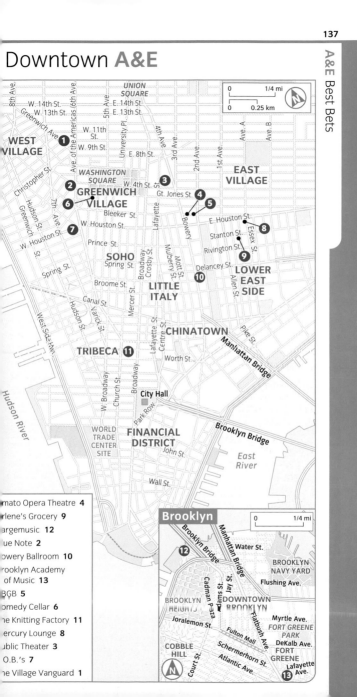

Midtown & Uptown **A&E**

Alvin Ailey American Dance Theater **8**
Apollo Theater **1**
B.B. King Blues Club & Grill **15**
Birdland **14**
Carnegie Hall **9**
Carolines on Broadway **13**
City Center **12**
Gotham Comedy Club **19**
Iridium **11**
Irving Plaza **18**
Jazz Standard **20**
Joyce Theater **17**
Juilliard School **6**
Lenox Lounge **2**
Lincoln Center **7**
Madison Square Garden **16**
92nd Street Y Tisch Center for the Arts **4**
Radio City Music Hall **22**
Roseland Ballroom **10**
St. Nick's Pub **3**
Symphony Space **5**
Town Hall **21**

The Best Arts & Entertainment

Broadway **Theaters**

Al Hirschfeld **19**	Gershwin **6**	New Amsterdam **38**
Ambassador **9**	Helen Hayes **27**	New Victory **37**
American Airlines **41**	Hilton Theatre **40**	Palace **32**
August Wilson Theater **4**	Imperial **18**	Plymouth **26**
Belasco **35**	John Golden **20**	Richard Rogers **17**
Biltmore **13**	Longacre **12**	Royale **24**
Booth **29**	Lunt-Fontanne **16**	St. James **22**
Broadhurst **23**	Lyceum **34**	Shubert **28**
Broadway **3**	Majestic **21**	Studio 54 **2**
Brooks Atkinson **15**	Marquis **31**	Vivian Beaumont **1**
Circle in the Square **8**	Minskoff **30**	Walter Kerr **11**
Cort **33**	Music Box **25**	Winter Garden **7**
Ethel Barrymore **14**	Nederlander **39**	
Eugene O'Neill **10**	Neil Simon **5**	

New York **Arts & Entertainment, A to Z**

Classical Music

★ **Bargemusic** BROOKLYN   Talk about original; this permanently docked barge is a primo chamber music concert hall. *At Fulton Ferry Landing (just south of the Brooklyn Bridge), Brooklyn.* ☎ *718/624-2083. www.bargemusic.org. Tickets $25–$40. Subway: 2/3 to Clark St.; A/C to High St. Map p 137.*

★★★ **Juilliard School** LINCOLN CENTER   America's premier music school sponsors more than 500 concerts a year, most at no charge. *60 Lincoln Center Plaza (Broadway at 65th St.).* ☎ *212/799-5000. www.juilliard.edu. Free admission to most shows; select performances $20. Subway: 1/9 to 66th St. Map p 138.*

★★★ **New York Philharmonic** LINCOLN CENTER   Founded in 1842, this is one of the best symphonies on the planet. *At Avery Fisher Hall, Lincoln Center, Broadway & 65th St.* ☎ *212/875-5656 for audience services, 212/875-5030 for box office information, or Center Charge at 212/721-6500 for tickets. www.newyorkphilharmonic.org. Tickets $36–$75. Subway: 1/9 to 66th St. Map p 138.*

Dance

★★ **Alvin Ailey American Dance Theater** MIDTOWN WEST This world-renowned modern dance company moved into a new permanent home in November 2004. Called the Joan Weill Center for Dance, it's the largest facility dedicated to dance in the country. *405 W. 55th St. (at Ninth Ave.).* ☎ *212/405-9000. www.alvinailey.org. Tickets $25–$110. Subway: 1/2/3/9/A/C to 59 St./Columbus Circle. Map p 138.*

Alvin Ailey American Dance Theater's first performance was at the 92nd Street Y in 1958.

★★ **City Center** MIDTOWN WEST Modern dance doesn't get any better than this, and the sightlines are terrific from all corners. *131 W. 55th St. (btwn Sixth & Seventh aves.).* ☎ *877/247-0430. www.citycenter. org. Tickets $15–$125. Subway: F/N/Q/R/W to 57th St.; B/D/E to Seventh Ave. Map p 138.*

★ **Joyce Theater** CHELSEA   Built as a movie house, the Art Deco Joyce has become a great modern dance center. Joyce SoHo has experimental works. *175 Eighth Ave. (at 19th St.).* ☎ *212/242-0800. www.joyce.org. Tickets $25–$40. Subway: C/E to 23rd St.; 1/9 to 18th St. Joyce SoHo at 155 Mercer St. (btwn Houston & Prince sts.).* ☎ *212/431-9233. Subway: N/R to Prince St. Map p 138.*

★★★ **New York City Ballet** LINCOLN CENTER   The legendary George Balanchine founded this stellar company. *At the New York State Theater, Lincoln Center, Broadway & 64th St.* ☎ *212/870-5570. www.nycballet.com. Tickets $30–$95. Subway: 1/9 to 66th St. Map p 138.*

Heavenly Sounds

While New York's churches may play traditional hymns during their religious services, many also offer afternoon and evening concerts in a variety of secular styles, from classical to opera, from purely instrumental to thrilling soloists. The price is right, too: A few concerts require tickets, but most have a "requested donation" that ranges from $2 to $10 (and they won't turn you away if you don't pay it). Check out the websites for schedules. My favorite spots are: **Church of the Transfiguration** (1 E. 29th St.; www.littlechurch.org); **St. Paul's Chapel and Trinity Church** (www.saintpaulschapel.org; p 8); **The Cathedral of St. John the Divine** (www.stjohndivine.org; p 67); **St. Ignatius Loyola** (980 Park Ave.; www.saintignatiusloyola.org); and **St. Bartholomew** (www.stbarts.org), which also has its own restaurant (p 117).

Landmark Venues

★★★ Apollo Theater HARLEM A legendary institution. *See p 68, bullet* ⑨.

★★★ Brooklyn Academy of Music BROOKLYN Just 25 minutes by subway from midtown, BAM is the place for cutting-edge theater, opera, dance, and music. *30 Lafayette Ave. (off Flatbush Ave.), Brooklyn.* ☎ *718/636-4100. www.bam.org. Ticket prices vary. Subway: 2/3/4/5/M/N/Q/R/W to Pacific St./Atlantic Ave. Map p 137.*

★★★ Carnegie Hall MIDTOWN WEST One of the world's most respected concert halls. *See p 26, bullet* ⑦.

★★★ Lincoln Center for the Performing Arts UPPER WEST SIDE *See p 26, bullet* ⑤.

Madison Square Garden GARMENT DISTRICT The most famous names in pop music play this cavernous 20,000-seat arena. *Seventh Ave. & 31st–33rd sts.* ☎ *212/465-MSG1. www.thegarden.com. Ticket prices vary. Subway: A/C/E/1/2/3/9 to 34th St. Map p 138.*

A performance at Carnegie Hall.

★ **92nd Street Y Tisch Center for the Arts** UPPER EAST SIDE Forget what you know about the "Y"—this Jewish community center offers top-notch cultural events. *1395 Lexington Ave. (at 92nd St.).* ☎ *212/415-5500. www.92ndsty.org. Tickets $15–$25. Subway: 4/5/6 to 86th St.; 6 to 96th St. Map p 138.*

★★ **Public Theater** NOHO Groundbreaking stagings of Shakespeare's plays as well as new plays, classical dramas, and solo performances. *425 Lafayette St. (btwn Astor Place and E. 4th St.).* ☎ *800/276-2392. www.publictheater.org. Ticket prices vary. Subway: 6 to Astor Place. Map p 137.*

★★ **Radio City Music Hall** MIDTOWN WEST This stunning 6,200-seat Art Deco theater is home to the annual Christmas Spectacular and the Rockettes. *See p 16, bullet* ❺.

★ **Symphony Space** UPPER WEST SIDE This innovative institution includes the Peter Jay Sharp Theater and the Leonard Nimoy Thalia Theater and offers a varied program of dance, film, readings, and music. *2537 Broadway (at 95th St.).* ☎ *212/864-1414. www. symphonyspace.org. Ticket prices*

Radio City Music Hall at Christmas.

vary. Subway: 1/2/3/9 to 96th St. Map p 138.

★ **Town Hall** MIDTOWN WEST A National Historic Site, this intimate space has outstanding acoustics, and performers ranging from Celine Dion to Ladysmith Black Mambazo, from Philip Glass to David Byrne. *123 W. 43rd St. (btwn Sixth & Seventh aves.).* ☎ *212/840-2824. www. the-townhall-nyc.org. Tickets $20–$80. Subway: N/Q/R/S/W/1/2/3/7/9 to 42nd St./Times Sq.; B/D/F/V to 42nd St. Map p 138.*

Broadway Theaters

In the Big Apple you'll find a kaleidoscopic mix of big-budget blockbusters and alternative, experimental shows. Broadway is the place to see glorious spectacles such as *The Producers,* classics like *12 Angry Men,* and first-run hits like *Proof.* Casts often include faces you'll recognize from the big screen: Kevin Spacey, Patrick Stewart, and Glenn Close, to name a few. And these days, the smaller and alternative shows are frequently lit by star power, too (Tim Robbins' Actors' Gang are regulars at the Public Theater (above). For information on tickets see "Getting Tickets" (p 147); for a list of theaters, see p 48 or the map on p 140.

Live Music

Arlene's Grocery LOWER EAST SIDE   A casual rock music club with a good sound system; great bang for the buck. *95 Stanton St. (btwn Ludlow & Orchard sts.).* ☎ *212/358-1633. www.arlenes-grocery.net. Up to $10 cover. Subway: F to Second Ave. Map p 137.*

B.B. King Blues Club & Grill THEATER DISTRICT   This 550-seat venue plays the blues (naturally) as well as pop, funk, and country. *237 W. 42nd St. (btwn Seventh & Eighth aves.).* ☎ *212/997-4144. www. bbkingblues.com. Tickets $20–$150. Subway: A/C/E/Q/W/1/2/3/7/9 to 42nd St. Map p 138.*

★★ Birdland MIDTOWN WEST A legendary jazz club and one of the city's favorites. *315 W. 44th St. (btwn Eighth & Ninth aves.).* ☎ *212/581-3080. www.birdlandjazz.com. Tickets $20–$50. Subway: A/C/E to 42nd St. Map p 138.*

Blue Note GREENWICH VILLAGE Soft-jazz fans take note: excellent sound system and sightlines, though you pay for them. *131 W. 3rd St. (at*

When the original Birdland opened in December, 1949, Charlie Parker was the headliner.

Check out the Rock and Roll Karaoke at Arlene's Grocery on Monday nights.

Sixth Ave.). ☎ *212/475-8592. www. bluenote.net. Tickets $10–$70. Subway: A/B/C/D/E/F/V to W. 4th St. Map p 137.*

Bowery Ballroom LOWER EAST SIDE   Another Art Deco wonder, this one with a big stage and good sightlines from every corner. Alt rockers like Patti Smith perform here and the Fab Faux, a Beatles tribute band, also makes frequent appearances. *6 Delancey St. (at Bowery).* ☎ *212/533-2111. www.bowery ballroom.com. Tickets $20–$40. Subway: F/J/M/Z to Delancey St. Map p 137.*

CBGB EAST VILLAGE   At press time, New York's most famous rock club was in danger of becoming obsolete. *315 Bowery (at Bleecker St.).* ☎ *212/982-4052. www.cbgb. com. Up to $12 cover. Subway: F to Second Ave.; 6 to Bleecker St. Map p 137.*

★ Iridium THEATER DISTRICT Guitar great Les Paul has played two sets at this glamorous jazz club every Monday for a long time, and the Iridium also hosts tributes to the likes of Thelonius Monk and Miles Davis. *1650 Broadway (at 51st St.).* ☎ *212/582-2121. www.iridiumjazzclub.com. Tickets $25–$35. Subway: 1/9 to 50th St. Map p 138.*

Irving Plaza GRAMERCY PARK This midsize music hall is a prime stop for national-name rock bands that aren't quite big enough yet (or anymore) to sell out Roseland. *17 Irving Place (1 block west of Third Ave. at 15th St.).* ☎ *212/777-1224. www.irvingplaza.com. Tickets $15–$45. Subway: L/N/R/4/5/6 to 14th St./ Union Sq. Map p 138.*

★★ Jazz Standard GRAMERCY/ MURRAY HILL One of the city's largest jazz clubs, Jazz Standard has a retro vibe and the best food of any club (it's part of, and downstairs from, Blue Smoke—see p 117). *116 E. 27th St. (btwn Park Ave. S. & Lexington Ave.).* ☎ *212/576-2232. www.jazzstandard.net. $15–$25 cover. Subway: 6 to 28th St. Map p 138.*

★ The Knitting Factory TRIBECA This famed avant-garde music venue has experimental jazz, acoustic folk,

Iridium hosts a jazz brunch buffet on Sundays.

On Sunday, kids can take part in the Jazz Standard's "Jazz for Kids" program.

poetry readings, and out-there multimedia art. *74 Leonard St. (btwn Broadway & Church St.).* ☎ *212/219-3055. www.knittingfactory.com. $5–$20 cover. Subway: 1/9 to Franklin St. Map p 137.*

★★ Lenox Lounge HARLEM This beautifully renovated and historically accurate gem features top jazz vocalists, trios, and quartets. *288 Malcolm X Blvd. (Lenox Ave. btwn 124th & 125th sts.).* ☎ *212/427-0253. www.lenoxlounge.com. $10–$15 cover. Subway: 2/3 to 125th St. Map p 138.*

★★ Mercury Lounge LOWER EAST SIDE The perfect live-music rock-'n'-roll bar. I've loved it since 1995, when a music-journalist friend took me here to listen to Cake. The music at the Merc is still that cool. *217 E. Houston St. (at Essex St./ Ave. A).* ☎ *212/260-4700. www.mercuryloungenyc.com. $8–$15 cover; some shows require tickets. Subway: F to Second Ave. Map p 137.*

Roseland Ballroom MIDTOWN WEST This 1919 ballroom's elegant days are firmly in the past; now it's a rockin' 2,500-capacity general-admission hall. *239 W. 52nd St. (btwn Broadway & Eighth Ave.).*

☎ 212/247-0200. www.roseland ballroom.com. Tickets $15–$70. Subway: C/E/1/9 to 50th St. Map p 138.

★★ St. Nick's Pub HARLEM Unpretentious St. Nick's in Harlem's Sugar Hill district has great live entertainment every night. It draws the famous (Roy Hargrove, James Carter) and many lesser-knowns, all of whom partake in the late-night jam session after the show. *773 St. Nicholas Ave. (at 149th St.).* ☎ *212/ 283-9728. Under $5 cover. Subway: A/C/D/B to 145th St. Map p 138.*

★★ S.O.B.'s SOHO This top world-music venue features Brazilian, Caribbean, and Latin beats. The music is so hot you won't be able to stay in your seat. *204 Varick St. (at Houston St.).* ☎ *212/243-4940. www. sobs.com. $8–$15 cover. Subway: 1/9 to Houston St. Map p 137.*

The Village Vanguard GREENWICH VILLAGE What CBGB is to rock, the Village Vanguard is to jazz. *178 Seventh Ave. S. (just below 11th St.).* ☎ *212/255-4037. www.village vanguard.net. Tickets $25–$30. Subway: 1/2/3/9 to 14th St. Map p 137.*

Opera
★ Amato Opera Theatre EAST VILLAGE This off-the-beaten-track find is a showcase for talented young singers. The theater barely seats 100, so buy tickets well in advance. *319 Bowery (at 2nd St.).* ☎ *212/228-8200. www.amato.org. Tickets $25–$45. Subway: F to Second Ave.; 6 to Bleecker St. Map p 137.*

★★★ Metropolitan Opera LINCOLN CENTER Opera aficionados know that this is one of the most electrifying companies in the world. *At the Metropolitan Opera House, Lincoln Center, Broadway & 64th St.* ☎ *212/362-6000. www.met opera.org. Tickets $25–$295. Subway: 1/9 to 66th St. Map p 138.*

★ New York City Opera LINCOLN CENTER The repertoire includes more modern and experimental works than at the Met, but singers are less well known. *At the New York State Theater, Lincoln Center, Broadway & 64th St.* ☎ *212/870-5570. www.nycopera.com. Tickets $25–$115. Subway: 1/9 to 66th St. Map p 138.*

★ New York Gilbert and Sullivan Players UPPER WEST SIDE Light-hearted operetta is the ticket here, and no one does it better. *At Symphony Space, Broadway & 95th St.* ☎ *212/864-5400. www.nygasp. org. Tickets $40–$65. Subway: 1/2/3/9 to 96th St. Map p 138.*

The Metropolitan Opera's first performances were in 1883.

Stand-up Comedy
★★ Carolines on Broadway

THEATER DISTRICT   Hot headliners come to this upscale club (Jerry Seinfeld, Rosie O'Donnell, and Tim Allen have all taken the stage; Colin Quinn is here frequently). *1626 Broadway (btwn 49th & 50th sts.).* ☎ *212/757-4100. www.carolines. com. $15–$40 cover. Subway: N/R to 49th St.; 1/9 to 50th St. Map p 138.*

★ Comedy Cellar GREENWICH

VILLAGE   This intimate subterranean club is a favorite among comedy cognoscenti. It gets names you'd expect (Dave Chapelle, Chris Rock) and a few you wouldn't (William Shatner). *117 Macdougal St. (btwn Bleecker & W. 3rd sts.).* ☎ *212/254-3480. www.comedycellar.com. $10–$20 cover. Subway: A/B/C/D/E/F/V/S to W. 4th St. Map p 137.*

★ Gotham Comedy Club FLAT-

IRON DISTRICT   Big names are frequently on the marquee, but the "New Comedy Showcase" is a staple. Gotham teaches would-be stand-ups the ropes through 1-day

TKTS is run by the country's largest not-for-profit performing arts service organization.

seminars and even multiweek courses, and you'll see some of the students take the stage. *34 W. 22nd St. (btwn Fifth & Sixth aves.).* ☎ *212/367-9000. www.gothamcomedy club.com. $10–$35 cover. Subway: F/N/R to 23rd St. Map p 138.*

Getting Tickets

If your heart is set on seeing a particular show, buy tickets in advance from **TeleCharge** (☎ **212/239-6200;** www.telecharge.com) or **Ticketmaster** (☎ **212/307-4100;** www.ticketmaster.com).

The free membership programs at **www.broadway.com**, **www.playbill.com**, or **www.theatermania.com** can save you up to 50% on tickets. For the best deals on **same-day tickets,** visit **TKTS** (47th St. and Broadway; open 3–8pm for evening performances, 10am–2pm for Wed and Sat matinees, 11am–8pm on Sun for all performances). Tickets are 25% to 50% off, plus a $2.50 per ticket service charge. You won't find seats to this season's smash hit, but most other shows are available. Only cash and traveler's checks are accepted. **Tip:** The lines are much shorter at **TKTS Lower Manhattan** in South Street Seaport (199 Water St. at the corner of Front and John sts.; open Mon–Fri 11am–6pm, Sat 11am–4pm; subway: 2/3/4/5 to Fulton St.). All the same policies apply. Visit www.tdf.org or call NYC/Onstage at ☎ 212/768-1818 for more information.

Broadway **Theaters**

Al Hirschfeld. *302 W. 45th St.* ☎ *212/239-6200.*

Ambassador. *219 W. 49th St.* ☎ *212/239-6200.*

American Airlines. *227 W. 42nd St.* ☎ *212/719-1300.*

August Wilson. *245 W. 52nd St.* ☎ *212/239-6200.*

Belasco. *111 W. 44th St.* ☎ *212/239-6200.*

Biltmore. *261 W. 47th St.,* ☎ *212/239-6222.*

Booth. *222 W. 45th St.* ☎ *212/239-6200.*

Broadhurst. *235 W. 44th St.* ☎ *212/239-6200.*

Broadway. *1681 Broadway.* ☎ *212/239-6200.*

Brooks Atkinson. *256 W. 47th St.* ☎ *212/719-4099.*

Circle in the Square. *1633 Broadway.* ☎ *212/239-6200.*

Cort. *138 W. 48th St.* ☎ *212/239-6200.*

Ethel Barrymore. *243 W. 47th St.* ☎ *212/239-6200.*

Eugene O'Neill. *230 W. 49th St.* ☎ *212/239-6200.*

Gershwin. *222 W. 51st St.* ☎ *212/586-6510.*

Helen Hayes. *240 W. 44th St.* ☎ *212/944-9450.*

Hilton Theatre. *213 W. 42nd St.,* ☎ *212/307-4100.*

Imperial. *249 W. 45th St.* ☎ *212/239-6200.*

John Golden. *252 W. 45th St.* ☎ *212/239-6200.*

Longacre. *220 W. 48th St.* ☎ *212/239-6200.*

Lunt-Fontanne. *205 W. 46th St.* ☎ *212/575-9200.*

Lyceum. *149 W. 45th St.* ☎ *212/239-6200.*

Majestic. *245 W. 44th St.* ☎ *212/239-6200.*

Marquis. *302 W. 45th St.* ☎ *212/239-6200.*

Minskoff. *200 W. 45th St.* ☎ *212/869-0550.*

Music Box. *239 W. 45th St.* ☎ *212/239-6200.*

Nederlander. *208 W. 41st St.* ☎ *212/921-8000.*

Neil Simon. *250 W. 52nd St.* ☎ *212/757-8646.*

New Amsterdam. *214 W. 42nd St.* ☎ *212/82-2900.*

New Victory. *209 W. 42nd St.* ☎ *646/223-3020.*

Palace. *1564 Broadway.* ☎ *212/730-8200*

Plymouth. *236 W. 45th St.* ☎ *212/239-6200.*

Richard Rodgers. *226 W. 46th St.* ☎ *212/221-1211.*

Royale. *242 W. 45th St.* ☎ *212/239-6200.*

St. James. *246 W. 44th St.* ☎ *212/239-6200.*

Shubert. *225 W. 44th St.* ☎ *212/239-6200.*

Studio 54. *254 W. 54th St.* ☎ *212/719-1300.*

Vivian Beaumont. *150 W. 65th St.* ☎ *212/239-6200.*

Walter Kerr. *219 W. 48th St.* ☎ *212/239-6200.*

Winter Garden. *1634 Broadway.* ☎ *212/239-6200.* ●

The Best **Lodging**

The Best Lodging

Lodging Best Bets

Most **Romantic**
★★★ Inn at Irving Place $$$
56 Irving Place (p 154)

Most **Historic**
★ The Peninsula–New York $$$$
700 Fifth Ave. (p 156)

Best **Boutique Hotel**
★★ Hotel Giraffe $$$ *365 Park Ave. S. (p 154)*

Best **Place to Channel Dorothy Parker**
★ The Algonquin $$ *59 W. 44th St. (p 154)*

Most **Luxurious Hotel**
★★ The Mark $$$$ *25 E. 77th St. (p 155)*; and ★★★ Ritz-Carlton New York $$$ *2 West St. (p 156)*

Best **Moderate Hotel**
★ The Melrose Hotel $$ *140 E. 63rd St. (p 156)*

Best **Budget Hotel**
★★ La Quinta Inn $ *17 W. 32nd St. (p 155)*

Best **for Kids**
★★ Red Roof Inn $ *6 W. 32nd St. (p 156)*; and ★★ The Regency $$$$ *540 Park Ave. (p 156)*

The Sofitel is close to Broadway theaters.

Best **Value**
★★ Belvedere Hotel $$$ *319 W. 48th St. (p 154)*

Best **Themed Hotel**
★ The Library Hotel $$$ *299 Madison Ave. (p 155)*

Most **Charming B&B**
★★ The Inn on 23rd $$ *131 W. 23rd St. (p 155)*

Best **for Hobnobbing with Celebrities**
★ The Mercer $$$ *147 Mercer St. (p 156)*; and ★ Soho Grand Hotel $$$ *310 W. Broadway (p 157)*

Best **European-Style Hotel**
★ Fitzpatrick Grand Central Hotel $$ *141 E. 44th St. (p 154)*; and ★ Larchmont Hotel $ *27 W. 11th St. (p 155)*

Best **View**
★★★ Ritz-Carlton New York $$$ *2 West St. (p 156)*

Best **for Business Travelers**
★ Wall Street Inn $$ *9 S. William St. (p 158)*

Most **Laid-Back Luxury Hotel**
★★ The Mark $$$$ *25 E. 77th St. (p 155)*

Most **Trendy**
★ W Union Square $$$ *201 Park Ave. S. (p 158)*

Most **Awe-Inspiring Modern Design**
Tribeca Grand Hotel $$$ *2 Sixth Ave. (p 157)*

Most **Glamorous**
★★ The Sherry-Netherland $$$$ *781 Fifth Ave. (p 157)*

Best **for Serenity Seekers**
★★ Sofitel New York $$$ *45 W. 44th St. (p 157)*

Downtown **Lodging**

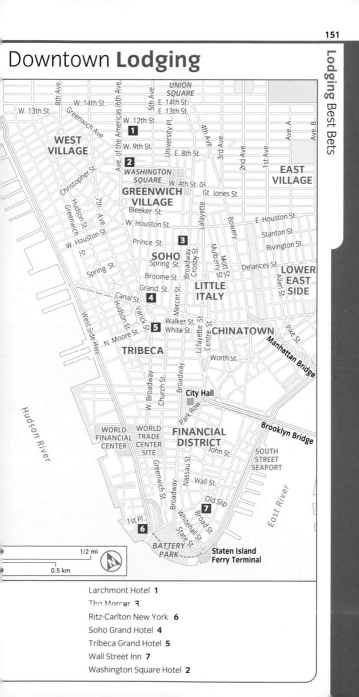

Larchmont Hotel **1**

The Mercer **3**

Ritz-Carlton New York **6**

Soho Grand Hotel **4**

Tribeca Grand Hotel **5**

Wall Street Inn **7**

Washington Square Hotel **2**

Midtown & Uptown **Lodging**

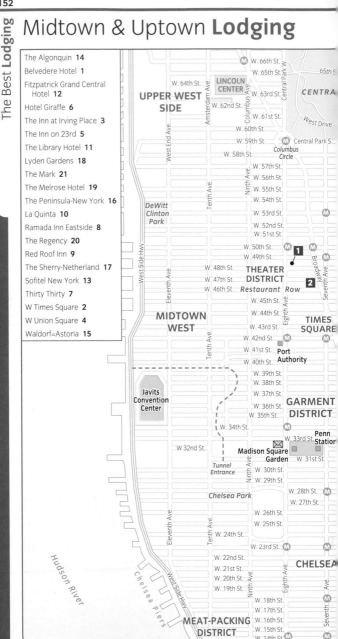

New York **Hotels, A to Z**

★ **The Algonquin** MIDTOWN WEST This 1902 hotel is a literary landmark (home of the Round Table, frequented by Dorothy Parker and other writers), and renovations have restored its splendor. *59 W. 44th St. (btwn Fifth & Sixth aves.).* ☎ *888/ 304-2047. www.algonquinhotel.com. 174 units. Doubles $159–$299. AE, DC, DISC, MC, V. Subway: B/D/F/V to 42nd St. Map p 152.*

★★ **kids Belvedere Hotel** MIDTOWN WEST The design here is sharp, especially in the public spaces, but the real reason to stay is in the amenities. Every room has a desk and a kitchenette with mini-fridge, sink, and microwave. This is ideal for travelers who don't want to eat every meal at a restaurant. *319 W. 48th St. (at Eighth Ave.).* ☎ *888/HOTEL58. www.belvedere hotelnyc.com. 400 units. Double $160–$450. AE, DC, DISC, MC, V. Subway: C/E to 50th St. Map p 152.*

★ **Fitzpatrick Grand Central Hotel** MIDTOWN EAST Attractive and intimate, this Irish-owned property is a terrific choice for those who seek the creature comforts a chain hotel offers but detest the blandness that's usually part of the deal. *141 E. 44th St. (at Lexington Ave.).* ☎ *800/ 367-7701. www.fitzpatrickhotels.com. 155 units. Doubles $249–$349. AE, DC, DISC, MC, V. Subway: 4/5/6/7/S to 42nd St./Grand Central. Map p 152.*

★★ **Hotel Giraffe** GRAMERCY/ MURRAY HILL The stylish guest rooms boast high ceilings, velveteen upholstered chairs, and black-and-white photos from the '20s and '30s. The lovely rooftop garden is another draw. *365 Park Ave. S. (at 26th St.).* ☎ *877/296-0009. www.hotelgiraffe. com. 73 units. Doubles $325–$425 w/breakfast. AE, DC, MC, V. Subway: 6 to 28th St. Map p 152.*

★★★ **Inn at Irving Place** GRAMERCY This 170-year-old town house offers 19th-century elegance. Spacious rooms have antiques and art, nonworking fireplaces, and big bathrooms. *56 Irving Place (btwn 17th & 18th sts.).* ☎ *800/685-1447. www.innatirving.com. 12 units. Doubles $325–$415. AE, DC, MC, V. Subway: N/R/4/5/6 to 14th St./Union Sq. Map p 152.*

The two town houses that make up the Inn at Irving Place have housed everything from apartments to a speakeasy.

The Larchmont Hotel is tucked in the residential section of historic Greenwich Village.

★★ **kids The Inn on 23rd**
CHELSEA   One of Manhattan's few full-service B&Bs, this inn offers individualized, spacious guest rooms decorated with a personal touch. *131 W. 23rd St. (btwn Sixth & Seventh aves.).* ☎ *877/387-2323. www.innon 23rd.com. 14 units. Doubles $175 $250. AE, DC, MC, V. Subway: F/1/9 to 23rd St. Map p 152.*

★★ **La Quinta Inn** MIDTOWN
WEST   Friends of mine have stayed here and loved it. The location is perfect (proximity to sights and on a nice street) and the decently sized rooms have amenities that you don't expect at a budget hotel, such as free high-speed Internet access. *17 W. 32nd St. (btwn Fifth Ave. & Broadway).* ☎ *800/551-2303. www. applecorehotels.com or www.lq. com. 182 units. Doubles start at $99. AE, DC, DISC, MC, V. Subway: B/D/ F/V/N/R to 34th St. Map p 152.*

★ **Larchmont Hotel** GREENWICH
VILLAGE   If you're willing to share a bathroom, it's hard to find a better priced option than this charming European-style hotel. *27 W. 11th St. (btwn Fifth & Sixth aves.).* ☎ *212/ 989-9333. www.larchmonthotel.com. 58 units. Doubles $90–$125. AE, MC, V. Subway: A/B/C/D/E/F/V to W. 4th St.; F to 14th St. Map p 151.*

★ **The Library Hotel** MIDTOWN
EAST   Each of the 10 floors is dedicated to a major category of the Dewey Decimal System. Lovely, but it's unlikely you'll have time to read the books in your room. *299 Madison Ave. (at 41st St.).* ☎ *877/793-7323. www.libraryhotel.com. 60 units. Doubles $295–$425. AE, DC, MC, V. Subway: 4/5/6/7/S to 42nd St. Map p 152.*

★ **kids Lyden Gardens** UPPER
EAST SIDE   Each suite includes a small but fully equipped kitchen so you can save money by preparing some of your own meals, and the one-bedrooms have more than enough space for families. *215 E. 64th St. (btwn Second & Third aves.).* ☎ *212/355-1230. 131 units. 1-bedroom suites $260–$330. AE MC, V, Disc. Subway: 4/5/6/N/R/W to 59th St. Map p 152.*

★★ **kids The Mark** UPPER EAST
SIDE   I love the motto: "No jacket, no tie, no attitude." Think impeccable service and comfort, but no stuffiness. *25 E. 77th St. (btwn Madison & Fifth aves.).* ☎ *800/THEMARK. www.mandarinoriental.com/themark. 180 units. Doubles $545–$695. AE, DC, MC, V. Subway: 6 to 77th St. Map p 152.*

★ **The Melrose Hotel** UPPER EAST SIDE   A $40-million renovation has turned the Barbizon hotel for women into a hotel for everyone. This lovely old building features an eclectic mix of Italian Renaissance, Gothic, and Islamic architecture. *140 E. 63rd St. (at Lexington Ave.).* ☎ *800/MELROSE. www.melrosehotel newyork.com. 306 units. Doubles $239–$399. AE, DC, MC, V. Subway: F to Lexington Ave. Map p 152.*

★ **The Mercer** SOHO   So hip it hurts. Forget the celebs and enjoy the high-ceilinged guest rooms, lush linens, and tile-and-marble bathrooms. *147 Mercer St. (at Prince St.).* ☎ *888/918-6060. www.mercerhotel. com. 62 units. Doubles $395–$440. AE, DC, DISC, MC, V. Subway: N/R to Prince St. Map p 151.*

★ **The Peninsula–New York** MIDTOWN   Housed in a 1905 landmark building, the Peninsula is now a state-of-the-art stunner. Guest rooms come with high-speed wiring and fabulous bathrooms. *700 Fifth Ave. (at 55th St.).* ☎ *800/262-9467. www.peninsula.com. 239 units. Doubles $590–$750. AE, DC, DISC, MC, V. Subway: E/F to Fifth Ave. Map p 152.*

★ **Ramada Inn Eastside** MIDTOWN EAST   My brother-in-law was skeptical about staying at a Manhattan Ramada, but one visit converted him. The neighborhood is a big selling point, as are the 24-hour business center and the 24-hour fitness center. And while the rooms are small, they are well organized. *161 Lexington Ave. (at 30th St.).* ☎ *800/625-5980. www.applecore hotels.com or www.ramada.com. 95 units. Doubles start at $89. AE, DC, DISC, MC, V. Subway: 6 to 28th St. Map p 152.*

★★ kids **Red Roof Inn** HERALD SQUARE   This former office building has more spacious rooms and

An executive suite at the Regency.

bathrooms than are usually found in this price category. *6 W. 32nd St. (btwn Broadway & Fifth Ave.).* ☎ *800/567-7720. www.applecorehotels.com or www.redroof.com. 171 units. Doubles $109–$300 w/breakfast. AE, DC, DISC, MC, V. Subway: B/D/F/V/N/R to 34th St. Map p 152.*

★★ kids **The Regency** UPPER EAST SIDE   A stay at the Regency can make you feel like a star: Guest rooms are big, service is grand, and there's even a kids' concierge. *540 Park Ave. (at 61st St.).* ☎ *212/759-4100. www.loewshotels.com. 351 units. Doubles $419–$499. AE, DC, MC, V. Subway: 4/5/6/N/R to 59th St. Map p 152.*

★★★ kids **Ritz-Carlton New York** BATTERY PARK   Divinely luxurious with large guest rooms, the Ritz has one drawback: its location on the extreme southern tip of Manhattan (however, you'll have magnificent views of New York Harbor and Lady Liberty). *2 West St. (at 1st Place).* ☎ *800/241-3333. www.ritzcarlton.com. 298 units. Doubles $350–$490. AE, DC, DISC, MC, V. Subway: 4/5 to Bowling Green. Map p 151.*

★★ The Sherry-Netherland
MIDTOWN This 1927 neo-Romanesque property is both a hotel and a residential building. The grandly proportioned rooms have high ceilings, big bathrooms, and walk-in closets. *781 Fifth Ave. (at 59th St.). ☎ 800/247-4377. www.sherrynetherland. com. 77 units. Doubles $425–$625. AE, DC, DISC, MC, V. Subway: N/R to Fifth Ave. Map p 152.*

★★ Sofitel New York
MIDTOWN WEST Built in 2000, the Sofitel blends Old World elegance with New World amenities. Rooms are spacious, adorned with art, and soundproofed. *45 W. 44th St. (btwn Fifth & Sixth aves.). ☎ 212/354-8844. www.sofitel.com.*

Many rooms at The Sherry-Netherland have either park or 59th Street views.

398 units. Doubles $229–$429. AE, DC, MC, V. Subway: B/D/F/V to 42nd St. Map p 152.

★ Soho Grand Hotel SOHO
Built as a modern ode to SoHo's cast-iron past, the Soho Grand attracts an entertainment-industry crowd. William Morris textiles and soft lighting abound. *310 W. Broadway (at Grand St.). ☎ 800/965-3000. www.sohogrand. com. 369 units. Doubles from $339. AE, DC, DISC, MC, V. Subway: A/C/E/N/R/1/ 9 to Canal St. Map p 151.*

Thirty Thirty
MURRAY HILL This is a good bet for travelers who want a budget hotel that also has a sense of style. The rooms, however, are small. *30 E. 30th St. (btwn Madison & Park aves.). ☎ 800/497-6028. www.thirty thirty-nyc.com. 243 units. Doubles $115–$145. AE, DC, DISC, MC, V. Subway: 6 to 28th St. Map p 152.*

Tribeca Grand Hotel TRIBECA
This hotel merges high style, luxury comforts, and a hip downtown location. Because guest rooms face the eight-story atrium, they can be loud, so each is equipped with a white-noise machine. *2 Sixth Ave. (btwn White & Church sts.). ☎ 877/519-6600. www.tribecagrand.com. 203 units. Doubles $259–$359. AE, DC, DISC, MC, V. Subway: 1/9 to Franklin St.; A/C/E to Canal St. Map p 151.*

Waldorf=Astoria MIDTOWN EAST
This massive Art-Deco masterpiece is a genuine New York landmark. But with over 1,000 rooms, the pace can be hectic, and the check-in lines daunting. *301 Park Ave. (btwn 49th & 50th sts.). ☎ 800/WALDORF.*

A "romance bath" at the Ritz-Carlton is sprinkled with rose petals.

Budget-Friendly Hotels

New York is one of the most expensive cities in the world, a fact you'll really appreciate when you try to book a hotel. To get the best price, follow these rules. **Schedule carefully,** because prices climb sky-high when events like the Marathon are on. **Don't feel you have to be in the center of town**—you can save money and get more space by staying uptown or downtown. **Look for deals online** on sites like www.orbitz.com, www.expedia.com, www.hotels.com, www.quikbook.com, and www.priceline.com, but don't overlook the hotels' own websites, which can offer exclusive deals. And **be flexible**—so what if your room is tiny, you're going to be too busy to spend much time there anyway.

www.waldorfastoria.com. 1,245 units. Doubles $229–$485. AE, DC, DISC, MC, V. Subway: 6 to 51st St. Map p 152.

★ **Wall Street Inn** FINANCIAL DISTRICT This intimate, seven-story Lower Manhattan oasis is warm, comforting, and serene. Friendly, professional, personalized service is the hallmark. *9 S. William St. (at Broad St.).* ☎ *212/747-1500. www.thewallstreetinn.com. 46 units. Doubles $249–$450. AE, DC, DISC, MC, V. Subway: 2/3 to Wall St.; 4/5 to Bowling Green. Map p 151.*

Washington Square Hotel GREENWICH VILLAGE The rooms are tiny, but pleasant in this afford-able hotel facing Washington Square Park. It's worth paying a few extra dollars for a south-facing room on a high floor. *103 Waverly Place (btwn Fifth & Sixth aves.).* ☎ *800/222-0418. www.wshotel.com. 165 units. Doubles $150–$179. AE, MC, V. Subway: A/B/C/D/E/F/V to W. 4th St. (use 3rd St. exit). Map p 151.*

★ **W Times Square** TIMES SQUARE Most rooms boast magnifi-cent views; thankfully, shades block out most of the neon at night and double-paned windows keep them relatively quiet. *1547 Broadway (at*

47th St.). ☎ 888/625-5144. www. whotels.com. 509 units. Doubles from $259. AE, DC, DISC, MC, V. Subway: N/R to 49th St. Map p 152.

★ **W Union Square** UNION SQUARE The 1911 Guardian Life Beaux Arts building has been revived with bold, clean-lined modernism. *201 Park Ave. S. (at 17th St.).* ☎ *212/ 253-9119. www.starwood.com. Dou-bles $239–$550. AE, DC, DISC, MC, V. Subway: N/R/W/6/5/4 to Union Sq. Map p 152.* ●

The Washington Square Hotel has been hosting travelers for over a century.

The
Savvy Traveler

Before You Go

Government Tourist Offices

IN THE U.S.: NYC & Company, 810 Seventh Ave., New York, NY 10019 ☎ 800/NYC-VISIT; www.nycvisit. com. **IN THE U.K.:** NYCVB Visitor Information Center, 36 Southwark Bridge Rd., London, SE1 9EU ☎ **020/7202 6368**.

The Best Time to Go

July and August are hot and humid, but because the local population tries to escape, the city is far less crowded and there are plenty of free alfresco events. December brings crowds and the highest prices; January and February are relatively cheap. But there's nothing like New York in spring or fall when the weather is mild.

Festivals & Special Events

WINTER. For information on the lighting of the **Rockefeller Center Christmas Tree** call ☎ 212/332-6868. On **New Year's Eve** the most famous party of them all takes place in Times Square (☎ 212/768-1560; www.timessquarealliance.org). During **Restaurant Week** (1 week in January and 1 in June), you can enjoy $20 prix-fixe menus at lunch or $35 for dinner at some of the best restaurants in the city (☎ 212/484-1222; www.nycvisit.com).

SPRING. The **Triple Pier Antiques Show,** the city's largest antiques show takes place in March (☎ 212/255-0020; www.antiqnet.com/Stella for this and additional shows) as does, of course, the **St. Patrick's Day Parade** (☎ 212/484-1222) on the 17th. The **Easter Parade** (☎ 212/484-1222), not a traditional parade, but a flamboyant fashion display along Fifth Avenue from 48th to 57th streets, is on Easter Sunday.

SUMMER. All summer long, the **Lincoln Center Festival** (☎ 212/546-2656; www.lincolncenter.org), celebrates the best of the performing arts from all over the world (tickets go on sale in late May). **SummerStage** (☎ 212/360-2756; www.summerstage.org) is a summer-long festival of outdoor performances in Central Park, featuring world music, pop, folk, and jazz artists, the New York Grand Opera, and the Chinese Golden Dragon Acrobats, among others. At the same time and also in Central Park well-known actors take on the Bard in the Public Theater's long-running **Shakespeare in the Park** series (☎ 212/539-8750; www.publictheater.org). The **Independence Day Harbor Festival and Fourth of July Fireworks Spectacular** (☎ 212/484-1222, or Macy's Visitor Center at 212/494-2922) takes place on July 4. **Lincoln Center Out of Doors** (☎ 212/546-2656; www.lincolncenter.org), a series of free music and dance performances, is held on the plazas of Lincoln Center.

FALL. The **West Indian–American Day Parade** (☎ 212/484-1222 or 718/625-1515), an annual Brooklyn event on Labor Day, is New York's best street festival. The **Greenwich Village Halloween Parade** (☎ 212/475-3333, ext. 14044; www.halloween-nyc.com) on October 31 is a flamboyant parade that everyone is welcome to join. Something everyone should do at least once is see the **Radio City Music Hall Christmas Spectacular** (☎ 212/247-4777; www.radiocity.com) and watch the **Macy's Thanksgiving Day Parade** (☎ 212/484-1222).

The Weather

The worst weather in New York is during that long week or 10 days

NEW YORK'S AVERAGE TEMPERATURE & RAINFALL

	JAN	FEB	MAR	APR	MAY	JUNE
Daily Temp. (°F)	38	40	48	61	71	80
Daily Temp. (°C)	3	4	9	16	22	27
Days of Precip.	11	10	11	11	11	10

	JULY	AUG	SEPT	OCT	NOV	DEC
Daily Temp. (°F)	85	84	77	67	54	42
Daily Temp. (°C)	29	29	25	19	12	6
Days of Precip.	11	10	8	8	9	10

that arrive between mid-July and August when the temperatures go up to 100°F (38°C) with 90% humidity. Another time when you might not want to stroll around the city is mid-winter when temperatures drop to around 20°F (–7°C) and the winds whip through the concrete canyons. If you want to know how to pack just before you go, check CNN's online 5-day forecast at *www.cnn.com/ weather*. You can also get the local weather by calling ☎ *212/976-1212*.

Useful Websites

- www.nycvisit.com: A wealth of free information about the city.

- www.nymetro.com and www. villagevoice.com: Good coverage of arts and events.

- www.timeoutny.com: Comprehensive listings, restaurant reviews, shopping, and nightlife.

- www.dailycandy.com: Sign up for daily e-mails listing sample sales.

- www.gocitykids.com: Information for families with young kids.

- www.broadway.com, www.play bill.com, www.theatermania. com: Offer membership programs that save you money on Broadway tickets.

- www.panynj.gov/ and www. mta.nyc.ny.us/index.html: Transit information.

- www.weather.com: Up-to-the-minute worldwide weather reports.

Restaurant & Theater Reservations

I can't say it enough: Book well in advance if you're determined to eat at a particular spot or see a certain show. For popular restaurants, if you didn't call in advance, try asking for early or late hours—often tables are available before 6.30pm and after 9pm. You could also call the day before or first thing in the morning, when you may be able to take advantage of a cancellation.

If you're interested in a popular show, call or go online for tickets well before your trip. Try **TELECHARGE** (☎ *212/239-6200*) or **TICKETMASTER** (☎ *212/307-4100; www.ticketmaster. com*). For last-minute theater seats, see the information about TKTS in the "Getting Tickets" box on p 147.

Cell (Mobile) Phones

In general it's a good bet that your phone will work in New York, although if you're not from the U.S., you'll be appalled at the poor reach of the **GSM (GLOBAL SYSTEM FOR MOBILES) WIRELESS NETWORK,** which is used by much of the rest of the world. (To see where GSM phones work in the U.S., check out *www.t-mobile.com/coverage/ national_popup.asp*). And you may or may not be able to send SMS (text messages) overseas. Assume nothing—call your wireless provider and get the full scoop.

In a worst-case scenario, you can always rent a phone from **INTOUCH USA** (📞 *800/872-7626; www.intouch global.com*) or a rental car location, but beware that you'll pay $1 a minute or more for airtime.

Getting **There**

By Plane

Three major airports serve New York City: **JOHN F. KENNEDY INTERNATIONAL AIRPORT** (📞 *718/244-4444*) in Queens, is about 15 miles (1 hr. driving time) from Midtown Manhattan; **LAGUARDIA AIRPORT** (📞 *718/533-3400*), also in Queens, is about 8 miles (30 min.) from Midtown; and **NEWARK INTERNATIONAL AIRPORT** (📞 *973/961-6000*) in nearby New Jersey, is about 16 miles (45 min.) from Midtown. Always allow extra time, though, especially during rush hour, peak holiday travel times, and if you're taking a bus. Information on all three is available online at *www.panynj.gov.*

Your best bet is to stay away from public transportation when traveling to and from the airport. **TAXIS** are a quick and convenient alternative. They're available at designated taxi stands outside the terminals. Fares, whether fixed or metered, do not include bridge and tunnel tolls ($3.50–$4) or a tip for the cabbie (15%–20% is customary). They do include all passengers in the cab and luggage (from 8pm–6am, a $1 surcharge also applies on New York yellow cabs). **FROM JFK:** A flat rate of $45 to Manhattan (plus tolls and tip) is charged. **FROM LAGUARDIA:** $17 to $27, metered, plus tolls and tip. **FROM NEWARK:** The dispatcher for New Jersey taxis gives you a slip of paper with a flat rate ranging from $30 to $38 (toll and tip extra), depending on where you're going in Manhattan. The yellow-cab fare from Manhattan to Newark is the meter amount plus $15 and tolls (about $45–$55, perhaps a few dollars more with tip).

PRIVATE CAR AND LIMOUSINE COMPANIES provide convenient 24-hour door-to-door airport transfers. They are a little more expensive than taxis, but they're a good idea if you're traveling at rush hour because they charge flat fees. Call at least 24 hours in advance and a driver will meet you near baggage claim. I use **ALLSTATE** (📞 *800/453-4099*) and **TEL-AVIV** (📞 *800/222-9888*).

AIRTRAINS are available at Newark and JFK but are a poor option if you have luggage or any mobility issues, and I strongly suggest that you avoid AirTrain JFK (www.airtrainjfk.com) altogether. The Newark AirTrain (📞 *888/EWR-INFO; www.airtrain newark.com*) will deposit you at a NJ Transit station, where you then take another train to Penn Station.

BUS AND SHUTTLE SERVICES provide a comfortable and less expensive (but usually more time-consuming) option for airport transfers than taxis and car services. The blue vans of **SUPER SHUTTLE** (📞 *212/258-3826; www.supershuttle.com*) serve all three airports. **THE NEW YORK AIRPORT SERVICE** (📞 *718/875-8200; www.nyairportservice.com*) buses travel from JFK and LaGuardia to the Port Authority Bus Terminal (42nd St. and Eighth Ave.), Grand Central Terminal (Park Ave. between

41st and 42nd sts.), and to select Midtown hotels. Fares run between $15 and $19 per person.

By Car

From the **NEW JERSEY TURNPIKE** (I-95) and points west, there are three Hudson River crossings into the city's west side: the **HOLLAND TUNNEL** (lower Manhattan), the **LINCOLN TUNNEL** (Midtown), and the **GEORGE WASHINGTON BRIDGE** (upper Manhattan). From **UPSTATE NEW YORK,** take the **NEW YORK STATE THRUWAY** (I-87), which crosses the Hudson on the Tappan Zee Bridge and becomes the **MAJOR DEEGAN EXPRESSWAY** (I-87) through the Bronx. For the east side, continue to the Triborough Bridge and then down the FDR Drive. For the west side, take the Cross Bronx Expressway (I-95) to the Henry Hudson Parkway or the Taconic State Parkway to the Saw Mill River Parkway to the Henry Hudson Parkway

south. From New England, **THE NEW ENGLAND THRUWAY** (I-95) connects with the **BRUCKNER EXPRESSWAY** (I-278), which leads to the Triborough Bridge and the FDR Drive on the east side. Note that you'll have to pay tolls along some of these roads and at most crossings.

Once you arrive in Manhattan, park your car in a garage (expect to pay $20–$45 per day) and leave it there. Don't use your car for traveling within the city.

By Train

AMTRAK (800/USA-RAIL; www. amtrak.com) runs frequent service to New York City's **PENN STATION**, on Seventh Avenue between 31st and 33rd streets, where you can easily pick up a taxi, subway, or bus to your hotel. To get the best rates, book early (as much as 6 months in advance) and travel on weekends.

Getting **Around**

By Subway

Run by the **METROPOLITAN TRANSIT AUTHORITY (MTA),** the subway system is the fastest way to travel around New York, especially during rush hours. The subway runs 24 hours a day, 7 days a week. The rush-hour crushes are roughly from 8 to 9:30am and from 5 to 6:30pm on weekdays. The fare is $2 (half price for seniors and those with disabilities); children under 44 inches tall ride free. Fares are paid with a **METROCARD,** a magnetically encoded card that debits the fare when swiped through the turnstile (or the fare box on any city bus). MetroCards also allow you free transfers between the bus and subway within a 2-hour period. There are Pay-Per-Ride and Unlimited Ride

MetroCards; both can be purchased at any subway station, and from many drugstores.

Once you're in town, you can stop at the MTA desk at the **TIMES SQUARE INFORMATION CENTER,** 1560 Broadway, between 46th and 47th streets (where Broadway meets Seventh Ave.) to pick up the latest subway map. (You can also ask for one at any token booth, but they might not always be available.)

Less expensive than taxis, better views than subways—buses would be the perfect alternative if they didn't sometimes get stuck in traffic. They're best for shorter distances or when you're not in a rush. Like the subway fare, bus fare is $2, payable with a **METROCARD** or **EXACT CHANGE.** Bus drivers don't make change, and fare boxes don't accept dollar bills or pennies. If you pay with a MetroCard, you can transfer to another bus or to the subway for free within 2 hours. If you pay cash, you must request a **FREE TRANSFER** slip that allows you to change to an intersecting bus route only (legal transfer points are listed on the transfer paper) within 1 hour of issue. Transfer slips cannot be used to enter the subway.

Yellow **TAXI CABS** are licensed by the Taxi and Limousine Commission (TLC). Base fare on entering the cab is $2.50. The cost is 40¢ for every ⅕ mile or 40¢ per 2 minutes in stopped or very slow-moving traffic (or for waiting time). There's no extra charge for each passenger or for luggage, but you must pay bridge or tunnel tolls. You'll also pay a $1 night surcharge after 8pm and before 6am. A 15% to 20% tip is customary. You can hail a taxi on any street. *Never* accept a ride from any other car except an official city yellow cab (private livery cars are not allowed to pick up fares on the street).

Fast **Facts**

APARTMENT RENTALS   Your best bets are **Manhattan Getaways** (☎ **212/956-2010;** manhattangetaways.com) with a network of unhosted apartments around the city that start at $145 per night, or **A Hospitality Company** (☎ **800/987-1235** or 212/813-2444; www.hospitalityco.com) which owns and manages 300 apartments around Manhattan starting at $125 per night.

ATMS   You'll find **automatic teller machines (ATMs)** on just about every block in Manhattan. Some ATMs will allow you to draw U.S. currency against your bank and credit cards. Check with your bank before leaving home and remember that you will need your personal identification number (PIN) to do so.

BABYSITTING   The first place to check is with your hotel. Many hotels have babysitting services or will provide you with lists of reliable sitters. If this doesn't pan out, call the **Baby Sitters' Guild** (☎ **212/682-0227;** www.babysittersguild.com). The sitters are licensed, insured, and bonded, and can even take your child on outings.

BANKING HOURS   Banks tend to be open Monday through Friday from 9am to 3pm and sometimes Saturday mornings.

B&BS   In addition to **Manhattan Getaways** (see "Apartment Rentals" above) you can try **As You Like It** (☎ **800/277-0413** or 212/695-0191; www.furnapts.com) or **Manhattan Lodgings** (☎ **212/677-7616;** www.manhattanlodgings.com).

BUSINESS HOURS   In general, retail stores are open Monday through Saturday from 10am to 6 or 7pm, Thursday from 10am to 8:30 or 9pm, and Sunday from noon to 5pm.

CLIMATE   See "The Weather" on p 160.

CONCERTS   See "Tickets" below.

CONSULATES & EMBASSIES   All embassies are located in Washington, D.C. All the countries listed below have consulates in New York, and most nations have a mission to the United Nations (also in New York). If your country isn't listed, call for directory information in Washington, D.C. (☎ **202/555-1212**), for the number of your national embassy. The embassy of **Australia** is at 1601 Massachusetts Ave. NW,

Washington, DC 20036 (☎ **202/ 797-3000;** www.austemb.org). The embassy of **Canada** is at 501 Pennsylvania Ave. NW, Washington, DC 20001 (☎ **202/682-1740;** www. canadianembassy.org). The embassy of **Ireland** is at 2234 Massachusetts Ave. NW, Washington, DC 20008 (☎ **202/462-3939;** www.irelandemb. org). The embassy of the **United Kingdom** is at 3100 Massachusetts Ave. NW, Washington, DC 20008 (☎ **202/588-7800;** www.britainusa. com/consular/embassy).

CREDIT CARDS   Credit cards are a safe way to "carry" money, they provide a convenient record of all your expenses, and they generally offer good exchange rates. You can also withdraw cash advances from your credit cards at banks or ATMs, provided you know your PIN.

CUSTOMS   Visitors arriving by air, no matter what the port of entry, should cultivate patience and resignation before setting foot on U.S soil. Getting through immigration control can take as long as 2 hours on some days, especially on summer weekends. People traveling by air from Canada, Bermuda, and certain countries in the Caribbean can sometimes clear Customs and Immigration at the point of departure, which is much quicker.

DENTISTS   If you have dental problems, a nationwide referral service known as **1-800-DENTIST** (☎ **800/ 336-8478**) will provide the name of a nearby dentist or clinic.

DINING   With a few exceptions at the high-end of the scale, dining attire is fairly casual. It's a good idea to make reservations in advance if you plan on eating between 7 and 9pm.

DOCTORS   The **NYU Downtown Hospital** offers physician referrals at ☎ **888/698-3362**.

ELECTRICITY   Like Canada, the United States uses 110 to 120 volts AC (60 cycles), compared to 220 to 240 volts AC (50 cycles) in most of Europe, Australia, and New Zealand.

If your small appliances use 220 to 240 volts, you'll need a 110-volt transformer and a plug adapter with two flat parallel pins to operate them here. Downward converters that change 220–240 volts to 110–120 volts are difficult to find in the United States, so bring one with you.

EMBASSIES   See "Consulates & Embassies" above.

EMERGENCIES   Dial ☎ **911** for fire, police, and ambulance. The **Poison Control Center** can be reached at ☎ **800/222-1222** toll-free from any phone. If you encounter serious problems, contact **Traveler's Aid International** (☎ **202/546-1127;** www.travelersaid.org) to help direct you to a local branch. This nationwide, nonprofit, social-service organization geared to helping travelers in difficult straits offers services that might include reuniting families separated while traveling, providing food and/or shelter to people stranded without cash, or even emotional counseling.

EVENT LISTINGS   Good sources include the **New York Times** (www.nytimes.com) with excellent arts and entertainment coverage, **Time Out New York** (www.timeout ny.com) with extensive weekly listings, and the weekly **Village Voice** (www.villagevoice.com) which you can pick up for free all over the city.

FAMILY TRAVEL   Good bets for timely information include the "Weekend" section of Friday's **New York Times,** which has a section dedicated to the week's best kid-friendly activities; the weekly **New York** magazine, which has a full calendar of children's events in its "Cue" section; and **Time Out New York Kids.** For more extensive recommendations, you might want to purchase a copy of **Frommer's New York City with Kids,** an entire guidebook dedicated to family visits to the Big Apple.

GAY & LESBIAN TRAVELERS The International Gay & Lesbian Travel Association (IGLTA) (☎ 800/448-8550 or 954/776-2626; www.iglta.org) is the trade association for the gay and lesbian travel industry, and offers an online directory of gay- and lesbian-friendly travel businesses. All over Manhattan, but especially in neighborhoods such as the **West Village** and **Chelsea,** shops, services, and restaurants cater to a gay and lesbian clientele. The **Lesbian and Gay Community Services Center** is at 208 W. 13th St., between Seventh and Eighth avenues (☎ 212/620-7310; www.gaycenter.org).

HOLIDAYS Banks, government offices, post offices, and many stores, restaurants, and museums are closed on the following legal national holidays: January 1 (New Year's Day), the third Monday in January (Martin Luther King Jr. Day), the third Monday in February (Presidents' Day, Washington's Birthday), the last Monday in May (Memorial Day), July 4th (Independence Day), the first Monday in September (Labor Day), the second Monday in October (Columbus Day), November 11 (Veterans' Day/Armistice Day), the fourth Thursday in November (Thanksgiving Day), and December 25 (Christmas). Also, the Tuesday following the first Monday in November is Election Day and is a federal government holiday in presidential-election years (held every 4 years, and next in 2008).

INSURANCE **Trip-Cancellation Insurance** helps you get your money back if you have to back out of a trip, if you have to go home early, or if your travel supplier goes bankrupt. Allowed reasons for cancellation can range from sickness to natural disasters to the State Department declaring your destination unsafe for travel. In this unstable world, trip-cancellation insurance is a good buy if you're getting tickets well in advance. Insurance policy details vary, so read the fine print—and especially make sure that your airline or cruise line is on the list of carriers covered in case of bankruptcy. For information, contact one of the following insurers: **Access America** (☎ 866/807-3982; www.accessamerica.com); **Travel Guard International** (☎ 800/826-4919; www.travelguard.com); **Travel Insured International** (☎ 800/243-3174; www.travelinsured.com); and **Travelex Insurance Services** (☎ 888/457-4602; www.travelex-insurance.com).

Although it's not required of travelers, **health insurance** is highly recommended. Unlike many European countries, the United States does not usually offer free or low-cost medical care to its citizens or visitors. Doctors and hospitals are expensive, and in most cases will require advance payment or proof of coverage before they render their services. Though lack of health insurance may prevent you from being admitted to a hospital in non-emergencies, don't worry about being left on a street corner to die: The American way is to fix you now and bill the living daylights out of you later.

Insurance for British Travelers: Most big travel agents offer their own insurance and will probably try to sell you their package when you book a holiday. Think before you sign. **Britain's Consumers' Association** recommends that you insist on seeing the policy and reading the fine print before buying travel insurance. **The Association of British Insurers** (☎ 020/7600-3333; www.abi.org.uk) gives advice by phone and publishes *Holiday Insurance,* a free guide to policy provisions and prices. You might also shop around for better deals: Try **Columbus Direct** (☎ 020/7375-0011; www. columbusdirect.net).

Insurance for Canadian Travelers: You should check with their provincial health plan offices or call **Health Canada** (☎ 613/957-2991; www.hc-sc.gc.ca) to find out the extent of your coverage and what documentation and receipts you must take home in case you are treated in the United States.

Lost-Luggage Insurance: On domestic flights, checked baggage is covered up to $2,500 per ticketed passenger. On international flights (including U.S. portions of international trips), baggage is limited to approximately $9 per pound, up to approximately $635 per checked bag. If you plan to check items more valuable than the standard liability, see if your valuables are covered by your homeowner's policy or get baggage insurance as part of your comprehensive travel-insurance package. Don't buy insurance at the airport, as it's usually overpriced. Be sure to take any valuables or irreplaceable items with you in your carry-on luggage, since many valuables (including books, money, and electronics) aren't covered by airline policies. If your luggage is lost, immediately file a lost-luggage claim at the airport, detailing the luggage contents. For most airlines, you must report delayed, damaged, or lost baggage within 4 hours of arrival. The airlines are required to deliver luggage, once found, directly to your house or destination free of charge.

INTERNET CENTERS The **Times Square Visitors Center,** 1560 Broadway, between 46th and 47th streets (☎ 212/768-1560; open daily 8am–8pm), has computer terminals that you use to send e-mails courtesy of Yahoo!. In Times Square, **easyInternetCafé,** 235 W. 42nd St., between Seventh and Eighth avenues (☎ 212/398-0775; www.easyeverything.com), is open 24/7. **Kinko's** (www.kinkos.com) charges 30¢ per minute ($15 per hour) and has numerous locations around town.

LIMOS Try **Allstate** (☎ 800/453-4099) or **Tel-Aviv** (☎ 800/222-9888).

LOST PROPERTY **Travelers Aid** (www.travelersaid.org) helps distressed travelers with all kinds of problems, including lost or stolen luggage. There is an office on the second floor of the International Arrivals Building at JFK Airport (☎ 718/656-4870), and one in Newark Airport's Terminal B (☎ 973/623-5052).

MAIL & POSTAGE The main post office is at 421 Eighth Ave. (33rd St.); other branches can be found by calling ☎ 800/275-8777 or logging onto www.usps.gov. Mail can be sent to you, in your name, c/o General Delivery at the main post office. Most post offices will hold your mail for up to 1 month, and are open Monday to Friday from 8am to 6pm, and Saturday from 9am to 3pm. At press time, domestic postage rates were 22¢ for a postcard and 37¢ for a letter. For international mail, a first-class letter of up to ½ ounce costs 60¢ (46¢ to Canada and 40¢ to Mexico); a first-class postcard costs 50¢ (including Canada and Mexico); and a preprinted postal aerogramme costs 50¢.

MONEY Don't carry a lot of cash in your wallet, but always have $20 on hand for taxi fare. Many small restaurants won't accept credit cards, so ask up front if you plan to pay with plastic. Traveler's checks are something of an anachronism from the days before ATMs; **American Express** (☎ 800/221-7282), **Visa** (☎ 800/732-1322), and **MasterCard** (☎ 800/223-9920) all offer them. If you choose to carry traveler's checks, be sure to keep a record of their serial numbers separate from your checks in the event that they are stolen or lost.

PASSPORTS Always keep a photocopy of your passport with you when you're traveling. If your passport is lost or stolen, having a copy significantly facilitates the reissuing process at your consulate. Keep your passport and other valuables in your room's safe or in the hotel safe.

PHARMACIES **Duane Reade** (www. duanereade.com) has 24-hour pharmacies in Midtown at 224 W. 57th St., at Broadway (**☎ 212/541-9708**); on the Upper West Side at 253 W. 72nd St., between Broadway and West End Avenue (**☎ 212/580-0497**); and on the Upper East Side at 1279 Third Ave., at 74th Street (**☎ 212/744-2668**).

SAFETY New York is one of the safest large cities in the United States, but crime most definitely exists here. Trust your instincts because they're usually right. You'll rarely be hassled, but it's always best to walk with a sense of purpose and self-confidence. Don't stop in the middle of the sidewalk to pull out and peruse your map. Anywhere in the city, if you find yourself on a deserted street that feels unsafe, it probably is; leave as quickly as possible. If you do find yourself accosted by someone with or without a weapon, remember to keep your anger in check and that the most reasonable response (maddening though it may be) is not to resist.

SENIOR TRAVELERS New York subway and bus fares are half price ($1) for people 65 and older. Many museums and sights (and some theaters and performance halls) offer discounted admittance and tickets to seniors, so don't be shy about asking and always bring an ID card. Many hotels offer senior discounts; **Choice Hotels** (www.hotelchoice.com) gives 30% off their published rates to anyone over 50, provided you book your room through their nationwide toll-free reservations number (that is, not directly with the hotels or through a travel agent). Members of **AARP** (formerly known as the American Association of Retired Persons), 601 E St. NW, Washington, DC 20049 (**☎ 888/687-2277** or 202/434-2277; www.aarp.org), get discounts on hotels, airfares, and car rentals. AARP offers members a wide range of benefits, including *AARP: The Magazine* and a monthly newsletter. Anyone over 50 can join.

SMOKING Smoking is prohibited on all public transportation, in the lobbies of hotels and office buildings, in taxis, bars, restaurants, and in most shops.

Spectator Sports You've got your choice of baseball teams, the **Yankees** (**☎ 718/293-6000;** www. yankees.com) and the **Mets** (**☎ 718/507-TIXX;** www.mets.com). For basketball there's the **Knicks** (**☎ 877/NYK-DUNK;** www.nyknicks.com) and the **New York Liberty** (**☎ 212/465-6080;** www.wnba.com/liberty).

TAXES **Sales tax** is 8.625% on meals, most goods, and some services. **Hotel tax** is 13.25% plus $2 per room per night (including sales tax). **Parking garage tax** is 18.25%.

TAXIS See "Limos" and "Getting Around" above.

TELEPHONE For directory assistance, dial **☎ 411;** for long-distance information, dial 1, then the appropriate area code and 555-1212. Pay phones cost 25¢ for local calls. There are four area codes in the city: two in Manhattan, the original **212** and the new **646,** and two in the outer boroughs, the original **718** and the new **347.** Also common is the **917** area code, which is assigned to cellphones, pagers, and the like. All calls between these area codes are local calls, but you'll have to dial 1 + the area code + the 7 digits for all calls, even ones made within your area code.

TICKETS Tickets for concerts at all larger theaters can be purchased through **Ticketmaster** (☎ 212/307-7171; www.ticketmaster.com). For advance tickets at smaller venues contact **Ticketweb** (☎ 866/468-7619; www.ticketweb.com). For theater tickets you can buy tickets in advance from **TeleCharge** (☎ 212/239-6200; www.telecharge.com) or **Ticketmaster** (☎ 212/307-4100; www.ticketmaster.com). If you're looking for last-minute tickets, check the "Getting Tickets" box on p 147.

TIPPING Tipping is ingrained in the American way of life. Here are some rules of thumb: In hotels, tip **bellhops** at least $1 per bag ($2–$3 if you have a lot of luggage) and tip the **chamber staff** $1 to $2 per day (more if you've left a disaster area for him or her to clean up, or if you're traveling with kids and/or pets). Tip the **doorman** or **concierge** only if he or she has provided you with some specific service (like calling a cab). In restaurants, bars, and nightclubs, tip **service staff** 15% to 20% of the check, tip **bartenders** 10% to 15%, and tip **checkroom attendants** $1 per garment. Tipping is not expected in cafeterias and fast-food restaurants. Tip **cab drivers** 15% of the fare and tip **skycaps** at airports at least $1 per bag ($2–$3 if you have a lot of luggage).

TOILETS Public restrooms are available at the **visitor centers** in Midtown (1560 Broadway, between 46th and 47th sts.; and 810 Seventh Ave., between 52nd and 53rd sts.). Grand Central Terminal, at 42nd Street between Park and Lexington avenues, also has clean restrooms. Your best bet on the street is **Starbucks** or another city java chain—you can't walk more than a few blocks without seeing one. The big

chain bookstores are good for this, too. You can also head to **hotel lobbies** (especially the big Midtown ones) and **department stores** like Macy's and Bloomingdale's. On the Lower East Side, stop into the **Lower East Side BID Visitor Center**, 261 Broome St., between Orchard and Allen streets (open Sun–Fri 10am–4pm, sometimes later).

TOURIST OFFICE NYC & Company, 810 Seventh Ave., New York, NY 10019 (☎ 800/NYC-VISIT; www.nycvisit.com).

TOURS **Big Apple Greeter** (☎ 212/669-8159; www.bigapple greeter.org) provides free neighborhood walking tours. If you'd rather get an overview of the city, you can try one of the hop-on, hop-off bus tours offered by **Gray Line** (☎ 800/669-0051; www.grayline newyork.com). They also have a host of other options—helicopter flights, museum admission, and guided visits of sights.

TRAVELERS WITH DISABILITIES **Hospital Audiences, Inc.** (☎ 212/575-7676; www.hospitalaudiences.org) arranges attendance and provides details about accessibility at cultural institutions as well as cultural events adapted for people with disabilities. Services include "Describe!," which allows visually impaired theatergoers to enjoy theater events; and the invaluable **HAI Hot Line** (☎ 212/575-7676), which offers accessibility information for hotels, restaurants, attractions, cultural venues, and much more. This nonprofit organization also publishes *Access for All,* a guidebook on accessibility, available by calling ☎ 212/575-7663 or by sending a $5 check to 548 Broadway, Third floor, New York, NY 10012-3950. Another terrific source for travelers with disabilities who are coming to New York City is **Big Apple Greeter** (☎ 212/669-8159; www.bigapplegreeter. org). All of its employees are extremely well versed in accessibility issues. They can provide a resource list of agencies that serve the city's community with disabilities, and sometimes have special discounts available to theater and music performances. Big Apple Greeter even offers one-to-one tours that pair volunteers with visitors with disabilities; they can even introduce you to the public transportation system if you like. Reserve at least 1 week ahead.

Public buses are an inexpensive and easy way to get around New York. All buses' back doors are supposed to be equipped with wheelchair lifts (though the city has had complaints that not all are in working order). Buses also "kneel," lowering their front steps for people who have difficulty boarding. Passengers with disabilities pay half-price fares ($1). The **subway** isn't yet fully wheelchair accessible, but a list of about 30 accessible subway stations and a guide to wheelchair-accessible subway itineraries are on the MTA website. Call ☎ **718/596-8585** for bus and subway transit info or go online to www.mta.nyc.ny.us/nyct and click on the wheelchair symbol.

A Brief **History**

1524 Giovanni da Verrazano sails into New York Harbor.

1609 Henry Hudson sails up the Hudson River.

1621 The Dutch West India Company begins trading from New York City.

1626 The Dutch pay 60 Guilders ($24) to the Lenape Tribe for the island of New Amsterdam.

1664 The Dutch surrender New Amsterdam to the British and the island is renamed after the brother of King Charles II, The Duke of York.

1765 The Sons of Liberty burn the British Governor in effigy.

1776 Independence from England is declared.

1789 The first Congress is held at Federal Hall on Wall Street, and George Washington is inaugurated.

1792 The first stock exchange is established on Wall Street.

1820 New York City is the nation's largest city with a population of 124,000.

1863 The draft riots rage throughout New York; 125 people die including 11 African Americans who are lynched by mobs of Irish immigrants.

1883 The Brooklyn Bridge opens.

1886 The Statue of Liberty is completed.

1892 Ellis Island opens and begins processing over a million immigrants yearly.

1904 The first subway departs from City Hall.

1920 Babe Ruth joins the New York Yankees.

1929 The stock market crashes.

1931 The Empire State Building opens and is the tallest building in the world.

1939 The New York World's Fair opens in Flushing Meadows, Queens.

1947 The Brooklyn Dodgers sign Jackie Robinson, the first African American to play in the Major Leagues.

1957 Elvis Presley performs live in New York on *The Ed Sullivan Show*.

1969 The Gay Rights movement begins with the Stonewall Rebellion in Greenwich Village.

1990 David Dinkins is elected as the first African-American mayor of New York City.

2000 The New York Yankees beat the New York Mets in the first Subway Series in 44 years. New York's population exceeds eight million.

2001 Terrorists use hijacked planes to crash into the Twin Towers of the World Trade Center, which brings both towers down and kills more than 3,000 people.

2003 Smoking is banned in all restaurants and bars.

2004 Ground breaks on the Freedom Tower to be built on the site of the World Trade Center.

Art & Architecture

New York is famous for its great buildings, but the truth is that the most interesting thing about its architecture is its diversity. From elegant Greek Revival row houses to soaring skyscrapers, the city contains excellent examples of every style. Constructed over 300 years, these buildings represent the changing tastes of the city's residents from Colonial times to the present.

Georgian (1700–76)

This style reflects Renaissance ideas made popular in England, and later in the United States, through the publication of books on 16th-century Italian architects. Georgian houses are characterized by a formal arrangement of parts employing a symmetrical composition enriched with classical details, such as columns and pediments.

EXAMPLE: ST. PAUL'S CHAPEL (p 8) the only pre-Revolutionary building remaining in Manhattan, is an almost perfect example of the Georgian style, with a pediment, colossal columns, Palladian window, quoins, and balustrade above the roof line.

Federal (1780–1820)

Federal was the first truly American architectural style. It was an adaptation of a contemporaneous English style called Adamesque, which included ornate, colorful interior decoration. Federal combined Georgian architecture with the delicacy of the French rococo and the classical architecture of Greece and Rome.

Typical Federal Exterior.

Lintel   Sash Window   Cornice

Side Light   Pilaster   Transom

The overall effect is one of restraint and dignity, and may appear delicate when compared to the more robust Georgian style.

EXAMPLES: In the **WEST VILLAGE**, near and along Bedford Street between Christopher and Morton streets, are more original Federal-style houses than anywhere else in Manhattan. House nos. 4 through 10 (1825–34) on Grove Street, just off Bedford, present one of the most authentic groups of late Federal–style houses in America. See p 77.

Greek Revival (1820–60)

The Greek Revolution in the 1820s, in which Greece won its independence from the Turks, recalled to American intellectuals the democracy of ancient Greece and its elegant architecture. At the same time, the War of 1812 diminished American affection for the British influence. With many believing America to be the spiritual successor of Greece, the use of classical Greek forms came to dominate residential, commercial, and government architecture.

EXAMPLE: Perhaps the city's finest Greek Revival building is **FEDERAL HALL NATIONAL MEMORIAL** (1834–42), at 26 Wall St., at Nassau Street. The structure has a Greek temple front, with Doric columns and a simple pediment, resting on a high base, called a plinth, with a steep flight of steps. See p 46.

Gothic Revival (1830–60)

The term *Gothic Revival* refers to a literary and aesthetic movement of the 1830s and 1840s that occurred in England and the United States. Adherents believed that the wickedness of modern times could benefit with a dose of "goodness" presumed to have been associated with the Christian medieval past. Architecture was chosen as one of the vehicles to bring this message to the people. Some structures had only one or two Gothic features, while others, usually churches, were copies of English Gothic structures.

EXAMPLE: TRINITY CHURCH, at Broadway and Wall Street (Richard Upjohn, 1846), is one of the most celebrated, authentic Gothic Revival structures in the United States. Here you see all the features of a Gothic church: a steeple, battlements, pointed arches, Gothic tracery, stained-glass windows, flying

Federal Hall National Memorial

Doric Entablature

Pediment

Doric Column

buttresses (an external bracing system for supporting a roof or vault), and medieval sculptures. See p 8.

Italianate (1840–80)

The architecture of Italy served as the inspiration for this building style, which could be as picturesque as the Gothic or as restrained as the classical. In New York, the style was used for urban row houses and commercial buildings. The development of cast iron at this time permitted the inexpensive mass production of decorative features that few could have afforded in carved stone. This led to the creation of cast-iron districts in nearly every American city. **EXAMPLES:** New York's **SOHO–CAST IRON HISTORIC DISTRICT** has 26 blocks jammed with cast-iron facades, many in the Italianate manner. The single richest section is **GREENE STREET** between Houston and Canal streets.

Early Skyscraper (1880–1920)

The invention of the skyscraper can be traced directly to the use of cast iron in the 1840s for storefronts, such as those seen in New York's SoHo. Experimentation with cast and wrought iron in the construction of interior skeletons eventually allowed buildings to rise higher. These buildings were spacious, cost-effective, efficient, and quickly erected—in short, the perfect architectural solution for America's growing downtowns. But solving the technical problems of the skyscraper did not resolve how the buildings should look. Most solutions relied on historical precedents, including decoration reminiscent of the Gothic, Romanesque (a style characterized by the use of rounded arches), or Beaux Arts. **EXAMPLES:** The **AMERICAN SURETY COMPANY,** at 100 Broadway (Bruce Price, 1895). The triangular **FLATIRON BUILDING,** at Fifth Avenue and 23rd

Street (Daniel H. Burnham & Co., 1902), has strong tripartite divisions and Renaissance Revival detail, see p 71. And, finally, the **WOOLWORTH BUILDING** (Cass Gilbert, 1913), on Broadway at Park Place, see p 7.

Second Renaissance Revival (1890–1920)

Buildings in this style show a definite studied formalism. A relative faithfulness to Italian Renaissance precedents of window and doorway treatments distinguishes it from the much looser adaptations of the Italianate. Scale and size, in turn, set the Second Renaissance Revival apart from the first, which occurred from 1840 to 1890. The style was used for banks, swank town houses, government buildings, and private clubs. **EXAMPLES:** New York's Upper East Side has two fine examples of this building type, each exhibiting most of the style's key features: the **RACQUET AND TENNIS CLUB,** 370 Park Ave. (McKim, Mead & White, 1918), based on the style of an elegant Florentine palazzo; and the **METROPOLITAN CLUB,** 1 East 60th St. (McKim, Mead & White, 1891–94).

Beaux Arts (1890–1920)

This style takes its name from the Ecole des Beaux-Arts in Paris, where a number of prominent American architects trained, beginning around the mid–19th century. These architects adopted the academic design principles of the Ecole, which emphasized the study of Greek and Roman structures, composition, and symmetry, and the creation of elaborate presentation drawings. Because of the idealized origins and grandiose use of classical forms, the Beaux Arts in America was seen as the ideal style for expressing civic pride. Grandiose compositions, an exuberance of detail, and a variety of stone finishes typify most Beaux Arts structures. **EXAMPLES:** The **NEW YORK PUBLIC**

LIBRARY (p 17), at Fifth Avenue and 42nd Street (Carrère & Hastings, 1911), is perhaps the best example. Others of note are **GRAND CENTRAL TERMINAL** (p 17), at 42nd Street and Park Avenue (Reed & Stem and Warren & Whetmore, 1903–13), and the **U.S. CUSTOM HOUSE** (Cass Gilbert, 1907) on Bowling Green between State and Whitehall streets.

International Style (1920–45)

In 1932, the Museum of Modern Art hosted its first architecture exhibit, titled simply "Modern Architecture." Displays included images of International Style buildings from around the world. The structures all share a stark simplicity and vigorous functionalism, a definite break from historically based, decorative styles. The International Style was popularized in the United States through the teachings and designs of **LUDWIG MIES VAN DER ROHE** (1886–1969), a German émigré based in Chicago. Interpretations of the "Miesian" International Style were built in most U.S. cities, including New York, as late as 1980.

EXAMPLES: Two famous examples of this style in New York are the **SEAGRAM BUILDING,** at 375 Park Ave. (Ludwig Mies van der Rohe, 1958), and the **LEVER HOUSE,** at 390 Park Ave., between 53rd and 54th streets (Skidmore, Owings & Merrill, 1952).

Art Deco (1925–40)

Art Deco is a decorative style that took its name from a Paris exposition in 1925. The jazzy style embodied the idea of

Lever House.

Chrysler Building.

modernity. One of the first widely accepted styles not based on historic precedents, it influenced all areas of design from jewelry and household goods to cars, trains, and ocean liners. Art Deco buildings are characterized by a linear, hard edge, or angular composition, often with a vertical emphasis and highlighted with stylized decoration.

EXAMPLES: Despite the effects of the Depression, several major Art Deco structures were built in New York in the 1930s, often providing crucial jobs.

ROCKEFELLER CENTER (Raymond Hood, 1932–40), p 16, includes 30 Rockefeller Plaza, a tour de force of Art Deco style, with a soaring, vertical shaft and aluminum details. The **CHRYSLER BUILDING'S**, p 17 (William Van Alen, 1930), needlelike spire with zigzag patterns in glass and metal is a distinctive feature on the city's skyline. The famous **EMPIRE STATE BUILDING,** p 18 (Shreve, Lamb & Harmon, 1931), contains a black- and silvertoned lobby among its many Art Deco features.

Art Moderne (1930–45)

Art moderne strove for modernity and an artistic expression for the sleekness of the machine age. Unbroken horizontal lines and smooth curves visually distinguish it from Art Deco and give it a streamlined effect. It was popular with movie theaters, and was often applied to cars, trains, and boats to suggest the idea of speed.

EXAMPLE: RADIO CITY MUSIC HALL, on Sixth Avenue at 50th Street (Edward Durrell Stone and Donald Deskey, 1932), has a sweeping art moderne marquee. See p 16.

Postmodern (1975–90)

Postmodernism burst on the scene in the 1970s with the reintroduction of historical precedents in architecture. With many feeling that the office towers of the previous style were too cold, postmodernists began to incorporate classical details and recognizable forms into their designs—often applied in outrageous proportions.

EXAMPLE: The **SONY BUILDING,** at 550 Madison Ave. (Philip Johnson/John Burgee, 1984), brings the distinctive shape of a Chippendale cabinet to the New York skyline.

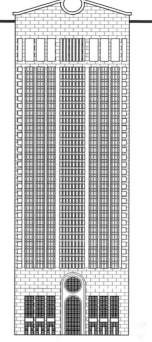

Sony Building

Toll-Free **Numbers & Websites**

Airlines

AER LINGUS

☎ 800/474-7424 in the U.S.

☎ 01/886-8844 in Ireland

www.aerlingus.com

AIR CANADA

☎ 888/247-2262

www.aircanada.ca

AIR FRANCE

☎ 800/237-2747 in the U.S.

☎ 0820-820-820 in France

www.airfrance.com

AIR NEW ZEALAND

☎ 800/262-1234 or -2468 in the U.S.

☎ 800/663-5494 in Canada

☎ 0800/737-000 in New Zealand

www.airnewzealand.com

AIRTRAN AIRLINES

☎ 800/247-8726

www.airtran.com

ALITALIA

☎ 800/223-5730 in the U.S.

☎ 8488-65641 in Italy

www.alitalia.it

AMERICAN AIRLINES

☎ 800/433-7300

www.aa.com

AMERICAN TRANS AIR

☎ 800/225-2995

www.ata.com

BMI

No U.S. number

☎ 0870/6070-222 in Britain

www.flybmi.com

BRITISH AIRWAYS

☎ 800/247-9297 in the U.S.

☎ 0870/850-9-850 in Britain

www.british-airways.com

CONTINENTAL AIRLINES

☎ 800/525-0280

www.continental.com

DELTA AIR LINES

☎ 800/221-1212

www.delta.com

EASYJET

No U.S. number

www.easyjet.com

The **Savvy** Traveler

IBERIA
☎ 800/772-4642 in the U.S.
☎ 902/400-500 in Spain
www.iberia.com

ICELANDAIR
☎ 800/223-5500 in the U.S.
☎ 354/50-50-100 in Iceland
www.icelandair.is

JET BLUE AIRLINES
☎ 800/538-2583
www.jetblue.com

KLM
☎ 800/374-7747 in the U.S.
☎ 020/4-747-747 in the Netherlands
www.klm.nl

LUFTHANSA
☎ 800/645-3880 in the U.S.
☎ 49/(0)- 180-5-838426 in Germany
www.lufthansa.com

NORTHWEST AIRLINES
☎ 800/225-2525
www.nwa.com

OLYMPIC AIRWAYS
☎ 800/223-1226 in the U.S.
☎ 80/111-444-444 in Greece
www.olympic-airways.gr

QANTAS
☎ 800/227-4500 in the U.S.
☎ 612/131313 in Australia
www.qantas.com

SCANDINAVIAN AIRLINES
☎ 800/221-2350 in the U.S.
☎ 0070/727-727 in Sweden
☎ 70/10-20-00 in Denmark
☎ 358/(0)20-386-000 in Finland
☎ 815/200-400 in Norway
www.scandinavian.net

SINGAPORE AIRLINES
☎ 800/742-3333 in the U.S.
☎ 65/6223-8888 in Singapore
www.singaporeair.com

SONG
☎ 800/359-7664
www.flysong.com

SWISS INTERNATIONAL AIRLINES
☎ 877/359-7947 in the U.S.
☎ 0848/85-2000 in Switzerland
www.swiss.com

TAP AIR PORTUGAL
☎ 800/221-7370 in the U.S.
☎ 351/21-841-66-00 in Portugal
www.tap-airportugal.com

THAI AIRWAYS INTERNATIONAL
☎ 800/426-5204 in the U.S.
☎ (66-2)-535-2081-2 in Thailand
www.thaiair.com

UNITED AIRLINES
☎ 800/241-6522
www.united.com

US AIRWAYS
☎ 800/428-4322
www.usairways.com

VIRGIN ATLANTIC AIRWAYS
☎ 800/862-8621 in continental U.S.
☎ 0870/380-2007 in Britain
www.virgin-atlantic.com

Index

Photo **Credits**

p viii: © Mitchell Funk/Getty Images; p 3 middle: © Richard Bryant/Arcaid/Alamy; p 3 bot-
tom: © Rudi Von Briel/Index Stock Imagery; p 4 top: © Allan Montaine/Lonely Planet
Images; p 5: © Michael Howell/Index Stock Imagery; p 7 bottom: © Goodshot/Alamy; p 8
top: © Norman Tomalin/Alamy; p 8 bottom: © Age Fotostock/SuperStock; p 9 bottom:
© Ace Stock Limited/Alamy; p 11 bottom: © Peter Hendrie/Lonely Planet Images; p 12 top:
© Barry Winiker/Index Stock Imagery; p 12 bottom: © Louie Psihoyos/Corbis; p 13 bottom:
© Alan Schein Photography/Corbis; p 15 middle: © Michael Kim/Corbis; p 16 top: © SCPho-
tos/Alamy; p 16 bottom: © Richard I'Anson/Lonely Planet Images; p 17 top: © Eric Kamp/
Index Stock Imagery; p 17 bottom: © Eric Kamp/Index Stock Imagery; p 18 top: © Louie Psi-
hoyos/Corbis; p 18bottom: © Jacob Halaska/Index Stock Imagery; p 19: © Digital Vision/AGE
Fotostock; p 21 bottom: © Comstock Images/Alamy; p 22 top: © Angus Oborn/Lonely
Planet Images; p 22 bottom: © Peter Bennett/Ambient Images Inc./Alamy; p 23 top:
© SuperStock/AGE Fotostock; p 23 bottom: © Michel Setboun/Corbis; p 25 bottom:
© Serge Hambourg/Louis Armstrong House & Archives; p 26 top: © Jan Halaska/Index Stock
Imagery; p 26 bottom: © Jon Wilton/Redferns Music Picture Library/Alamy; p 27 bottom:
© Colin Paterson/SuperStock; p 29 bottom: The Metropolitan Museum of Art, Purchase,
Isabel Shults Fund and Martin and Caryl Horwitz and Hearst Corporation Gifts, 1995
(1995.178.3) Photograph © 1997 The Metropolitan Museum of Art; p 30 top: © Vlad
Riabov/Alamy; p 30 bottom: © Chip East/Reuters/Corbis; p 33 bottom: © Greg Gawlowski/
Lonely Planet Images; p 34 bottom: © Michael S. Yamashita/Corbis; p 35 top: © SuperStock,
Inc./SuperStock; p 37 middle: © Paul Katz/Index Stock Imagery; p 38 top: © Richard Bryant/
Arcaid/Alamy; p 38 bottom: Harold Pestana's Soldiers of the Queen, © The Forbes Collec-
tion, New York All Rights Reserved; p 39 top: © Rudy Sulgan/AGE Fotostock; p 39 bottom:
© Kevin Foy/Alamy; p 41 bottom: © Peter Bennett/Ambient Images Inc./Alamy; p 42 bot-
tom: © Courtesy Algonquin Hotel; p 43 top: © Comstock Images/Alamy; p 45 bottom:
© Jeff Greenburg/Index Stock Imagery; p 46 bottom: © Peter Bennett/Ambient Images
Inc./Alamy; p 47 top: © Comstock Images/Alamy; p 49 middle: © Steve Sands/New York
Newswire/Corbis; p 49 bottom: © Marc Asnin/Corbis; p 50 top: © Omni Photo Communica-
tions Inc./Index Stock Imagery; p 51 bottom: © Barry Winiker/Index Stock Imagery; p 53
bottom: Carrie Walter Stettheimer, Stettheimer Doll House, left side 1920's, © Museum of
the City of New York, Gift of Miss Ettie Stettheimer, 45.125.1; p 54 top: © Dan Herrick/Lonely
Planet Images; p 54 bottom: © Heungman Kwan/Index Stock Imagery; p 55 top: © Jason
Klein/Trapeze School New York; p 57 bottom: © Omni Photo Communications Inc./Index
Stock Imagery; p 58 bottom: © Milu Cugar/Reuters/Corbis; p 59 top: © Eric Kamp/Index
Stock Imagery; p 60 top: © Paul Katz/Index Stock Imagery; p 61 top: © Chuck Pefley/Alamy;
p 63 bottom: © Lauree Feldman/Index Stock Imagery; p 64 top: © Lauree Feldman/Index
Stock Imagery; p 64 bottom: © Lauree Feldman/Index Stock Imagery; p 65 top: © Lauree
Feldman/Index Stock Imagery; p 67 bottom: © Omni Photo Communications Inc./Index
Stock Imagery; p 68 top: © Lee Snider/Photo Images/Corbis; p 68 bottom: © Dan Herrick/
Lonely Planet Images; p 69 bottom: © Matt Moyer/AP; p 71 middle: © Keate/Masterfile;

p 71 bottom: © Omni Photo Communications Inc./Index Stock Imagery; p 72 bottom: © Omni Photo Communications Inc./Index Stock Imagery; p 73 top: © Courtesy of Chelsea Piers; p 75 bottom: © Lee Snider/Photo Images/Corbis; p 76 bottom: © Peter Bennett/Ambient Images Inc./Alamy; p 77 top: © Steve Hamblin/Alamy; p 79 bottom: © Brooklyn Museum of Art/Corbis; p 80 top: © David Forbert/SuperStock; p 80 bottom: © Mark Gidson/Index Stock Imagery; p 81 top: © SuperStock, Inc./SuperStock; p 81 bottom: © Lauree Feldman/Index Stock Imagery; p 83 bottom: © Heungman Kwan/Index Stock Imagery; p 84 top: © Ace Stock Limited/Alamy; p 84 bottom: © Jochen Tack/Das Fotoarchiv/Black Star/Alamy; p 85 top: © Lauree Feldman/Index Stock Imagery; p 86 top: © Robert Holmes/Corbis; p 87: © Jochen Tack/Das Fotoarchiv/Black Star/Alamy; p 88 bottom: © Dan Herrick/Lonely Planet Images; p 92 bottom: © Heungman Kwan/Index Stock Imagery; p 93 top: © Frances Roberts/Alamy; p 94 top: © Kim Grant/Lonely Planet Images; p 94 bottom: © Ian Dagnall/Alamy; p 95 bottom: © Chris Gascoigne/VIEW Pictures Ltd./Alamy; p 96 bottom: © Angus Oborn/Lonely Planet Images; p 97 top: © Neil Setchfield/Alamy; p 98 top: © Heungman Kwan/Index Stock Imagery; p 99: © Michael Dwyer/Alamy; p 101 bottom: © Rudi Von Briel/Index Stock Imagery; p 102 bottom: © Comstock Images/Alamy; p 103 top: © AM Corporation/Alamy; p 105 bottom: © Jeff Richman, Green-Wood Cemetery Historian; p 106 top: © Lauree Feldman/Index Stock Imagery; p 106 bottom: © Jeff Richman, Green-Wood Cemetery Historian; p 107 top: © Margot Weiss; p 109 bottom: © Keith Levit/Alamy; p 110 top: © Bernd Obermann/Corbis; p 111: © Courtesy Baltz & Company/Guastavino's Restaurant; p 112 bottom: © Wyatt Counts; p 116 bottom: © Najlah Feanny/Corbis; p 117 top: © Courtesy Balthazar Restaurant; p 118 bottom: © davidburke & donatella; p 119 top: © Eric Laignel; p 119 bottom: © Courtesy Jean-Georges; p 120 bottom: © Andy Levin/Alamy; p 121 top: © Mark Peterson/Corbis; p 122 bottom: © Rosa Mexicano Restaurants; p 123 top: © Suba Archives; p 124 middle: © Walter Bibikow/Jon Arnold Images/Alamy; p 125: © Courtesy Bowlmor Lanes & Pressure Lounge; p 126 bottom: © Richard Drew/AP; p 130 bottom: © Joe Kohen/AP; p 131 top: © Dan Herrick/Lonely Planet Images; p 131 bottom: © Thomas A. Kelly/Corbis; p 132 top: © Gail Mooney/Corbis; p 133 top: © Dan Herrick/Lonely Planet Images; p 133 bottom: © PCL/Alamy; p 134 top: © Kim Grant/Lonely Planet Images; p 135: © Marty Lederhandler/AP; p 136 bottom: © Bartomeu Amengual/AGE Fotostock; p 141 top: © Kathy Willens/AP; p 142 bottom: © Bettmann/Corbis; p 143 top: © Barry Winiker/Index Stock Imagery; p 144 top: © Omni Photo Communications Inc./Index Stock Imagery; p 144 bottom: © Viviane Moos/Corbis; p 145 top: © Courtesy Jazz Standard; p 145 bottom: © Dan Herrick/Lonely Planet Images; p 146 bottom: © Bo Zaunders/Corbis; p 147 top: © Rudi Von Briel/Index Stock Imagery; p 149: © The Ritz-Carlton New York, Battery Park; p 150 bottom: © Mike Wilson/ Photos Accor; p 154 bottom: © Roy Wright ; p 155 top: © Omni Photo Communications Inc./Index Stock Imagery; p 157 top: © Lauree Feldman/Index Stock Imagery; p 157 bottom: © The Ritz-Carlton New York, Battery Park; p 158 bottom: © Washington Square Hotel; p 159: © Fabrik Studios/Index Stock Imagery.